D1623027

THE
COLORADO
TRAIL

SEVENTH EDITION

THE COLORADO MOUNTAIN CLUB PRESS
GOLDEN, COLORADO

The Colorado Trail
   The Official Guidebook of
   The Colorado Trail Foundation
   Seventh Edition, Revised
   ISBN # 0-9760525-2-0

Printed in China
Text copyright 2008 by The Colorado Trail Foundation.
Copyright (c) 2008 by The Colorado Mountain Club Press.
Published by The Colorado Mountain Club Press.
710 10th Street, Suite 200, Golden, CO 80401
(303) 279-3080   1 (800) 633-4417
email: cmcoffice@cmc.org
website: http://www.cmc.org/cmc

Editor: Terry Root.
Graphics Design and Maps: Steve Meyers
   and Terry Root.
Proofing: Joyce Carson and Linda Grey.
Project Liaison for CTF: Merle McDonald.
Publisher: Alan Stark.
GPS Data: courtesy of Jerry Brown,
   Bear Creek Survey Service, Inc.
Front cover photo: "Descending Elk Creek", CT Segment
   24, courtesy Colorado Mountain Expeditions.
Facing page photo: "Rolling Mountain",
   CT Segment 25 by Aaron Locander.

Contacting the editors:
We would appreciate it if readers would alert
us to any errors or outdated information by
contacting us at the address above.

Warning: Although there has been a effort to make the trail descriptions in this book as accurate as possible,
some discrepancies may exist between the text and the lay of the trail in the field. This book is not intended to be
instructional in nature, but rather, a guide for users of The Colorado Trail who already have the requisite training,
experience and knowledge. Before you begin a trek on The Colorado Trail, users need to be capable of inde-
pendent backcountry travel and be experienced in relevant mountaineering and orienteering techniques. Failure
to have the necessary knowledge, equipment and conditioning may subject users of The Colorado Trail to physical danger, injury or death. Some routes described in this book have changed and others will change; hazards
described may have expanded and new hazards may have formed since the book's publication. Each user of The
Colorado Trail may be held responsible and liable for all costs which may be incurred if a rescue is necessary.
(The State of Colorado pays the cost of rescuing anyone in possession of a valid Colorado fishing license, hunting license or CORSAR hiking certificate.)

THE CONTRIBUTORS:

This book is the result of a collaborative effort by volunteers from The **Colorado Trail Foundation**, the builders and stewards of the 485-mile Colorado Trail. To find out more about the CTF, or to join their efforts in preserving and maintaining the CT, see page 254.

Principal writer for the trail descriptions was **Jerry Brown** who spent nearly two months in the summer of 2005 in walking the entire trail, checking water sources, locating camp sites, and recording GPS data. Brown has hiked and biked the trail several times from his home at the trail's terminus in Durango. Acting as CTF's liaison to the publisher, **Merle McDonald** kept the flow of information coming and edited Brown's material. As a former CTF president and with years on CTF organized trips, McDonald was well-qualified to write the introductory sections for all the chapters. With over 25 years working on Colorado Mountain Club publications, **Terry Root** stepped in as editor, graphic designer, indexer; and wrote about everything from history-along-the-CT to pocket gophers in the book's sidebars. The late **Hugo Ferchau**, as professor of biology and botany at Western State in Gunnison, passed on his enthusiasm for the CT by writing about natural history for this book. **Denise R. Mutschler** and **David L. Gaskill** drew on their invaluable experience for their chapter on geology along the trail. Current CTF president (2005) **Marilyn Eisele** wrote the fine tribute about Gudy Gaskill. **Andrew Skurka**, the first person to complete the 7,700-mile, Sea-to-Sea Route (Quebec to Washington) offered insights on "lite-hiking". **Joyce Carson** found 99.9% of the mistakes (her estimate) as proofer. Other contributors were Steve Cave, Tom Brooksher, Andy Riach, Diane Parker, Suzanne Reed, Ken Swierenga, Jon Greeneisen, Chuck Lawson, George Miller, Ken Stagner, Sam Davis, Mark & Joellen Foken, Barney Barnett, Ernie Norris, Larry Mack, Ted LaMay, Bill Manning, Roger Gomas, Glen Kepler, Rolly Rogers, John Lipe, and Ernie Werren. The list on page 253 credits the many gifted photographers who captured the beauty and joy of hiking on the CT for this project.

⚠ TABLE OF CONTENTS

For ease of navigating *The Colorado Trail, The Official Guidebook*, sections of the guide are organized by the colors shown.

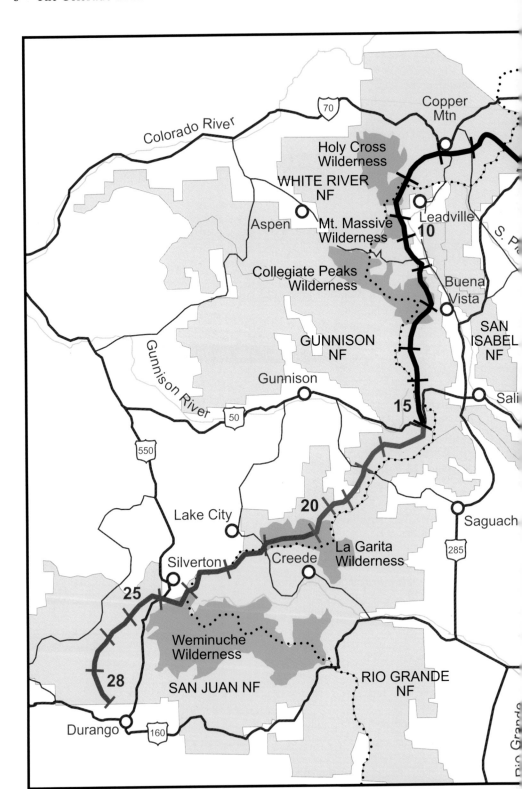

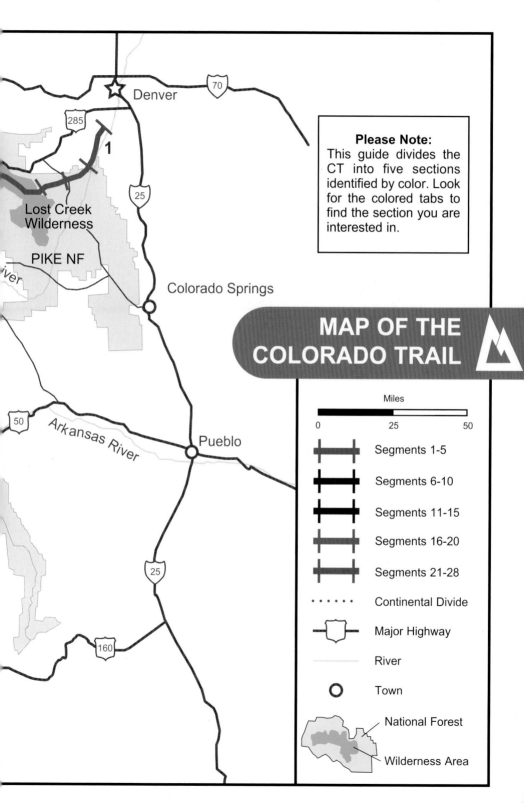

Please Note:
This guide divides the CT into five sections identified by color. Look for the colored tabs to find the section you are interested in.

MAP OF THE
COLORADO TRAIL

Miles

0   25   50

Segments 1-5

Segments 6-10

Segments 11-15

Segments 16-20

Segments 21-28

Continental Divide

Major Highway

River

Town

National Forest

Wilderness Area

Denver

Lost Creek Wilderness

PIKE NF

Colorado Springs

Arkansas River

Pueblo

ABOVE: *Eldorado Lake, Segment 24.*

FOREWORD ⚠

by GUDY GASKILL

Colorado! The name rolls off the tongue and brings to mind visual images of red rock walls, cascading waterfalls, lofty peaks, alpine meadows bedecked with wildflowers, and a unique outdoor lifestyle. This lifestyle has created a state of vigorous, healthy, and robust men and women, who flock to the mountains to practice their climbing and mountain biking skills in the summer and a multitude of snow sports in the winter. They live sincerely, work longer, and play harder. It is truly a magnificent state.

I have traveled all over the world, climbed and hiked in many different climates and environments, but each time as the plane brings me safely down to terra firma, my mind always comes back to the same question. Why did I ever leave Colorado? Colorado is home, a big friendly state with such a variety of scenery. Who could ever forget the azure blue sky, the color deepening as the day draws to an end, the spectacular cumulus clouds that billow up before the afternoon showers, and the show of golds, oranges, and crimsons in the sky on a late summer evening? Who could forget the tunnel of golden aspen, with a treasure of gold coins covering the fragrant earth on a crisp autumn day? Or the brilliance of ice crystals, shimmering a million colors in the early morning sun? This is heaven underfoot!

The Colorado Trail, a wilderness path designed to traverse some of the most scenic areas of the Rockies and the Continental Divide, is a unique experience for both body and soul. This revised guidebook to the trail describes all the wonders and beauty that you will see along The Colorado Trail. It chronicles the trees, flora, and fauna that you will encounter along the way. It will stir your imagination with the geological observations, creating a desire to know more of the area's ancient history and the powers of nature that formed this landscape. The Colorado Trail has also become a living history lesson, as it relates the tales of its earliest inhabitants, from Indians to turn-of-the-century miners and railroad barons. This guidebook makes the trail an educational reality.

We have received many wonderful letters from trail users from all over the world. The peace, solitude, and beauty have given us all a new look at our place on the earth. The Colorado Trail has changed many lives. Our daughter, Polly, who just recently came off the trail, wrote these words in one of her journal entries: "I walk the spine of rocks around the curve of the mountains. Awareness vibrates — colors, textures of plants radiate from the earth with vibrancy and life. Rock gardens of immense beauty gift my eyes. Tufts of shimmering bird feathers alight on rough bark. Rusted lichen paint the granite, life's green light dances on the ground. The smell of nature's perfume rises from the earth. The sound and touch of changing wind breathe against every hair on my body. Aliveness. Gratitude."

That is the effect the trail has on body and soul. That is the Colorado Trail!

GUDY GASKILL AND THE CT

by MARILYN EISELE

The "Trail to Nowhere" — that is how the *Empire Magazine* section of the Denver Post characterized the Colorado Trail in 1984.   Bill Lucas of the United States Forest Service had conceived the idea of a long distance trail between Denver and Durango in 1973.   In 1974, numerous focus groups were held to develop a plan for building this trail.   Gudy Gaskill, an active member of the Colorado Mountain Club since 1952 and later the first women president of the Colorado Mountain Club, attended that first focus meeting for the Colorado Trail.   Subsequently, she never missed a planning meeting in those early years.   The Colorado Mountain Trails Foundation was formed to plan, develop and manage the Colorado Trail, and Gudy Gaskill was asked to chair this committee.

The task ahead was immense; a route had to be drawn through several Forest Service Districts, linking early trails with existing mining and logging roads. Invitations had to be sent to thirteen Forest Service Districts to see if the trail could be built through their district. If a forester did not want the trail, Gudy would make numerous trips to persuade the district ranger of the value of the trail. After a year of extensive effort, most of the districts were in agreement. At the same time, Gudy was recruiting and training volunteers, leading trail crews, and purchasing supplies. In spite of the massive effort on the part of Gudy Gaskill and her "dirt digging volunteers", the Colorado Trail seemed to languish.

Hence the *Empire Magazine* article "Trail to Nowhere" by Ed Quillen. The article was just what the Colorado Trail needed. It caught the attention of the then Governor Dick Lamm and his wife Dottie. They spent time with a trail crew, hosted a fundraiser and rekindled support and cooperation between the state and the Forest Service.

In 1986, Gudy founded the non-profit Colorado Trail Foundation, whose focus and responsibility was the completion of the Colorado Trail, education along the trail and maintenance of the trail.   Gudy realized that with volunteer effort the trail could be built for approximately $500 per mile, compared to an estimated Forest Service cost of $25,000 per mile.

Gudy was a true visionary in realizing that volunteers were the heart, soul and future of outdoor stewardship. With the Forest Service providing the technical assistance, Gudy's volunteers provided the manual labor. The 468-mile long trail between Denver and Durango was completed in 1987. Through Gudy's vision of the value of volunteers, the trail is continuously updated and maintained and is one of the premier long distance trails in the nation.

Today Gudy is still very active in the Colorado Trail Foundation and volunteerism. She spends approximately eight weeks every summer at the Colorado Trail Educational Facility in the mountains above Lake City, managing the Foundation's educational programs. Classes in wildflowers, painting, geology, storytelling, pho-

Gudy Gaskill

tography and Wilderness First Aid are now offered by the Colorado Trail Foundation. This aspect of the Colorado Trail's mission and vision statement has now become her focus.

Today the Colorado Trail Foundation is still a "all volunteer " organization. The officers, Board of Directors, and thousands of other volunteers give unselfishly of their time. It is Gudy's inspiration that p e r m e a t e s throughout this massive volunteer effort and makes the organization f u n c t i o n . Volunteers come from all over the world to partici- pate in the legacy of the Colorado Trail.   In 2004, on September 25th, the Colorado Trail celebrated it's 30th anniversary. This is a real tribute to one individual to see her little band of volunteers grow into the wonderful organization that we know today.

Gudy has been recognized for her contributions to outdoor stewardship. She has been honored by two U.S. presidents and in 2002 was inducted into the Colorado Women's Hall of Fame.

Gudy Gaskill was "The Colorado Trail" champion and preserved through many obstacles in her dream to make it a reality. The "Mother of the Colorado Trail" inspires us all with a "Can Do" attitude.

HOW TO USE THIS GUIDE

The Colorado Trail is divided up into 28 individual **segments**, each of which is represented by a chapter in this guide. Segments have been established based on convenient access points to the trail. Most can conceivably be hiked in a day, although some would be a very long day, even with a light pack. The **Map of the Colorado Trail** on page 6-7 shows the entire length of the CT; plus major highways, towns, national forests and wilderness areas along the route.

This guide also divides the CT into five color-coded sections. Look for the colored tabs to find the section you are interested in.

- Segments 1-5
- Segments 6-10
- Segments 11-15
- Segments 16-20
- Segments 21-28

"Introduction" Page

Each segment (chapter) begins with an *introduction* page containing pertinent information summarizing that segment. The start and end points, plus one-way distance and approximate elevation gain, are shown in a box; along with a photograph taken along that segment. The elevation gain is the sum of major ascending portions and is a general indicator of how much extra effort will be required to deal with the ascent.

Beneath this is a general information box, including a list of available maps that cover each segment. The first is a *vicinity map*, based on **United States Forest Service (USFS) maps**, useful for general orientation purposes. These maps are reproduced in this guide, with page numbers leading you to them. United States Geological Survey (USGS) **topographic maps** are listed next in this box. These are the most detailed maps available, at a scale of 1:24,000. However, nearly 50 maps are required to cover the entire CT. Finally, *Trails Illustrated* **brand maps** are also available that encompass nearly all of the CT. These maps are of a smaller scale than the USGS topos, but are "field-ready," being water proof and tear-resistant.

Beneath the map listings are the **jurisdictions**, or appropriate USFS ranger districts, for that segment. Contact addresses for these are provided on page 243. Since most of the Colorado Trail passes through these federally-managed public lands, you'll want to contact them if you have a question about regulations.

Symbols for **Access From Denver** and **Access From Durango** indicate the normal condition of roads accessing the trail from the Denver-end of that section and the Durango-end of that section, respectively. (For through-hikers going from Denver to Durango, the first is the start of that segment and the latter is the end of that segment.) Please note that a dirt or gravel road that is listed as easily negotiable by a normal passenger car can become impassible after wet weather. Also, except for major highways, most of these are secondary roads that are not kept open during winter.

 Paved or graded-dirt access road

 Rough, dirt access road

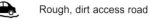 4-wheel drive access road

🥄	Plentiful water sources
🥄	Scattered water sources
🥄	Water is difficult to obtain
🚲	Suitable for bicycles
🚲	Recommended detour
🚲	Mandatory detour

Next are symbols that indicate the likely availability of **water** for this segment during late summer. More detailed information about the location of water sources is often provided in the *trail descriptions* section.

Finally, a symbol shows information for **mountain bikers**. If a detour is recommended or mandatory, a page number leads you to the detour's description and map. Cyclists are not allowed to travel the CT where it traverses a designated wilderness area and should likewise avoid other segments where terrain dictates it.

Gudy's Tip

Be sure to check out **Gudy's Tips**, useful insider information about that segment from the champion of the Colorado Trail, Gudy Gaskill. No one knows the CT better!

About This Segment

The next major section provides general information, interesting facts, and local history about each segment. Especially important here for long-distance hikers are the indications of where water and camping are available.

Trailhead/Access Points

Instructions for reaching the trailheads and trail access points are given in this section, along with symbols that indicate the normal condition of the roads (for definition of symbols, see page 13). All the segments described in this guide begin and end at points accessible by vehicle. Many have additional trail access points within the segment. Generally, *trailhead* refers to an official access point with a parking area, which sometimes can be primitive and skimpy. *Trail access* refers to a point where the trail crosses or approaches a road, but where no official parking is provided. One of the continuing priorities of the Colorado Trail Foundation is to increase and improve the number of trailheads on the Colorado Trail. In the meantime, be careful where you park your car.

Supplies, Services and Accommodations

A short paragraph describes supply points and services nearby to the CT. For major supply points, a town or city map is included that pinpoints services such as grocery stores, showers, post offices, and laundries. Larger towns will have multiple lodging and dining accommodations — check with the local Chamber of Commerce for more information. It should be noted that for some remote segments of the CT, no convenient points of re-supply are available.

Trail Description

Be alert for this symbol and box! It highlights a particular caution or warning that you should be aware of.

The detailed trail descriptions are laid out progressing from Denver to Durango. The descriptions indicate the distance of recognizable landmarks (indicated in **bold**) from the beginning of the trail segment. Often accompanying the mileage count, in parentheses, is the altitude of that landmark. These mileages were obtained using sophisticated, professional-quality GPS devices and are more accurate than mileages generated by measuring distances on maps and by using a mechanical measuring device.

Maps, Elevation Profiles and GPS

Each chapter ends with its *vicinity map*, a reproduction of the Forest Service map for that segment. Each map shows the CT segment in red, with adjacent segments dashed. Alternative trails to the main line of the CT are shown in blue and dashed as well. Key **landmark locations** are also shown on the maps — usually trail intersections, stream crossings, and trail access points.

CT (current segment)
CT (adjacent segment)
Alternate CT Route
Ⓗ   Landmark Location

In the bottom corner of each *vicinity map* page, a *trail elevation profile* shows the ups and downs encountered along that segment, including a graphic display of the steepness of individual portions and the position of the landmark locations. A chart in the opposite bottom corner summarizes these landmark locations. The distance of these locations from both the start of the segment and the Denver end of the CT are indicated, along with Global Positioning System coordinates designating the Latitude and Longitude. If you are entering these coordinates by hand into your GPS unit, set the unit to decimal degrees format (hddd.ddddd) and NAD27 CONUS datum. For more info about using the GPS waypoints, see pages 22-23.

For more precise orienteering purposes, the Colorado Trail Foundation recommends their *Official Colorado Trail GIS Reference Map Series* on CD ROM, including viewing software showing the CT positioned precisely on topographic maps, plus GPS generated data. Inquire with the CTF office (see page 254).

And There's More!

Additional *information* boxes provide interesting facts or useful information for specific segments, in order to help you get the most out of your CT experience.

| Indicates **helpful tips** for CT hikers, plus highlights other hikes or climbs in this segment. | Indicates a **viewing opportunity** in this segment, such as interesting places or wildlife. | Indicates information for **mountain bikers**, including other rides in the area that might be of interest. |

PLANNING FOR THE COLORADO TRAIL

Winding through the magnificent heart of the southern Rockies for 485 miles from Denver to Durango, the Colorado Trail is one of the nation's most beautiful and varied long-distance trails. For recreationalists — hikers, backpackers, mountain bikers, and horsepackers — the CT offers an unparalled path into the scenic wonders of Colorado's mountains, crossing eight mountain ranges, six national forests, and countless streams and rivers. The topography encountered by the CT hiker ranges over an enormously varied landscape from the edge of the high plains to the summits of alpine peaks along the Continental Divide. For those who are drawn to the wonder and beauty of the CT, their enjoyment of their experience is dependent on their ability to respond to the demands, challenges and even dangers imposed by this remarkable path through the wilderness.

Probably only a few people will consider hiking the entire route straight through, from one end to another. Through-hiking the Colorado Trail is not for the unprepared or out-of-shape. Most will opt for traveling segment by segment, either through day-hikes or by backpacking short portions for a few days at a time. Whether out for a day-hike or committed to through-hiking the entire trail, planning for your trip is crucial.

Planning a Hike on the CT

The Colorado Trail traverses a landscape ranging in altitude between 5,800 feet at its eastern end in Waterton Canyon to over 13,000 feet in the lofty San Juan Mountains of the southwestern corner of the state. Much of the trail ranges above 9,000 feet in altitude where winters are long and extreme. Snow covers the trail for much of the year, often persisting even into July along high ridges or in shady ravines. For that reason, it's important to give careful consideration to the time of year for your trek. (That's not to say that it is impossible to travel on some segments of the CT in the winter. Segment 9 at Tennessee Pass is the start of several classic ski tours, bolstered by the area's popular Tenth Mountain Division Hut System.) Except for the few places where major highways cross the trail, most of the access roads mentioned in this guide remained closed to traffic throughout the winter and well into the spring.

The Colorado Trail Foundation recommends the wisest strategy for terminus - to-terminus hikers is to begin their trek from the eastern end, starting from Segment 1 and ending at Segment 28, as laid out in the pages of this guide. Beginning at the relatively lower, Denver-end of the trail assures that the hiker will not encounter treeline until Georgia Pass in Segment 6, some 80 miles into the trek; whereas, treeline is met barely 20 miles into Segment 28 for the Durango-to-Denver bound hiker. Also, the average elevation for the eastern half of the CT is much lower than the higher western half, which is dominated by long alpine sections through the San Juan

Range, some of the loftiest mountains in the state. Through-hikers can set out from the Denver end by the first week in June, while east-bound hikers shouldn't begin from Durango until the beginning of July because of lingering snow. By early-to-mid October, winter can return to the high country, making it imperative to finish your trek well before then.

Day-hikers have more latitude to pick and choose individual segments to hike, based on seasonal snow cover. Segments 1 through 3 can have scant snow cover (or none at all) between winter storms. By early May, these low-elevation sections in the Front Range are often snow-free and showing their early wildflowers. Likewise, the first half of Segment 28 at the western end is low enough in altitude to be hiked in late spring. By early-June, significant portions of the trail at 9,000 feet in elevation and lower are mostly free of snow, including Segments 4 and 5, as well as that part of the CT traversing the lower flanks of the Sawatch Range in Segments 13 and 14. Last to be free of the icy grip of winter are the high reaches of the western half of the trail, especially Segments 20 through 28, where snow can linger well into July. Prior to that, icy slopes and cornices make travel difficult and dangerous, suitable only for those trained and equipped for winter mountaineering.

Getting To or From the CT

Both Denver and Durango are well served by air service from several national and regional carriers. Express bus and van service links travelers from Denver International Airport (DIA) with several of the resort communities close to the CT including Breckenridge, Frisco, Copper Mountain and Vail. Denver has its Regional Transportation District (RTD), an intra-urban bus and light-rail system that provides service between DIA and the rest of the metro area, including weekday service to near Waterton Canyon (the eastern terminus of the CT) on line 75X. Commercial, regularly-scheduled bus lines run between some of the towns and cities mentioned as re-supply points in this guide. However, note that schedules change frequently, sometimes eliminating stops entirely. Inquire about bus service well in advance. A few towns have shuttles that a CT hiker may use to get between the trail and town; notably, the Summit County Stage in Segments 6 and 7. Phone the various Chambers of Commerce mentioned in the **Supplies, Services and Accommodations** section of each chapter for info about local shuttle services or taxis. Those wishing for a unique way to access Segment 24 from either Durango or Silverton will find the historic Durango and Silverton Railroad to be a fascinating experience. You can book fares and check schedules at *www.durangosilvertonrailroad.com* or call 1-888-TRAIN07.

Re-Supplying on the CT

For those planning an extended trip on the CT, it will be unlikely, if not impossible to carry all the food needed for your trek from the start. Re-supply points are noted in the **Supplies, Services and Accommodations** section of each chapter. Many of these small towns will have limited supplies, often lacking the light-weight food stuffs needed for long-distance trekking. You may mail ahead supplies in your name, care of "General Delivery," to post offices listed in this guide, or you may arrange to meet someone bringing supplies to where the CT crosses a major highway or other access point. While some of the re-supply points listed have well-equipped hardware or sporting goods stores, other points are limited to small, general stores where small items like toggles or tent stakes may be difficult to find. Bring along extras of any small, unique items that are crucial parts of your kit. Also, please note that there are several long stretches of the CT in remote wilderness settings where convenient re-supply is not possible.

Equipment for the CT

The Colorado Trail traverses a wide range of lifezones from the hot, dry foothills of the Front Range to the harsh alpine tundra of the high mountains, where cold and wind can challenge anyone's gear. Effective, good-quality clothing and other gear will often determine the difference between a safe, enjoyable day in the mountains and an unpleasant, or even potentially disastrous, experience.

When preparing for a hike on the CT, always start with the *Ten Essentials* as your foundation (see page 20). Boots can be lightweight, but sturdy, for most day trips. But backpackers will usually want heavier, stiffer boots for good ankle support. For clothing, modern synthetics, like polypropylene and pile, are light, insulate well and dry quickly. But traditional wool clothing is still effective, even when damp. Avoid cotton entirely, as it loses all insulating ability when wet. Good-quality rain gear must be waterproof and breathable.

Study the recommended equipment list on page 20 for information for both day-hikers and through-hikers. With the recent emphasis on long-distance hiking, the so-called "go-lite" movement has gained enthusiastic adherents. With its long trekking distances and high-altitude hill climbs, the CT lends itself well to this phi-losophy.   The article on pages 20-21   gives innovative tips and   suggestions   for   the weight   con-scious packer.

RIGHT: *Sisters loaded up for their CT trek.*

Equipment Checklists

For Day Hikes

Day-pack:1500 to 3000 cubic inches
Insulating layer: poly tops and bottoms
Shirt or sweater: poly or wool
Pants: poly or wool
Parka shell: waterproof, windproof
Pants shell: waterproof, windproof
Hat: stocking cap or balaclava
Gloves: poly or wool
Extra socks

For Backpacking

Backpack: 3500 cubic inches or more
Pack cover: waterproof
Sleeping bag
Sleeping pad
Extra clothing
Stove and fuel
Cooking gear
Eating utensils
Food and food bags
Tent or bivy sack
Groundcloth: waterproof
Personal toiletries
Camp shoes
Headlamp

The Ten Essentials

Food
Water
Emergency shelter
Extra clothing
First aid kit
Flashlight
Map and compass
Matches/fire starter
Pocket knife
Sunglasses/sunscreen

Repair kit and sewing kit
Water filter and/or iodine tablets
Plastic trowel: for catholes
Plastic bags: for garbage
Rope or cord
Optional Gear:
Pillow
Camera gear and film
Reading material and/or journal
Fishing gear
Binoculars
Camp chair
Radio and cell/sat. phone
Walking stick/ski pole(s)

Why & How to Go Light on the CT by Andrew Skurka

"What a shame," I thought to myself, as I listened to Dana rant about the awful time he was having on the Colorado Trail, "all this amazing scenery, and an opportunity to be out here, and he is unable to appreciate any of it." Dana had started almost two weeks ago from Waterton Canyon and he was just now lumbering down from Georgia Pass, a mere 80 miles in. He told me that his knees had been bothering him since the end of Day 1, and that early on he had been forced to stop for 3 days because of too-painful-to-walk-on blisters and severe dehydration that almost put him in the hospital. And he reported that the climb up to the pass was another close call. "Nope, this is not fun at all. In fact, this pretty much stinks. The only reason I am out here now is to lose some weight." "You might want to start with your pack," I helpfully suggested from behind, while gazing at the overstuffed monstrosity he was carrying. "I think the 50-lbs of stuff in it is a big source of your problems, and that's why you are not enjoying yourself." Dana would have none of that: "This is the Colorado Trail. I need all of this." I tried to explain otherwise, but soon realized that it would be easier to convince a pack mule that "light is right" and that "lighter is better." And so, I quickened my pace and pushed on with my 10-lb pack, safely reaching Durango 16 days after the start of what I consider one of my most exhilarating and enjoyable outdoor experiences.

Lightweight backpacking is the fastest growing trend in backpacking – and for some darn good reasons. Baby boomers, families, couples, and strapping 24 year-olds with strong legs are lightening their once-heavy loads, choosing to be more comfortable, more mobile, less injury-prone, and safer; and they are making better use of their limited free time, seeing more because they can hike faster. I think that most of us enter the backcountry in order to enjoy the beauty and simplicity of the outdoors, and to get away from florescent lights, deadlines and suffocating development. Don't be like Dana and ruin the experience by carrying a motor home on your back.

I would argue that it is even more important to "go light" on the Colorado Trail than on most other hiking trails. A light pack will make the trail's numerous, multi-thousand-foot climbs and high elevations less taxing. Your pack weight will still be manageable, even after loading up on food and water before long stretches between re-supply points and water sources. Since a light pack allows you to move faster, you can more quickly get down from exposed places like Snow Mesa and the Tenmile Range when afternoon thunderstorms develop or as night approaches. Also, you are less injury prone with a light pack, and therefore less likely to become completely, or partially immobile in remote places that are difficult for you to exit or for rescue teams to access. Okay, so you have "seen the light." Now what is the best approach to start paring down pack weight?

First, **don't take stuff you don't need**. At the end of every outing, spread gear out on the floor and toss everything you didn't use (or could have done without) into a pile. Did you use the flashing mirror or the third set of clothes? Could you have done without the 500mm zoom lens?

Second, **replace heavy items with lighter and more functional ones** (then sell all the heavy stuff on eBay to someone less enlightened than you.) Start with the big items – replace your tent (with a tarp or tarp-like shelter), your overbuilt mountaineering pack (with a lightweight framed or frameless model), and your heavy sleeping bag (with a bag with high-loft insulation and a lightweight shell fabric).

Third, **use items that have multiple functions**. Your pack can be used as a sleeping pad. Your trekking poles can be used to pitch your shelter. And your soft-sided, plastic water containers make a good pillow when combined with a spare piece of clothing.

Fourth, **modify your gear to make it lighter and to work better** for you. Remove the ounces of extraneous, extra-long straps and belts from your pack. Cut out the guidebook pages you need and leave the rest at home (mail the other sections ahead if you are through-hiking).

Fifth, **refine, refine, refine**. Critically assess your gear, thinking about what you could do without, what would work better or be lighter, and what might be more appropriate for your particular style and preferences. Study the gear lists that others have put online, and seek feedback in online forums. You will continually find ways to lighten and improve your system, and your trips will become increasingly more enjoyable as you do.

That assumes that with your lighter pack you haven't made yourself unprepared for the conditions you may encounter. In fact, if you choose to "save" weight in ill-advised ways, you may find yourself colder, wetter, and more miserable – or worse – than if you'd huffed around everything-but-the-kitchen-sink. Lightweight backpacking does not mean "doing without," but rather "doing more or the same with less." It's a revolutionary change in the way we think about what we "need" in the outdoors. Dana didn't "need" that 4-season tent, full rainsuit, rugged hiking boots, and Maglite – what he needed was shelter, raingear, footwear, and an illumination device. A tarp-poncho, trail running shoes, and a 1-LED light would have been just as effective, but much lighter.

Your gear is not the only determinant in whether you are prepared. Knowledge – like how to stay warm and dry in inclement weather, to stay well nourished and hydrated, and to safely cross lingering snowfields – is the other critical component. Unlike gear, knowledge weighs nothing, and in bad situations it can supplement for equipment you do not have with you. The more time spent in the backcountry, the more you learn about lightweight travel and the less you need to comfortably enjoy yourself in the outdoors – and enjoyment is what this is all about, right? Check out these online resources for traditional, lightweight, and ultralight gear lists developed specifically with the CT in mind: *BackpackingLight.com, Backpacking.net* and *BackpackGearTest.org.*

Maps and Trail Markings Along the CT

Whether just out for the day or committed to through-hiking the entire route, every hiker on the CT should carry adequate maps and be proficient with navigating with map and compass. The maps in each segment of this guide are intended for informational purposes only. These are reproductions of Forest Service maps with the line of the CT marked in red and annotated with significant landmark locations. FS maps show highways, roads, trails, streams and rivers, towns and cities and other important features. They are useful for getting to access points for the trail and for portraying a general feel for the area; but for accurate navigation, you'll want to acquire detailed USGS topographic maps for each segment that you wish to hike. Or you can purchase the *Official Colorado Trail GPS Map Series* on CD-ROM from the Colorado Trail Foundation, based on the USGS map series and annotated with the trail and waypoints.

Over the several years that the Colorado Trail was developed, a variety of signage was used to mark the physical location of the trail from simple creosote posts to triangular, plastic markers to expensive redwood signs to reflective metal markers and even to blazes on tree trunks. All of them have one thing in common: displaying the instantly recognizable, mountain-shaped **CT-logo**. In some cases, the CT is co-linear with another developed trail, and thus shares signage with that trail. For instance, in some places, the markers and signs of the Continental Divide Trail, which is co-linear with the CT for over 100 miles, may be as conspicuous as that of the CT. In other sections, routes marked with blue diamonds may denote cross-country ski trails that may join the CT for (usually) a short distance before veering off.

Unfortunately, some signs have become the targets of souvenir hunters or vandals. Both the tread itself and the signs are susceptible to the harsh elements of nature; overgrowing vegetation, downed trees and avalanches. With many confusing intersections, indistinct or spotty trail tread in places, and the sporadic placing of trail signs, it is doubly important to carefully read the descriptions in this guidebook and to use all the navigational aids currently available to the CT hiker.

Using GPS Along the CT

A lightweight, economical GPS receiver can be an invaluable tool to navigating the Colorado Trail. A GPS receiver can be loaded with waypoints, either manually or by download from a PC. Waypoints organized sequentially form a route, like a series of invisible cairns along the trail. Since a GPS receiver always knows exactly (to within a few meters) where it is, it can easily and automatically calculate the bearing and distance to any waypoint stored in its memory. So, you might know how far is it to a campsite, which fork should you follow, or what is the bearing and distance to a reliable water source. The CT has been accurately mapped and a database of waypoints established. This guidebook lists waypoint locations for over 300 **landmark locations** along the CT; usually trail and road intersections, stream crossings or other important features along the trail. You can load these manually into your GPS unit or download the entire database by going to *www.bearcreeksurvey.com* or through purchasing the *Official Colorado Trail GPS Map Series* on CD-ROM from the Colorado Trail Foundation.

The data used to map the trail was obtained by traveling the trail while carrying professional, engineering-grade GPS equipment. Data was measured at set intervals of every five seconds as the trail was hiked. The data was post-processed and bad data was culled from the database. Whenever a feature such a trailhead, stream, intersection, etc. was encountered, the receiver was positioned at the feature and data was measured for 60-90 seconds. This results in much better accuracy than the line points themselves, since multiple GPS observations are made on one position. For the most part, we feel that most waypoints are within 6-12 feet. This provides a remarkably accurate database of the trail alignment. Note, however, that consumer-grade GPS units will not be as accurate, especially at the 5th and 6th decimal. For that reason, consider the last two decimals given here as "for informational purposes only."

The waypoint database for the CT is currently around 1,250 points. Recreational GPS units will not hold that many points, usually holding a maximum of 500. If you plan to use the full database, you will need to reload your GPS a couple of times along the way. The easiest way to do this is to re-load at libraries or Internet coffee shops along the way. Break the file into three, roughly equal parts. Create a CD with the data and your loading program and carry it, or e-mail the components to yourself before beginning your hike. You will need to carry the CD and the appropriate cable for your GPS.

The Colorado Trail waypoints are designed to match the datum of maps created by the US Geological Survey. When you first turn a GPS on, it will probably be set up in WGS84 (World Geodetic System of 1984). This has to be changed to NAD27 (North American Datum of 1927) to match our local system. Our waypoint lists are in a decimal degrees format, so that if your unit isn't already set to that, you'll have to change it. If you are reading this because you already loaded some points and didn't get satisfactory results, then delete the data you have in the GPS before proceeding. The GPS **must be set up** for the correct "Units" and "Coordinate System" before you load any waypoint data!

1. Find and select the "Setup" menu on your GPS.
2. Find and select the "Units" menu
3. Set the "Positions Format" to hddd.ddddd (decimal degrees). Magellan units may call this DEG.DDDDD.
4. Set the "Map Datum" to NAD27 CONUS (North American Datum of 1927, Continental US). Magellan units may just say AD27.
5. Load the data, either via a cable (preferred), or manually.

Remember: whenever you load data into a GPS, the data entered must match whichever format the GPS is configured for — or you may be miles off!

Water Along the CT

For the most part, drinking water is readily available along most segments of the CT, and we indicate in the text of this guide many potential water sources. On the first page of each segment, we indicate by symbol whether water sources are scarce, abundant or scattered in a typical year. However, there are some segments of the CT where careful planning of your water use is strongly advised. In these cases, reliable sources may be up to 20 miles apart, especially during drought years or in late summer when many seasonal streams have dried up.

Except for potable water from campgrounds, picnic areas and the like, all water sources should be treated as suspect. Most watersheds in Colorado see activity from beavers, and the grazing of livestock, mostly sheep and cattle, is common even at higher elevations. You should treat all drinking water for protozoa and bacterial organisms by one of the three recommended methods — boiling, filtration, or chemical disinfectant. Practice **Leave No Trace** procedures that safeguard the water supply for other users, including camping at least 100 feet from any stream, lake or spring.

Cycling on the CT

The popularity of mountain biking has grown enormously in Colorado over the last decade and it is common to encounter cyclists on certain portions of the CT. In particular, the designated cycling trails in the Pike National Forest around Segments 2 and 3, the dramatic ride over Searle and Kokomo Passes in Segment 8, the nationally-known ride along the Continental Divide in Segments 16 and 17, and the pedal through flower-filled meadows west of Molas Pass in Segment 25 are all popular with summer fat-tire enthusiasts. Cyclists wanting to experience the Colorado Trail need to be aware that not the entire trail is open to cycling. The CT passes through six, federally-designated wilderness areas that are closed to mechanical transport. In this guide we have put together **mandatory** detours to avoid these areas, as well as *recommended optional* detours that route cyclists past technically difficult sections or around sensitive and fragile alpine vegetation that could be damaged by knobby tires. A summary of the bicycle detours listed include:

♦A **mandatory** detour around the Lost Creek Wilderness Area, using a series of Forest Service roads around the southeast corner of the WA (page 70-71).

BELOW: *Engineer Mountain looms ahead of a rider in Seg. 25.*

♦A highly *recommended*, optional detour of the alpine route over the Tenmile Range, using the Tenmile Bike Path (page 92).

♦A **mandatory** bypass around the Holy Cross and Mount Massive Wilderness Areas using Forest Service roads and a section of US-24 (page 115).

♦A **mandatory** detour around the Collegiate Peaks Wilderness Area using county roads and a section of US-24 (page 131).

♦An *optional* detour around Raspberry Gulch using county roads Page 139).

♦A **mandatory** detour around the La Garita Wilderness Area using a section of CO-149 and a Forest Service road over Los Piños Pass (page 168-169).

♦A highly *recommended* detour around Coney Summit using a section of CO-149, county roads and Forest Service roads (page 194-195).

♦A **mandatory** bypass around the Weminuche Wilderness Area using US-550 and Forest Service roads (page 209).

♦An *optional* detour around the Junction Creek gorge using a Forest Service road (page 239).

While small portions of these detours do involve riding on busy highways, the majority of the miles are spent on little-used back roads and jeep trails, through country as every-bit as scenic and interesting as the route of the main CT.

With increased use of the Colorado Trail by mountain bikers, so also have conflicts between riders and other users escalated. Riders are reminded to ride ethically and responsibly, preserving the physical character of the CT (see page 63).

Horses and the CT

The Colorado Trail is open to horses and their riders for the entire 483 miles with a few restrictions in wilderness areas. The usual restrictions are controls on group size and the need for certified, weed-free feed. Check with the appropriate ranger district for specific regulations for each wilderness area.

While many riders have completed the CT without problems, others have reported some difficulties to the Colorado Trail Foundation. The CTF's trail maintenance guidelines call for the trail corridor to be cleared of vegetation 4 feet on either side of the centerline of the tread, to a height of 10 feet. This has not been achieved in some places. For the rider, ducking the head can usually solve the problem of low branches. Also, there is almost always the possibility to guide the horse around a tree to keep it from brushing it's leg. For the pack animal, the problem is a bit more serious. There still may be some cases where the CT trail corridor may be too narrow for a heavily-loaded pack animal. There are a couple of possible solutions: either remove the offending tree, or off-load the pack animal, proceed through the narrow section and reload. There is one location on the CT where off-loading is the only solution at this time. That is at the Gudy Gaskill Bridge across the South Platte River at the beginning of Segment 2. The heavy steel guardrail at the east end of the bridge will not allow a loaded pack animal to pass. The CTF will try to get that corrected in 2006. Fallen trees are a continuing maintenance problem and it is almost certain you will find some trees across the CT. A small saw could be a helpful tool to carry.

RIGHT: *Horsemen on the CT.*

In CT segments close to Denver, motorized vehicle barriers are used to remind vehicle operators that the CT is not open to motorized use. These barriers typically consist a steel pipe installed across the trail at a height of about 18 inches. Hikers and most horses easily step over them without breaking stride. However, some horses have become panicky when urged toward the pipe barrier. If you are planning horseback trip in Segments 1 and 2, it might be worthwhile to familiarize your horse with the concept of stepping over a low pipe barrier. Some horses become upset when encountering a person wearing a large backpack or even seeing a backpack sitting beside the trail. It is sometimes helpful to engage the backpacker in conversation. Explain that your horse becomes upset upon encountering unfamiliar sights in unfamiliar terrain. Ask the backpacker if he would mind stepping back off the trail a few feet while the horse passes.

Most of the streams that cross the CT have a suitable ford around the foot bridges. A few of the larger streams have sturdy wooden bridges suitable for horses. Some horses seem to panic at the sound of their steel shoes on a wooden bridge. Familiarization with these types of obstacles may reduce excitement on the trail.

The Colorado Trail has proven to be much harder on horseshoes than one would suspect. In a group of 20 horses on a weeklong ride on the CT, at least one horse required shoe repair every evening for loose or lost shoes. Repair tools were essential.

Homeland security requirements have caused the CT to be moved away from the Twin Lakes Reservoir dam (Segment 11). After crossing the bridge on CO-82, the CT curves to the south through a barbed wire maze that precludes horses. If you follow CO-82 another quarter mile east, the fence ends and it is easy to follow the road up to the south side of Twin Lakes to rejoin the CT. And Elk Creek (Segment 24) has another challenge for the horseman. In the summer of 2003, a flood severely damaged a narrow, steep section of the CT in the most spectacular canyon on the trail. Since it is in a wilderness area, the CTF has been unable to get permission to re-route the CT. It is passable, but it requires care. Be careful and good luck. The Colorado Trail on horseback is a great experience!

Safety on the CT

Along the more isolated portions of the Colorado Trail, assistance may be many hours, even days, away. Travelers should keep the following points in mind:

•*Be aware of weather and conditions:* Hypothermia, dehydration, lightening hazards on exposed ridges and altitude sickness are all potential hazards.

•*Start hiking early:* Summer afternoon thunderstorms are common in the high country. Start early and plan to be off exposed ridges before storms brew.

•*Don't travel alone:* It's safest to hike with companions; or at the very least, make sure that you leave a detailed itinerary with others.

•*Be in shape:* Get yourself in condition for your planned trip and acclimatize yourself to altitude before beginning your trek.

To activate a rescue group, contact the nearest county sheriff. See page 243 for a list of contact phone numbers for each segment. Counties and other jurisdictions may pass along the costs incurred while conducting search and rescue to the persons involved. To protect yourself and to keep search and rescue efforts at a high standard, the Colorado Trail Foundation recommends purchasing a *Colorado Outdoor Recreation Search and Rescue* (CORSAR) card, which establishes a fund to reimburse local sheriffs for costs incurred and protects the bearer against being held liable for such costs. The CORSAR card costs $3 for one year or $12 for five years, available through the CTF office. (If you already have a Colorado fishing, hunting or snowmobile, ATV, or boat registration, you are already covered in this program by a surcharge on those licenses.) Be aware that cell phones are not likely to operate in the wilderness. With recent technological advances that have greatly reduced the weight and the cost to affordable levels, consider investing in a satellite phone or an EPIRB (Emergency Position Indicating Radio Beacon) for peace of mind.

Backcountry Ethics and the CT

The Colorado Trail lies almost entirely on National Forest lands. In some areas, the trail route uses rights-of-way and easements across or adjacent to private property and patented mining claims. Negotiations for certain easements are still under way. Keep in mind that rights-of-way can be withdrawn by owners if problems associated with their use arise. Please respect any private property and no trespassing postings. Remember also that federal law protects cultural and historic sites on public lands, such as old cabins, mines and Indian sites. These historic, cultural assets are important to us all as a society, and are not meant to be scavenged for personal gain or enjoyment.

Practicing the **Leave No Trace** ethics and principles listed on pages 246-247 will ensure that our public lands remain pristine for others to enjoy. It is your responsibility to be aware of rules and regulations in force in public jurisdictions crossed by the CT. Contact the agencies listed on page 243 for more information.

Wilderness Area Regulations

Colorado has 36 designated wilderness areas, encompassing over 3 million acres. The Wilderness Act of 1964 prohibits logging, mining, permanent structures, commercial enterprises, and motorized and mechanical transport (including bicycles) in these protected areas. The CT passes through six wilderness areas, including **Lost Creek, Holy Cross, Mt. Massive, Collegiate Peaks, La Garita, and Weminuche**.

Trekkers can minimize impact on these pristine and spectacular places by adhering to the *Leave No Trace* principles outlined on page 246, and by following these general rules governing wilderness areas: 1. Camp at least 100 feet from lakes and streams. 2. Use a stove rather than building a fire. 3. Bury human waste six inches deep and 200 feet from water sources. Pack out toilet paper. 5. All dogs must be leashed (or are prohibited in some areas). 6. Pack out your trash. 7. Mountain biking is prohibited.

Each wilderness area will also have specific rules that apply to that area. Check with the appropriate Forest Service office (see pg. 243) for additional regulations that may apply.

Mt. Massive Wilderness, CT Segments 10 & 11.

ABOVE: *A rusting steam boiler and windlass lie next to an abandoned mine near Carson Saddle.*

COLORADO TRAIL HERITAGE

For thousands of years, this land was their land — the towering peaks, the expansive inter-mountain parks full of game, the cool mountain streams. The southern Rockies were home to a succession of cultures that left little impact upon the land other than the trails and paths through the mountains that defined their seasonal wanderings, some of which we still travel on today as part of the Colorado Trail.

By the 1600s, the Utes, whose people probably arrived from the Great Basin a few centuries earlier, had established themselves in the mountains of west-central Colorado. Perhaps the first tribe to acquire horses, they pursued a nomadic life following the movement of game, seeking spiritual guidance on mountain-top vision quests and engaging in sporadic warfare with other tribes — the Arapahos, the Navajos and the Comanches — who encroached on their mountain fastness.

At the time of the arrival of white settlers, two tribes of the several bands of Utes dominated the region of western Colorado — the Tabegauche and the Uncompahgre. A succession of mostly-failed treaties began that would eventually exile these bands to a small corner in the southwest part of the state and to a reservation in Utah. A treaty negotiated in 1858 restricted the Utes from entering areas where mineral had been discovered to that point — in effect, limiting the Indians to the Western Slope and southern Colorado. Soon, as miners continued to push west, conflicts erupted, resulting in the so-called Kit Carson Treaty of 1868, negotiated between a delegation of Utes, including Chief Ouray, led to Washington D. C. by the famed scout and Indian fighter. This treaty further pushed the Utes into an area corresponding to the San Juan Mountains, west of the Continental Divide. Two agencies were set up to distribute goods to the Indians; the White River Agency to the north and the Los Pinos Agency, west of Cochetopa Pass.

But blatant trespassing continued, as prospectors probed the mineral rich lands of the San Juans; and the infamous Brunot Treaty of 1873, once again facilitated by Chief Ouray and assisted by his friend Otto Mears, tried to settle the matter. The precious San Juans were ceded to the eager miners, and the Utes were settled on reservations with an attempt to change their life from a nomadic existence to that of farming. Not suited to this life and still pressured by white settlers who coveted the land north of the San Juan Mountains, pressure boiled over into the Meeker Massacre of 1878 at the White River Agency. A final treaty from an enraged white populace banished the Uncompahgre band to a new reservation in Utah and the long occupation of Colorado's mountain region by the Utes had ceased.

Chief Ouray, who had attempted to walk the fine line between two clashing cultures, never saw the heartbreaking removal of Utes from Colorado. He died while traveling to confer with other tribal leaders and is commemorated by having his name attached to a mountain peak along the Continental Divide near Marshall Pass.

The first white explorers in Colorado were Spanish, whose knowledge of the vast region north of their empire to the south was limited. In 1765, Juan Maria de Rivera explored the San Juan country on his way out to Utah, describing to his backers the favorable mineral wealth of the region. Others followed in 1776 in the persons of two friars, Fathers Dominquez and Escalante, charged with finding a route to California. Their intricate wandering throughout the Southwest, including through the present-day Durango area, had a great influence on subsequent travelers through the detailed maps that they produced. A few years later, an expeditionary force led by Juan Bautista de Anza entered the region in pursuit of raiding Comanche bands. He traveled through the San Luis Valley, noting the topography of the eastern flank of the San Juan Mountains and the Cochetopa Hills, and crossed over Poncha Pass, viewing the skyscraping Sawatch Range. Others followed, and by the early 1800s, the Spanish Trail wound a circuitous route through southwest Colorado on its way with caravans of goods from Sante Fe to California.

With the completion of the Louisiana Purchase in 1802 and the treaty of Guadalupe Hidalgo after the war with Mexico in 1848, exploration of the region shifted to American interests. Trappers and mountain men penetrated the southern Rockies, following the ancient Indian trails and using the same low passes over the Continental Divide that would later facilitate wagon roads, railways, highways and the Colorado Trail. Government sponsored expeditions set out to discover what was the character of this new land, determined by Manifest Destiny to become part of the country, and what lay beyond that seemingly impenetrable barrier, then know as the "Shining Mountains." The 1820 expedition led by Major Stephen Long crossed the plains and tentatively explored along the Rocky Mountain front, including a few days spent at present-day Waterton Canyon (the start of today's Colorado Trail) investigating the source of the South Platte River.

Soon after the conclusion of the Mexican War, Congress planned five expeditions to study proposed routes for a transcontinental railroad at different latitudes. Influential senator and strong proponent of Manifest Destiny, Thomas Hart Benton provided the financial backing on several subsequent expeditions led by his son-in-law, Captain John C. Fremont, already known for his trailblazing in California. His ill-fated fourth expedition in the winter of 1848 attempted to cross the Divide at the Cochetopa Hills and ended in disaster in the snowy mountains. Despite that setback, Benton and others pushed to find a feasible rail route through the southern Rockies. In 1852, Captain John W. Gunnison, an officer with considerable experience in exploring and surveying in the west, was dispatched to explore a mid-latitude rail route that would cross the Sangre de Cristo Mountains, pass through the San Luis Valley, cross the Continental Divide via one of the low passes in the Cochetopa Hills and continue on out to Utah and the Great Basin.

After considerable difficulty hacking a wagon road over Cochetopa Pass from a scant Indian trail, felling trees, moving large rocks and lowering wagons on ropes down the steep, western side, Gunnison's party finally emerged only to find the way blocked by an impassable gorge, the Black Canyon of the Gunnison. Convinced now that a rail route through the area was not practical, Gunnison, nevertheless, pushed on into Utah, only to be killed with several of his companions by a band of Piutes. His second-in-command, Lieutenant E. G. Beckwith continued west, completing the survey the following year. While the Gunnison Expedition met with tragedy, it was to have an important effect, providing information about the country that would influence settlement. Eventually, rails would cross the Divide at Marshall Pass, just a few miles east of Gunnison's crossing.

Following the Civil War, the government turned its attention to the rapid settlement of the West by sending out surveys to explore the country's resources and produce maps that would be useful to the miners, farmers, ranchers and town builders that were clamoring for information. The two most important of these in Colorado were the War Department-led Wheeler and civilian-based Hayden Surveys. Both surveys ranged widely over the Colorado mountains, occupying summits for triangulations stations, naming topographic features, analyzing the geology and mineral deposits, and studying the agricultural potential. Many of the prominent features encountered today by the CT hiker bear names recorded by the men of these surveys, including scores of peaks, rivers and streams, and mountain passes. Though Colorado was already well on its way to development because of the mining boom, the maps and reports completed after the end of the surveys in 1879 were valuable in guiding the wave of railroad builders, water project developers and entrepreneurs that followed.

Most of the Colorado Trail winds through the southern Rockies along the so-called "Mineral Belt", a band of territory trending from the northeast to southwest that contains the riches that attracted the early prospectors and mining men. After gold was first discovered in Colorado in 1858, boom towns sprang up overnight, and many, just as quickly, disappeared as the next big strike occurred. By the early 1870s, when big silver finds began to stabilize the mining industry in the state, more permanent towns and cities began to thrive. And though the eventual collapse of silver prices in the late 1890s mightily threatened the economy of these young settlements, many live on to this today as shells of their former rip-roaring glory, offering re-supply points to the CT hiker — places like, Breckenridge, Leadville, Creede, Lake City and Silverton. Those that didn't survive, disappeared entirely, engulfed again by nature; or left their rusting relics behind — dilapidated cabins and hulking steam boilers — for the CT hiker to explore and ponder. What was fortuitous for the eventual creation of the Colorado Trail was the network of foot paths, wagon roads, and rail lines built through the mountains as lifelines linking the remote communities together.

One of the most successful of the road builders was Otto Mears, a Russian emigrant, who after drifting into the San Luis Valley after the Civil War, decided to go into road building on the advice of territorial governor William Gilpin. Mears' initial venture, over Poncha Pass, was the first toll road in southwestern Colorado and launched the career of the "Pathfinder of the San Juan." Mears built roads over Cochetopa Pass and to Ouray, and as well, went on to construct railroads throughout the San Juan Mountains.

Railroads quickly became the key to development of the mining towns and cities, and entrepreneurs vied in grand schemes to be the first to penetrate the mountain barriers and reach the new diggings. The competition was fierce in the early 1880s between two narrow-gauge lines, John Evans' Denver South Park & Pacific and General William J. Palmer's Denver Rio Grande & Western, to tap into the quickly growing Gunnison and San Juan mining districts. Today's CT hiker follows the original path of the DSP&P as it once chugged into Waterton Canyon, then catches up with it again at the crossing of Kenosha Pass. Finally, you'll encounter the old roadbed left behind at Chalk Creek, where the line once snaked up the valley to bore under the Divide at the famous Alpine Tunnel. Likewise, the old roadbed of the D&RGW is crossed by the CT hiker at Tennessee and Marshall Passes. While these lines are long gone, a remnant of the D&RGW, re-christened as the Durango and Silverton Railroad, still crosses the CT daily in the scenic Animas Canyon as a tourist train. The Colorado Midland Railroad was another, short-lived line whose remains the CT visits near Mount Massive, where the Hagerman Tunnel once carried the rails under the Continental Divide at 11,500 feet. With the waning of mining in the first half of the 20th Century as a dominant industry in the state, the rails were torn up and a colorful time in the state's history vanished forever.

The abandoned railbeds and old wagon roads often have become roads and highways for autos, many times serving as the CT access routes listed in this guide. Beginning in the 1930s, with workers from the Civilian Conservation Corps and other Depression-era programs, a wave of trail building began that lasted into the 1950s; and, which was to provide ready-made tread for many miles of the CT. These trails were primarily constructed for fire management, often following parallel to a mountain range over a great distance with many side trails. The Main Range Trail, co-linear for large sections of the CT on the eastern slope of the Sawatch Range, is an example. Other trails and paths were built to facilitate fish stocking operations of high country lakes and streams. With the spectacular growth of interest in backpacking, hiking and other recreational pursuits, starting in the 1960s, these forgotten Indian trails, wagon roads, logging tracks, abandoned railbeds, and fire trails became the new highways for taking people on foot, horseback or mountain bike into Colorado's spectacular backcountry. Linked with miles of new tread built by thousands of dedicated volunteers, the Colorado Trail has become part of this rich heritage.

The facing page offers a sampling of **historical highlights** that are found along each of the five sections of the Colorado Trail delineated in this guide.

Kassler to Kenosha Pass (Seg. 1-5)

In its first few miles in Waterton Canyon, the CT follows the roadbed for the **Denver South Park & Pacific Railroad**, an early narrow-gauge line built by former territorial governor John Evans, barely a year after statehood in 1877. Just downstream of the Gudy Gaskill Bridge sits the shuttered South Platte Hotel, once a busy stopover for travelers on the line to the mines of Leadville and Gunnison. The DSP&P is encountered again at Kenosha Pass, where an interpretative display notes the switch-yard and maintenance shops once built in the meadows atop the pass. The DSP&P lost its famous race to reach Gunnison to the D&RGW, only achieving its loftier goal of reaching the Pacific when it was sold in foreclosure to the UP. The tracks over the pass were torn up in the 1930s.

Kenosha Pass to Halfmoon Creek (Seg. 6-10)

In 1942, a new city sprang up practically overnight in the mountain wilderness of Colorado. **Camp Hale**, needed to provide winter and mountain warfare training during World War II, was established in the East Fork Valley because of the natural setting of a large, flat valley, surrounded by steep hill-sides suitable for training in skiing, rock climbing, and cold weather survival skills.The famed 10th Mountain Division trained here. A little-known fact is that from 1959 to 1965, the site was used by the CIA to secretly train Tibetan rebels. Though there's little to see today for the CT hiker (the camp was deactivated in 1965), its legacy lives on at the commemorative plaque atop Tennessee Pass, the training site-turned-ski area Ski Cooper, and even in the nearby 10th Mountain Division Hut System.

Halfmoon Creek to Marshall Pass (Seg. 11-15)

Three distinct peaks frame the view on route to Marshall Pass — Mount Ouray (13,971), named for **Chief Ouray**; Chipeta Mountain, named after Ouray's wife; and Pahlone Peak, named for their son. Depending on your point of view, this great chief of the indigenous Utes is either a hero or a sell-out. From this point west, the CT largely travels through the Ute's ancestral lands and the story of these mountain Indians and Chief Ouray is one of loss of land and relocation, as whites ignored treaties and encroached into Ute territory. Ouray followed a path along the middle ground, trying to mediate conflicts and, in the end, mostly ceding to white demands. Today, he is considered one of Colorado's "pioneers" with a portrait hung in the State Capitol and with the lofty peak that bears his name.

Marshall Pass to San Luis Pass (Seg. 16-20)

Winding along that long section of the Divide know as the **Cochetopa Hills**, the CT crosses sever-al historic passes. These low points on the continent's backbone were used for centuries by Indians, as well as animals - "Cochetopa" means buffalo, presumably because the beasts migrated to and from the San Luis Valley through here. Whites also were attracted to these easy crossings, some-times with bad results. Explorer John C. Fremont's expedition to cross the Divide here in the winter of 1848 led to disaster, with rumors of cannibalism — not the last time that charge was heard in these mountains. In 1874, a party of miners disappeared into nearly the same area and months later, only Alferd G. Packer emerged. Packer was later convicted of murdering and dining on his companions.

San Luis Pass to Junction Creek (Seg. 21-28)

You'll hear it long before you reach the bottom of Elk Creek and the Animas River Canyon in Segment 24 — the long, mournful whistle of the **Durango and Silverton train**. Completed in 1881, only nine months after construction began out of Durango, the then-known Denver and Rio Grande Railroad carried passengers and freight to the booming, but isolated silver mines at Silverton. Through the years, slides, floods, snow, war and financial instability threatened the line, only to have it be saved by tourism. This historic train has been in continuous operation for over 124 years, car-rying passengers behind vintage steam locomotives and rolling stock indigenous to the line.

NATURAL HISTORY OF THE COLORADO TRAIL

by Hugo A. Ferchau
Past Thornton Professor of Botany, Western State College

This brief look at Rocky Mountain ecology is intended for those who wish to enjoy the Colorado Trail country but have previously had no contact with it, as well as for locals who have only rarely ventured into its vastness. Veterans of these wilds could probably write an equally good account of the inhabitants of the open spaces. Regardless, there is no question that the natural history of this region is the prize, the reward for the effort made in hiking the trail. This opportunity to observe the Rocky Mountain ecosystem also underscores the need to walk, not run, while making one's daily tour on the trail. In ten years of leading groups of students through the Rockies, it has been my experience that hikers who reach camp two hours before the rest can rarely relate any interesting observations. They might as well have worked out in a gym. To get the most out of your sojourn on the Colorado Trail, take the time to look, to sit, to let nature present itself to you, and to soak up all that it has to offer — you may pass this way but once.

Observing Wildlife

For some reason, we commonly use the term "wildlife" to refer only to animals. Plants, evidently, are considered to be somewhat trapped or tamed, or at least subdued. There is less drama associated with plants because we can prepare for our encounters with them, whereas animals tend to take us by surprise — they are there all of a sudden, and gone all of a sudden. As a botanist, I must recognize that most people would rather talk about a bear than about the bearberry.

The native fauna of the Rockies may readily be viewed from the Colorado Trail. At this point, I should make a digression concerning the domestic dog. Some hikers feel the hiking experience is not complete without their dog. To be sure, when a backpacker is on the trail alone, companionship is pleasant. When hiking in a group, however, a dog can be a nuisance. If you are interested in being a part of the surrounding ecosystem, your dog (which is not a part of that ecosystem) should be left at home.

But back to the question of those birds, bees, and the larger and more impressive animals you may encounter. Having been over most of the Colorado Trail, I cannot think of a single day's hike which did not reveal much of the Rocky Mountain fauna. By the same token, I have seen students hide for days without seeing a single animal. This apparent contradiction can be explained by the fact that native animals are not in a zoo. They have learned behavior and instincts which assure them of

FACING PAGE: *Rosy Paintbrush and Alpine Avens in an alpine meadow (Segment 25).*

avoiding threatening outsiders, such as hikers. You must meet the animals on their own terms. Several general rules may be followed. Dawn and dusk are when animals tend to be most active. Animals require water regularly. Many animals will learn to ignore you if you are part of the scenery, which means being relatively quiet and still. Do not try to see all of the fauna in a single sitting. Obtain some of the local texts and become familiar with the behavior of the animal or group of animals you wish to observe, and make a conscious effort to make the observations. You will probably have the most success with birds. Also, do not discount what might be considered the less dramatic animals, such as the small nocturnal rodents. A log to sit on at night and a flashlight will often allow you some captivating moments. Rising early in the morning and getting on the trail ahead of the group can also increase your chances of seeing wildlife. Early season hikers should note that fawning of deer and calving of elk occur in June. Try to avoid being disruptive if traveling during this time of year.

Some hikers may be fearful of encountering wildlife, but there is little need for worry. After taking students into the Rockies for more than ten years, we have never been attacked by anything. I have seen mountain lion and bear at reasonable distances, and I am sure they have observed me from distances which, were they known, would have excited me. I have seen bear droppings on the trail on a cold morning that were so fresh the steam was still rising off them. My wife woke up from a nap one afternoon, and there were fresh bear claw marks on a tree over her head. Good judgment will discourage you from being molested. An animal seeks food, not your company. If you have no food in your presence, you will generally not be bothered. If you choose to keep food, even nuts or a candy bar, in your tent, you may wake up at night to find a hole cut in the floor and confront the steely eyes of a mouse or pack rat. After arriving in camp, place your food away from the sleeping area—75 to 100 yards is a good distance.

LEFT: *Meadow napping in Segment 25.*

Plant Communities

The highly variable topography of the central Rocky Mountains provides for a kaleidoscopic variety of vegetation. The accompanying diagrams give some indications of the vegetation types encountered on the Colorado Trail, as well as their relationships to each other. Note that the zones are not defined by elevation alone, but depend also on local climatic factors. In the field, of course, matters can be even more complicated. In areas that have been disturbed, for example, as by fire or logging, different types of vegetation will exist in different relationships. Diagram 1 (page 38) shows the relationships between various plant communities in a "climax" situation, that is, in an ecologically stable, undisturbed environment. When the land has been disturbed, the plants proceed through a "succession" phase before eventually evolving back into a climax state. Diagram 2 (page 39) shows the relationships between various types of vegetation during succession. Because of the severe climate and short growing season in the Rockies, successional vegetation patterns may persist for more than a hundred years. In addition, a single hillside may be covered with successional vegetation in one place and climax vegetation in another.

Riparian Vegetation: This is the vegetation found along streambanks, and it plays a variety of important roles, such as controlling erosion and providing cover and feed for wildlife. On the western slope, lower elevation streambanks are dominated by assorted cottonwood trees, alder, maple and red-osier dogwood. With increasing elevation the cottonwoods become less evident, while the shrubs persist, eventually being dominated by willows. On the eastern slope, the cottonwoods are not as evident but, as on the western slope, a mixture of shrubs prevails, becoming increasingly dominated by willows at higher elevations.

Despite what appears to be very aggressive growth by riparian species, they are among the most sensitive to human activity. And because of their proximity to water, they are typically among the most threatened and endangered.

Sagebrush: The sagebrush, the cold desert scrubland of the Rockies, can be found from low to surprisingly high elevations. It is interspersed with grasses, and is the primary grazing land of central and western Colorado. It is also quite dry, with little water available for hikers; ranchers typically maintain water supplies in stock tanks for their cattle, but those supplies are definitely not recommended for humans. During the day, this environment can become quite hot, while at night even summertime temperatures can drop to near freezing. During June, watch out for ticks.

Scrub Oak and Piñon-Juniper Woodland: This dryland plant community is most evident along the Colorado Trail where it climbs through the foothills above Denver. It will also be seen occasionally at higher elevations, on the driest and most stressed sites, until near Kenosha Pass. Junipers tend to be widely spaced, with grasses interspersed in between, while the scrub oak tends to be clumped together so closely as to be almost impenetrable. This sort of vegetation makes for good game habitat, and hikers should be prepared for deer to pop up most anywhere, particularly in early June. In late summer, the scrub oak/piñon-juniper woodland is prone to wildfire, which can move rapidly through the dry terrain. Such fires are often started by lightning strikes, and occasionally by hikers, who are reminded to pay attention to their campfires.

Ponderosa Pine: This is the lowest elevation timber tree. Because of its good lumber quality and proximity to civilization, it has been the most extensively cut. Thus you may see large, old ponderosa stumps among woodland vegetation, indicating a logged ponderosa forest where the tall pines have not yet returned. These long needled pines tend to grow well spaced, with grasses flourishing between trees. As a result, ranchers like to graze their stock among the ponderosa, particularly in early spring. On the eastern slope, ponderosa pine is found on less stressed south facing hillsides. On the western slope, it is the tree one encounters above the open, arid countryside of the sagebrush community.

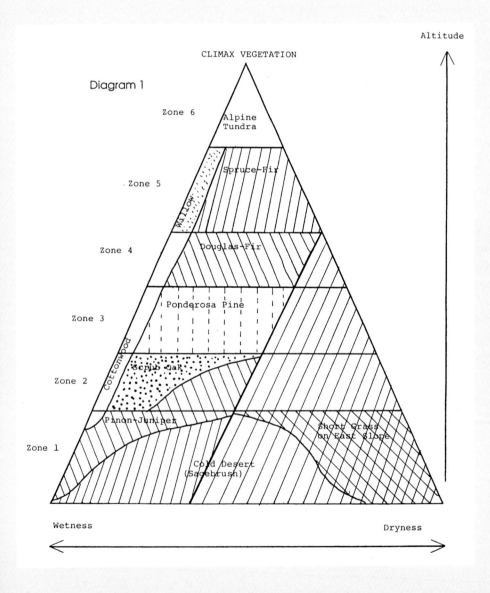

Douglas Fir: This predominant tree is not to be confused with the giant firs of the Pacific Northwest, though it is related to them. Here in the Rockies, we have the runts of the litter. The Douglas fir occupies moist, cool sites. On the eastern slope it is found on the slopes opposite the ponderosa pine, and on the western slope it grows above the level of the ponderosa. In either case, as a result of the moister environment and shorter growing season, Douglas fir trees tend to grow closer together, with little ground cover underneath. Much of both the eastern and western slopes is Douglas fir habitat, but because it is also the type most likely to be burned, much of that habitat is occupied by successional vegetation. Hikers, again, should remember to be careful with fire.

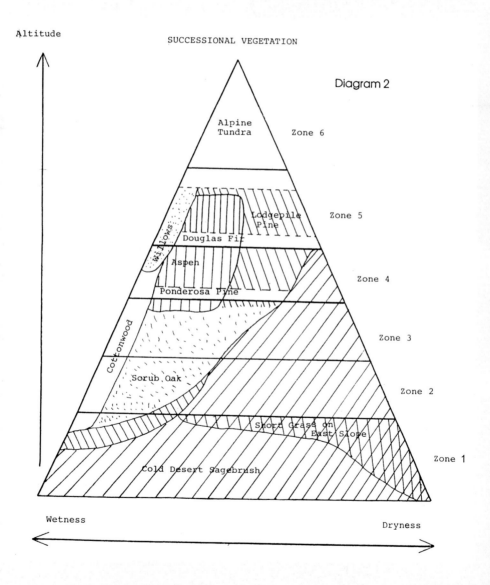

ABOVE: *Gaines Gulch (Seg. 28).*

Spruce-Fir Forest: This, the highest elevation forest, is composed of Engelmann spruce and subalpine fir. Because of the late snowmelt, moist summertime conditions and early snowfall, this vegetation type has been least altered by fire. Many of the spruce-fir forest in the Rockies are as much as 400 years old. These dense forests tend to contain many fallen logs, which can be a real deterrent to hiking. The logs are typically moist, and hikers walking over them may be surprised when the bark slips off and they lose their footing. Ground cover may be lacking, and a thick humus layer may be present.

As one approaches timberline, the spruce-fir stands tend to be more open. The trees are clustered, with grasses and beautiful wildflowers interspersed between them. These tree clusters provide refuges for elk during the night. At the timberline itself, the trees are bushlike, weatherbeaten and windshorn. They often grow in very dense clumps which can provide an ideal refuge for hikers. Winds of 50 mph can whistle by virtually unnoticed while you sit in a clump of timberline trees. Animals are aware of this, too, and thus, while waiting out a storm, you may have the pleasure of observing a great deal of small mammal activity.

Lodgepole Pine and Aspen: These are ordinarily successional species which can occupy a given site for up to 200 years. The lodgepole pine often succeeds disturbed Douglas fir and spruce-fir communities and grows on the driest sites. Its seeds are opened by fire, and a wildfire will cause the deposition of thousands of seeds— and, a few years later, the appearance of many dense stands of seedlings and saplings. These pine stands are often referred to as "horsehair." There is virtually no ground cover in the deep shade beneath the saplings, and competition is fierce between the closely spaced trees. The dryness of the site encourages repeated fires.

The aspen occupies moister sites. A clump of aspen among lodgepole pines suggests a potential source of water. Aspen reproduce from root suckers, and any ground disturbance, such as a fire, causes a multitude of saplings to appear. On drier sites, aspen is typically interspersed with Thurber fescue, a large bunchgrass. In moderately moist sites the ground cover will consist of a multitude of grasses, forbs and shrubs. Wet site aspen often has a ground cover dominated by bracken fern. Aspen

RIGHT: *A butterfly feeds off an Alpine Sunflower in the Trail Creek Valley.*

groves can be attractive for camping, but during June and July may be infested with troublesome insects.

Alpine Tundra: Though it strikes many people as odd, the tundra can be likened to a desert because it enjoys only minimal precipitation. During the winter, fierce winds prevent snow from accumulating anywhere except in depressions. During the summer, the snowmelt drains quickly off the steeper slopes, leaving the vegetation there to depend for survival on regular afternoon showers. Despite the harsh conditions, the alpine tundra is quite diverse, and includes such different environments as meadows, boulder fields, fell fields, talus and both temporary and per-manent ponds. The cushion-like meadows are a favorite site for elk herds. The boulder fields provide homes for pikas, marmots and other animals, and the protected spaces between the boulders can produce some of the most beautiful wildflowers. The fell fields are windswept sites from which virtually all mineral soil has been blown away, leaving behind a "pavement" which, despite its austerity, may have some interesting plants. The talus fields consist of loose rock; they also host some interesting plants and animals. The ponds often teem with invertebrates and can provide good sites for observing the fascinating bird known as the ptarmigan.

LEFT: *Yellow-bellied Marmot*

Wildflowers Along the Colorado Trail

Who can resist the elegant grace of Colorado's state flower, the **Blue Columbine**, or not be moved by nature's showy display blanketing the slopes astride the CT in mid-summer? There are hundreds of species of flowering plants of *conspicuous varieties* (actually thousands, including inconspicuous plants such as grasses and sedges) along the path of the Colorado Trail, as it winds its way through all five of the major *lifezones* identified in Colorado. Lifezones are delineated by elevation and are defined by their unique ecosystems and plant communities. Beginning on the margin of the high plains at 5,800 feet at Kassler (Seg. 1), the Colorado Trail climbs to a lofty 13,270 feet on the flanks of Coney Summit (Seg. 22). In the process, it ascends through the Plains (3,500-6,000 feet), Foothills (6,000-8,000 feet), Montane (8,000-10,000 feet), Subalpine

ABOVE: *Near Lime Creek (Seg. 25).*

(10,000-11,500 feet) and Alpine (11,500-14,400 feet) zones. An alert hiker will notice this progression of plant communities along the way, which is driven by changes in climate, soil chemistry, seasonal snow accumulation and other factors.

As the season unfolds, the colorful pageantry climbs up the slopes, along with the CT hiker. A Durango-bound, through-hiker starting among late-May, blooming cactus and bright, spring-green slopes in Waterton Canyon will reach Georgia Pass in a few weeks, treeline still blanketed deep in snow. By the time he climbs atop Indian Trail Ridge near the end of his trek in mid-July, his stroll through the tundra will be carpeted with an incredibly colorful display of alpine flowers.

The list on the facing page offers a sampling of some of the more common wildflowers that are prevalent in each of the five sections of the Colorado Trail delineated in this guide. In general, each major section of the trail has characteristics that dictate the types of flowering plants that a hiker may encounter; including altitude, soil types, accumulation of moisture, etc. However, most of these plants are not unique to any one portion of the CT and can be expected to be found in any suitable habitat along the trail. (For instance, **Indian Paintbrush** is a common plant whose colorful

bracts nearly any hiker can identify since its many species and subspecies exists throughout the state in a variety of habitats.) For each plant listed, you will find one of its common names, along with its scientific name (*genus species*). A plant can have several different common names, often varying by region, and the existence of a myriad of subspecies can frustrate precise identification for the amateur. You'll need to get a good hand lens for close examination of biological features and any of the excellent flower guides available for Colorado plants. *Rocky Mountain Flora* by James Ells (Colorado Mountain Club Press) is an excellent field guide with over 1,200 color photos of plants likely to be found along the CT.

Kassler to Kenosha Pass (Seg. 1-5)

Most of this section is at lower elevations. Plants from the *Plains zone* merge in Platte Canyon with *Foothills zone* residents. Blooms begin as early as late April and extend well into June. Look for **Prickly Pear Cactus** (*Opuntia macrorhiza*), Yucca *(Yucca glauca)*, tiny Filaree *(Erodium caepitosa)* and showy Prickly Poppy *(Argemone polyanthemos)*. The dry, gravelly soils beyond the canyon support Sand Lily *(Leucocrinum montanum)*, while you may find Pasqueflower *(Anemone patens)* in damp ravines. Close to Kenosha Pass, Wild Iris *(Iris missouriensis)* bursts forth in the meadows of South Park.

Kenosha Pass to Halfmoon Creek (Seg. 6-10)

Most through-hikers will cross the high passes of the Continental Divide and Tenmile Range too soon for most flowers to appear. However, look for sweet-smelling Alpine Forget-me-not (*Eritrichium elongatum*) and for Alpine Springbeauty *(Claytonia megarhiza)* in fellfields and rock crevices. As the snow melts along the trail, Snow Buttercup *(Ranunculus adoneus)* and **Globeflower** *(Trollius albiflorus)* spring out of retreating snowbanks. Once in the shadow of Mount Massive, Alpine Wallflower *(Erysimum capitatum)* and Rydberg Penstemon *(Penstemon rydbergii)* are common.

Halfmoon Creek to Marshall Pass (Seg. 11-15)

For this section, the CT runs largely through thick *Montane* forests; alternating between that of rather barren lodgepole stands and some lovely aspen forests. In aspen glens and forest clearings, tall Heart Leaved Arnica (*Arnica cordifolia*), Larkspur *(Delphinium nuttallianum)*, Red Columbine *(Aquilegia elegantula)* and **Monkshood** *(Aconitum columbianum)* rise above undergrowth. Sharing sunny benches above the reservoirs with ubiquitous sage are Shrubby Cinquefoil *(Pentaphylloides floribunda)* and Rabbitbrush *(Chyysothamnus nauseosus)*. The latter is a late bloomer and harbinger of fall.

Marshall Pass to San Luis Pass (Seg. 16-20)

For the CT hiker on this high, lonely section along the Divide, the mid-summer wildflowers are your cheerful companion. Grasses and sedges dominate the sweeping ridgetop panoramas, punctuated by **Alpine Sunflower** *(Rydbergia grandiflora)*, with huge heads all turned to the rising sun, and the more understated American Bistort *(Bistorta bistortoides)*. Further west, the Divide rises to true alpine tundra near San Luis Peak and the slopes are carpeted with dwarf plants like Alpine Avens *(Acomastylis rossii turbinata)*, Alpine Phlox *(Phlox condensata)* and Moss Campion *(Silene acaulis subacaulescens)*.

San Luis Pass to Junction Creek (Seg. 21-28)

For the through-hiker, the best is saved for last! West of Molas Pass, the CT enters a verdant landscape of rolling mountains, rising above lush *Subalpine* meadows and culminating by mid-July in spectacular displays on Indian Trail Ridge. Blue Columbine *(Aquilegia coerulea)*, **Wild Geranium** *(Geranium caespitosum)*, and Silky Phacelia *(Phaecelia sericea)* nod in the breeze. Along the rushing streams, Monkeyflower *(Mimulus guttatus)*, Parry Primrose *(Primula parryi)* and Kingscrown *(Rhodiola integrifolia)* dip roots in cold melt water.

GEOLOGY ALONG THE COLORADO TRAIL

by Denise R. Mutschler and David L. Gaskill

To venture along the Colorado Trail is to catch a glimpse of Colorado's history, a great deal of which is linked to the extraction of mineral wealth. For more than a hundred years Colorado towns have prospered and declined according to the fortunes of the mining industry. A far earlier history, however, is that of the land through which the trail passes. Much of the natural beauty of Colorado can be attributed to the geologic forces that have shaped the varied landscapes of this Rocky Mountain state.

In eastern Colorado lies the westernmost edge of the Great Plains, a rolling landscape that abruptly gives way to mountains at an altitude of about 5000 feet. Underlying the plains are interlayered beds of a variety of rocks: shale, sandstone, conglomerate, limestone, coal, and volcanic ash. These beds vary in age from the geologically recent to as much as 570 million years old. In the Denver Basin (see Figure 1) this 13,000-foot-thick sequence of sediments lies above a still older Precambrian basement consisting of crystalline granitic and metamorphic rocks. Geologists learn much about the earth by "reading" the rocks, and they postulate a history here that dates back 1.8 billion years.

Some of the sedimentary rocks are visible along the Front Range, where they have been bent, broken, and brought to the surface by the forces that pushed the mountains upward. Most notable are the Fountain Sandstone flatirons, which make up the Red Rocks amphitheater and other points of interest, and the hogbacks of the Dakota and Morrison formations seen from Interstate 70. This dramatic meeting of plains and mountains provides a fine setting for the Colorado Trail as it begins its winding course through the ranges and valleys of western Colorado.

At the start, the trail moves westward across the Front Range, the core of which is made of basement rocks that have been uplifted again and again during the past 330 million years. In many places the older rocks — schists, gneisses, quartzites, marbles, and metamorphosed volcanics — have been intruded by younger granitic bodies, such as the Pikes Peak batholith.

West of the Front Range, the Colorado Trail passes to the north of South Park, a wide basin underlain by sedimentary rocks like those of the plains. These rocks were intruded by mineralized stocks of granodiorite porphyry during a mountain-building period known as the Laramide Orogeny, which occurred 40 to 70 million years ago.

The trail continues through part of the Breckenridge mining district, a region famous for its gold. The largest gold nugget ever discovered in Colorado was found here and can be seen today at Denver's Museum of Natural History. The mining of

FACING PAGE: *Eroded formations of metamorphosed volcanics near Snow Mesa (Segment 21.)*

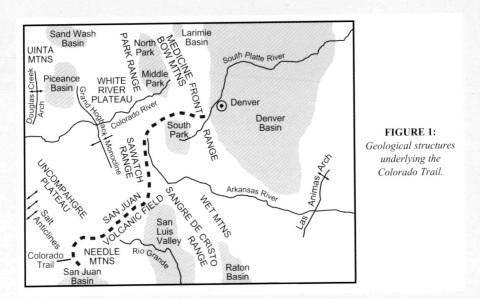

FIGURE 1:
*Geological structures
underlying the
Colorado Trail.*

gold and silver was Colorado's principal industry in the late 1800s, when placer gold in streambeds lured eager prospectors into the mountains in search of source veins and lodes. Today we recognize far more diversity in the state's mineral wealth: limestone, sand, gravel, building stone, lead, molybdenum, zinc, coal, oil (including oil shale), and natural gas. One more commodity ought to be acknowledged—snow! Obviously, the winter sports industry depends on this annual accumulation in the mountains; less obvious, perhaps, but incredibly important, is the fact that each year as the snowpack melts, water is stored in forest soils, alluvium, and porous rocks, ready to supply the needs of every living thing.

The trail goes up and over the Tenmile Range, a block of uplifted, ancient metamorphic rocks. Beyond Copper Mountain it passes through an area of layered rocks that have been intruded by quartz monzonite and granodiorite porphyry dikes and sills. It crosses a 20-million-year-old rhyolite near Camp Hale and goes on to Tennessee Pass and the gold-bearing strata of the Cambrian, Devonian, Mississippian, and Pennsylvanian periods.

South of the pass, ancient gneisses and schists (1.7 billion years old) are cut by silver-producing veins of the St. Kevin-Sugar Loaf mining district. Early Indians once extracted turquoise from deposits in this area. The trail skirts Turquoise Reservoir on a 1.4-billion-year-old granite batholith and crosses moraines left behind by now-extinct Sawatch glaciers. At one time glaciers dammed the Arkansas River, forcing it to carve out a new channel on the east side of the valley.

The upper Arkansas Valley, part of the long, north-south Rio Grande rift, is bounded by a steplike series of parallel faults on the east and by the Sawatch fault zone on the west, along which many hot springs are located. One of these springs is at Mount Princeton, where the trail passes the Chalk Cliffs, a hydrothermally altered part of a 30-million-year-old quartz monzonite batholith. Farther south, near the summit of Mount Antero, aquamarine (beryl), topaz, garnet, and other rare minerals are found. Topaz and garnet are also found in the valley near the town of Nathrop.

Southwest of Marshall Pass is the San Juan Volcanic Field, a point of considerable geologic interest. Between 35 and 22 million years ago, this area was the scene of violent eruptions from many enormous craters. These craters, or calderas, are the present-day sites of such gold and silver mining camps as Creede, Silverton, and Lake City. Layers of volcanic rock from both passive and explosive eruptions cover the area to a depth of thou-

ABOVE: *Conglomerate boulder, La Plata Mountains.*

sands of feet. Younger volcanic rocks, about 3.5 million years old, are also present.

Along the north flank of the Needle Mountains uplift, the trail passes through spectacular Precambrian terrain in the Grenadier Range. This includes upthrust beds of quartzite, slate, and phyllite. An erosional nonconformity between 1.4-billion-year-old Precambrian rocks and an overlying layer of quartzite represents a gap in time of about 600 million years.

Beyond Molas Lake the trail works upward through successively younger sedimentary rock layers. Some of these are different from the rock units found in eastern Colorado. Others, such as the Dakota, Morrison, Entrada, and Leadville formations, are equivalent to formations found elsewhere. The Mancos Shale of western Colorado, for instance, was deposited in the same sea as the Pierre Shale of eastern Colorado, but the western rocks are older than the eastern ones. This is because the ancient sea gradually migrated eastward, altering both the time and place of deposition.

The ridge south of Grizzly Peak consists of clays and marlstones of the Morrison Formation (well known as a source of dinosaur bones) and also of the ancient beach and lagoon deposits that comprise the Dakota Sandstone. These are intruded by igneous rocks in the form of dikes, sills, and laccoliths. From this divide, the trail affords splendid views of the area's mountain ranges: the San Miguel, the San Juan, the La Plata, and the Needles.

Heading southward to the La Plata Mountains, the trail crosses red shales, siltstones, mudstones, grits, and conglomerates. The La Plata Range consists of sedimentary rocks that were domed up during the Laramide Orogeny by the intrusions of sills, laccolith, and stocks. The dome was subsequently dissected by erosional forces and is the location of a mining district that has produced gold and silver-bearing telluride, ruby silver, copper, and lead ores since 1873.

The trail continues to wend its way southward to Junction Creek and descends by way of successive younger strata to arrive at the trail's southern terminus — Junction Creek Trailhead outside of Durango.

Segment 1
Kassler to
South Platte Canyon

BELOW: *South Platte Canyon.*

Distance: 16.8 miles
Elevation Gain: approx 2160 ft

USFS Maps: Pike National Forest, see pages 52-53.

USGS Quad Maps: Kassler, Platte Canyon.

Trails Illustrated map: # 135.

Jurisdiction: South Platte Ranger District, Pike NF.

Access from Denver: 🚗

Access from Durango: 🚗

Availability of Water: ☕

Bicycling: 🚲

Gudy's Tip

"*A broken toggle or cotter pin may be difficult to replace along the trail, as sporting goods stores are far apart. Make sure your backpack is in excellent condition before setting off.*" If you are a through-hiker, you need to make sure your gear is in top shape. Although in this guide we do point out towns along the way for re-supply, they are few and far between. Carry spares of small, critical items.

About This Segment

This first segment of the Colorado Trail begins at the Waterton Canyon Trailhead next to the South Platte River. This is a very popular day use area and, undoubtedly, the busiest segment of the entire Colorado Trail. The trail follows gravel roads for the first 7 miles. These roads, used by the Denver Water Board to access Strontia Springs Dam, have some use restrictions. Dogs are not allowed and the roads are closed from ? hour after sunset until ? hour before sunrise. Camping is not permitted along the first 7 miles. The road is only open to official motorized vehicles, which keeps the traffic count pretty low. In the first 6 miles, the road only gains about 40 feet per mile, which allows for a very pleasant walk, hike, jog or bicycle ride; and lots of people take advantage of it every day. After the first 7 miles, the trail gets a lot more vigorous; the domain of determined backpackers, expert mountain bikers and masochistic trail runners.

Camping is NOT permitted in sight of the river along the first 7 miles of Segment 1. Also, dogs are not permitted on the Denver Water Board Road.

The only good campsites on this segment are around Bear Creek, which normally has water available. The camping problem is further exacerbated by the prohibition of overnight camping within 0.25 mile of either side of the South Platte River. The irony of this is that there are lots of good sites along the river, with plenty of good water and even a Forest Service-provided toilet, but overnight use is prohibited and rigorously enforced within sight of the road. One solution is to use one of the few poor campsites available above the river, featuring an uncomfortable night's sleep on a 10-degree slope.

For those wishing to share the trail with their canine companion, the best solution is to arrange to have someone deliver your dog to you at the beginning of Segment 2. Another possibility, for hard-core dog lovers, is to start your hike with your dog at the Indian Creek Campground, located beside CO-67 at about 10 miles southwest of Sedalia. Follow the Indian Creek Equestrian Trail until it intersects with the CT at Bear Creek (mile 8.8). From there on, dogs are permitted on the trail. See Trails Illustrated Map # 135 for details. (Note than the Colorado Trail Foundation does not monitor the condition of the Indian Creek Equestrian Trail.)

Trailhead/Access Points

Kassler-Waterton Canyon Trailhead : Take I-25 south out of Denver to CO-470. Turn west on CO-470 for 12.5 miles to CO-121 (Wadsworth Blvd.). Go south (left) on CO-121 for 4.5 miles, then turn left onto a road marked as Waterton Canyon. Continue 0.3 miles to the large trailhead parking area on the left. If this parking area is full, there is another parking area located 0.25 mile north up the Waterton Canyon Road, connected to the lower parking lot by a trail.
Douglas CO RD-97 : See Segment 2.

Supplies, Services and Accommodations

Denver and its southern suburbs have the full array of services expected in a metropolitan area.

Trail Description

Begin your trip at the parking area at **mile 0.0** (5,520) **Ⓐ**. There are picnic tables, outdoor toilets, and several interpretive displays. Cross the road from the parking area and follow the route through another parking area that is closed to the public. At **mile 0.4**, a road forks off to the left. Ignore this choice and stay on the main road. Another intersection is encountered at **mile 0.9** **Ⓑ**. Continue ahead into the canyon. Pass some houses at **mile 3.2** (5,630) **Ⓒ** and stay on the main road to **mile 6.4 Ⓓ**. Here, at a fork in the road (5,800), you can see the Strontia Springs Dam to your right.

Continue ahead to **mile 6.6** and encounter another intersecting fork with a Forest Service sign (5,840). Keep bearing to the right to a well-identified intersection at **mile 6.8** and leave the main road on a jeep trail to the left. Continue ahead to **mile**

Waterton Canyon

A favorite with Denver-area day-hikers, bike riders, fisherman, birders and others, Waterton Canyon can be a sometimes unpleasant, crowd-filled beginning to a 482-mile trek through the heart of the Colorado Rockies. The CT follows a service road of the Denver Water Board for the first 6.5 miles; itself once the road bed of the Denver, South Park, and Pacific Railroad, built in 1877.

But water is the driving force that has influenced the development of the canyon. Explorer Major Stephen Long camped here in 1820, charged with finding the headwaters of the Platte. Years later, the town of Waterton sprang up, headquarters for the Water Board's decades-long effort to harness the resource for a thirsty city developing on the plains. Near the mouth, the Kassler Treatment Plant stands as a recognized National Landmark, with its technologically advanced (for 1912) slow-sand filtration method. Further up the road, you can see the original diversion dam for the 130-year old High-Line Canal. Other diversion dams also take water from the Platte to Marston Reservoir. Finally, at mile 6.4, the massive, 243-foot high Strontia Springs Dam soars above the river. Finished in 1983, its 1.7-mile long lake and extensive tunnel system tie together elements of the huge metro-area water delivery network. And if the water developers had had their way, an even more immense reservoir, Twin Forks, would have been built upstream, threatening the canyon and inundating a portion of the CT. This challenge was beat back in 1990; and for now, once past the dam, civilization is left behind and the canyon seems much as Major Long must have found it — with cool fir and pine sheltering the slopes and elusive bighorn sheep frolicking on the crags.

BELOW: *Waterton Canyon.*

Viewing Bighorn Sheep

The Rocky Mountain Bighorn Sheep, selected as the state mammal, is a fitting symbol of Colorado. With their massive curving horns, rams present a majestic silhouette that matches the grandeur of their rugged surroundings. Waterton Canyon is home to a band of bighorn that have been increasingly threatened by encroaching human activities.

The Waterton band is very unique in existing at lower elevations and so close to a major city. Before settlement, bighorns often wintered in the foothills and even ventured out into the Great Plains; but they now occur mostly at higher elevations in the state, often near or above treeline, usually avoiding forested country and civilization.

Bighorn are susceptible to lungworm and associated pneumonia, the spread of which is apparently facilitated by persistent crowding by visitors causing unobservable stress in the animals. Also, traditional routes to salt licks, important to meet the animal's mineral requirements, may be cut off. The construction of the Strontia Springs Dam in

ABOVE: *Bighorn sheep in the La Garita Wilderness Area.*

the 1980s severely impacted the Waterton band, which has recovered somewhat since.

The sheep can often be spotted by visitors, sometimes moving right down to the service road in the canyon. CT users should not harry, startle, or attempt to feed the animals. Through-hikers will have other chances to view this magnificent animal along the CT, usually near or at treeline in open, rolling terrain; such as along the Continental Divide in Segments 15 and 16, and then again, in the high fastness of the La Garita and Weminuche Wilderness Areas.

7.0 **ⓔ** , where the single-track trail finally begins (6,040). The trail ascends sharply to **mile 8.0 ⓕ** , where the Roxborough Trail leaves to the left, connecting to Roxborough State Park. There is a bench here known as "Lennys Rest" (6,536), a popular destination for day users. Stay on the right fork, follow the trail to **mile 8.8** and cross Bear Creek (6,215).

There is a good campsite along the creek at **mile 9.0** (6,247). In dry years, this may be the last available water until the South Platte River; so, it is advisable to fill up here. Continue to **mile 9.8 ⓖ** where the trail joins FS-692, a former motorcycle trail, now closed. Continue ahead on the rough trail, following a small stream that begins at **mile 10.0** for about 0.5 mile. At **mile 10.6**, the Colorado Trail leaves FS-692 and continues its climb. There is a nice, dry campsite at mile **11.0** (7,200). At mile **11.3 ⓗ** , cross FS-692 once again, continuing straight ahead through the intersection (7,228). Follow the trail as it reaches a high point at about **mile 12.9** (7,495) **ⓘ** . A dry campsite, with views of the Buffalo Creek fire area, is passed at **mile 13.0**. From here, the trail begins a rolling descent to **mile 16.8 ⓚ** at the South Platte River (6,130) and the end of Segment 1. Camping is not permitted at the river. The trail continues across the river on the Gudy Gaskill Bridge.

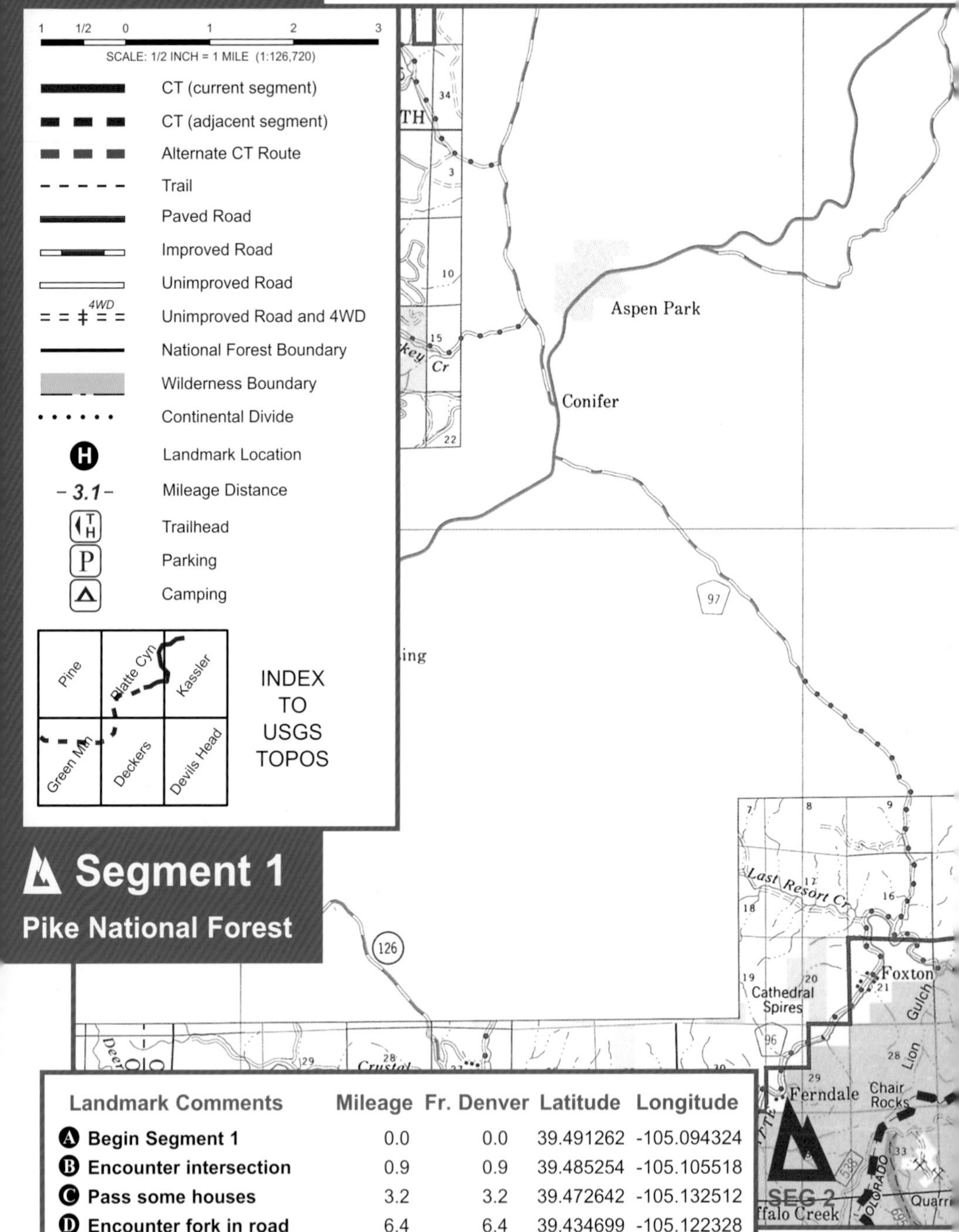

Scale					
1	1/2	0	1	2	3

SCALE: 1/2 INCH = 1 MILE (1:126,720)

▬▬▬▬	CT (current segment)
▬ ▬ ▬	CT (adjacent segment)
▬ ▬ ▬	Alternate CT Route
- - - - -	Trail
▬▬▬▬	Paved Road
⊏▭▭⊐	Improved Road
══════	Unimproved Road
= = ‡ = =	Unimproved Road and 4WD
▬▬▬▬	National Forest Boundary
▓▓▓▓	Wilderness Boundary
• • • • • •	Continental Divide
H	Landmark Location
– 3.1 –	Mileage Distance
(T H)	Trailhead
(P)	Parking
(△)	Camping

INDEX TO USGS TOPOS

Pine	Platte Cyn	Kassler
Green Mtn	Deckers	Devils Head

◭ Segment 1
Pike National Forest

Aspen Park

Conifer

97

126

97

8   9

Last Resort Cr   17

18   16

19   20   Foxton   21

Cathedral Spires   96

SEG 2   Quarr

Buffalo Creek   COLORADO   33

29   Ferndale   Chair Rocks

28   Lion Gulch

Landmark Comments	Mileage	Fr. Denver	Latitude	Longitude
A Begin Segment 1	0.0	0.0	39.491262	-105.094324
B Encounter intersection	0.9	0.9	39.485254	-105.105518
C Pass some houses	3.2	3.2	39.472642	-105.132512
D Encounter fork in road	6.4	6.4	39.434699	-105.122328
E Begin single track	7.0	7.0	39.428630	-105.119052
F Intersect Roxborough Tr.	8.0	8.0	39.424081	-105.120209
G Join FS-692	9.8	9.8	39.413526	-105.125073
H Cross FS-692	11.3	11.3	39.411188	-105.133591
J Reach high point	13.0	13.0	39.405848	-105.152497
K End of Segment 1	16.8	16.8	39.400472	-105.167169

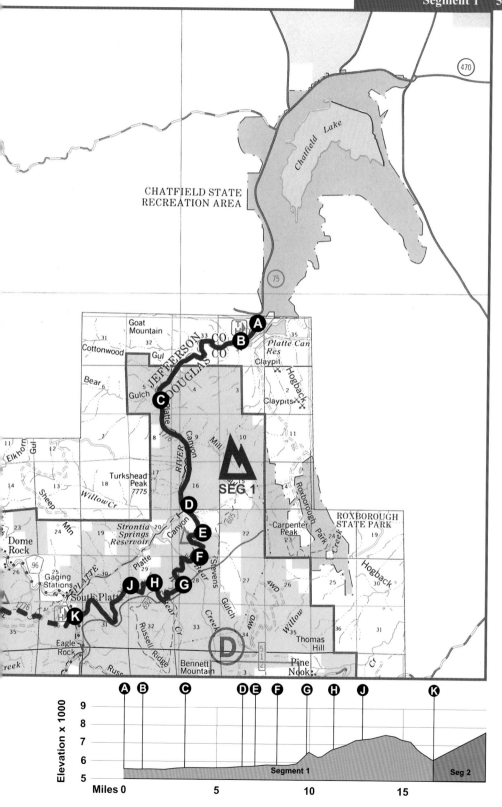

Segment 2
South Platte Canyon to Colorado Trailhead FS-550

BELOW: *A hiker passes through the burn area.*

Distance: 11.5 miles
Elevation Gain: approx 2200 ft

USFS Maps: Pike National Forest, see pages 58-59.

USGS Quad Maps: Platte Canyon, Deckers.

Trails Illustrated map: # 135.

Jurisdiction: South Platte Ranger District, Pike NF.

Access from Denver:

Access from Durango:

Availability of Water:

Bicycling:

Gudy's Tip

"*When you reach the South Platte River, fill up on water as it is a long, dry climb to Top-of-the-World ridge. There is emergency water at the fire station, a short distance from where the trail nears County Rd-126.*" As this segment is relatively low in elevation and shade is scarce due to the fire, it can be brutally hot. Plan your water carefully and hike early in the day when it is cooler.

About This Segment

Segment 2 is one of the driest sections along the trail. There is NO reliable source of water after leaving the South Platte River until reaching mile 1.3 of Segment 3. Much of this segment is in the Buffalo Creek burn area and little shade is available. Persons traveling this section should be sure to fill their water bottles at the South Platte River. Complicating the situation, camping is not allowed along the river, most likely necessitating having a dry camp somewhere in Segment 2. The good news is that, after completing this section, water is more plentiful and regulations become less worrisome as the Denver area is left behind.

> **!**
> There is EMERGENCY drinking water available at a unmanned fire station located a short walk north of where the CT first approaches CO-126. There is a water faucet at the rear of the fire station. Fill your water bottle, TURN OFF THE WATER and leave the area immediately.

An interesting deviation from the CT, with enhanced vistas, is available as a result of the 1996 Buffalo Creek fire. The CT crosses closed FS-538 at mile 5.8. The CT then parallels this road for the next 3 miles. The road follows the crest of the ridge, while the CT is below the crest by 20 to 100 feet on the east side of the road. Therefore, the road route has much greater views. One can return to the CT at any time by hiking east for a few minutes to intersect the CT. Often one can see the CT from the top of the ridge. The ridge road goes through the area where the burned-out Top of the World Campground used to be. From this high point, one should return down to the CT since the jeep road soon turns away from paralleling the CT and ends at CO-126.

Trailhead/Access Points

One other caution; private property owners along this segment tend to zealously guard their privacy. Don't trespass or park your vehicle on private land.

Douglas County Rd-97 Trailhead : From Denver, drive southwest on US-285 for about 20 miles to the mountain town of Conifer. One-quarter-mile past the end of town, exit the highway to your right. At the stop sign turn left, proceed under the highway, turn right, proceed a few feet to the stop sign, and turn left. This is Jefferson Co Rd-97, better known as Foxton Road. Proceed about 9 miles down Foxton Road to a stop sign at an intersection with Jefferson Co Rd-96. Turn left on Co Rd-96 for 10.6 miles to the boarded-up South Platte Hotel. Cross over the bridge and the road becomes Douglas County Rd-97. Seven-tenths of a mile further on, you will see on your right the 141-foot long, steel Gudy Gaskill Bridge crossing the river. This is the South Platte River Trailhead for Segment 2 of the Colorado Trail.

This trailhead can also be reached from the south via Woodland Park and north on CO-67 to Deckers (a one-store town). Then, follow the river via Douglas Co Rds-67/97 to the trailhead.

Colorado Trailhead on FS-550 : See Segment 3.

Trail Description

The segment begins by crossing the South Platte River, **mile 0.0** (6,128) **Ⓐ** , on

ABOVE: *Through-hiker on Segment 2.*

a steel bridge erected by The Colorado Trail Foundation in 1999. After crossing the bridge, turn to the right briefly, head down towards the river and pass under the bridge to the east. After 300 feet, the trail begins climbing the steep hillside above the river.

Pass an abandoned quartz mine **B** at **mile 1.1** (6,600) and enter the Buffalo Creek fire area at **mile 1.2**. Cross an old jeep road at **mile 1.3**. The trail continues within the burn area, passing by cliffs of pink granite at **mile 2.5**, before briefly entering an unburned forest at **mile 2.6**. There are good, dry campsites at **mile 3.6** (7,326) **C** . Cross another old jeep road at **mile 4.0**. At **mile 4.5** (7,560) **D** , the trail briefly joins a old jeep road for about 200 feet, then leaves the road to the right. A good view rewards the traveler at **mile 5.0** (7,744) with Chair Rocks just to the north of the trail. Raleigh Peak (8,183) is about a mile to the south, with Long Scraggy Peak (8,812) about 4 miles south.

Cross the Top of the World Campground Road at **mile 5.8** (7,690) **E**. The campground was destroyed by the 1996 fire. Cross an old jeep road at **mile 7.1** (7,610), then re-enter the burn area. Follow the trail through the burn area to **mile 10.0**, then turn sharply left just before reaching Jefferson Co. Rd.-126 (7,622). Follow the trail as it parallels the road. Cross Spring Creek Road at **mile 10.1** **F** , then turn west and cross Jefferson Co. Rd.-126 at **mile 10.3**. Pass by a gate and follow a small dirt road to **mile 10.5** (7,714). Turn left here on a Forest Service road. Follow the road to the end of the segment at **mile 11.5** (7,842) **G** , where there is a large parking area and toilet.

One note of caution: this trailhead is operated by the Forest Service as a pay facility. Those who park or use any other amenities of the facility are expected to pay a fee. Camping is prohibited inside the fee area. Camping outside the fee area, in the vicinity of the CT, is permitted. Please follow the "Leave No Trace" guidelines.

Groceries/Post Office
J. W. Green Mercantile Co
17706 County Rd 96
(303) 838-5587

Medical
Park County Health Center
Hwy 285 (in Bailey)
(303) 838-7653

Buffalo Creek Services

Distance From CT:	
	3.2 miles
Elevation:	6,750
Zip Code:	80425
Area Code:	303

Supplies, Services and Accommodations

Buffalo Creek town, approximately 3.2 miles north on Jefferson County Road 126 from the trail at mile 9.5, was once a whistle stop on the DSP&PRR. It survives with a few cabins, a small general store (very unique!), a pay phone, and a Forest Service work center.

Fire!

On May 18, 1996, a human-induced wildfire burned through nearly 12,000 acres of the Pike National Forest, including most of the western half of this segment and, subsequently, nearly destroyed the small mountain community of Buffalo Creek. Following the fire, several torrential rainstorms swept the area, including one on July 12 that dumped almost 5 inches of rain on the denuded slopes, causing severe flash flooding. Two people died and millions of dollars in property damage occurred. Downstream, some 300,000 cubic yards of sediment was swept into the Strontia Springs Reservoir and miles of riparian habitat was lost along area creeks and rivers.

The fire torched Top of the World Campground and other features along the CT in Segment 2, dramatically changing the character of the surrounding landscape. Once a walk through pleasant pine forests, the now-exposed CT in Segment 2 has expansive views under a hot summer sun. Nearly ten years later, grasses and small plants are well established; but few trees survived the inferno and it will be centuries before the area recovers to a mature forest.

It's little consolation to the victims; but wildfire can be a good thing. In a normal forest before human settlement, it naturally occurred on a frequent basis, clearing out debris, rejuvenating the soil with nutrients and keeping the amount of fuel low, which meant that rarely would a fire burn large enough or hot enough to destroy mature trees. Decades of fire suppression, and perhaps, a decrease in logging contributed to a disaster-in-the-making. In fact, the Buffalo Creek area is part of an almost continuous 2,500-square mile swath of ponderosa pine forest that's primed for catastrophic fires, as was born out only a few years later by the even more apocalyptic 138,000-acre Hayman Fire which struck only a few miles to the south.

If there is an unintended boon for the CT hiker or rider, it is the vistas which have opened up of this country, dotted with its weathered domes of rough, Pikes Peak granite - including Cathedral Spires, Raleigh Peak, Long Scraggy Peak — all striking sights from the trail. Early season CT hikers will be rewarded with wildflowers in the newly opened-up slopes, such as Sand Lily and Paintbrush on the dry, gravelly areas with Pasqueflower and Spring Beauty in the damper ravines.

BELOW: *Spring growth on the newly opened-up slopes.*

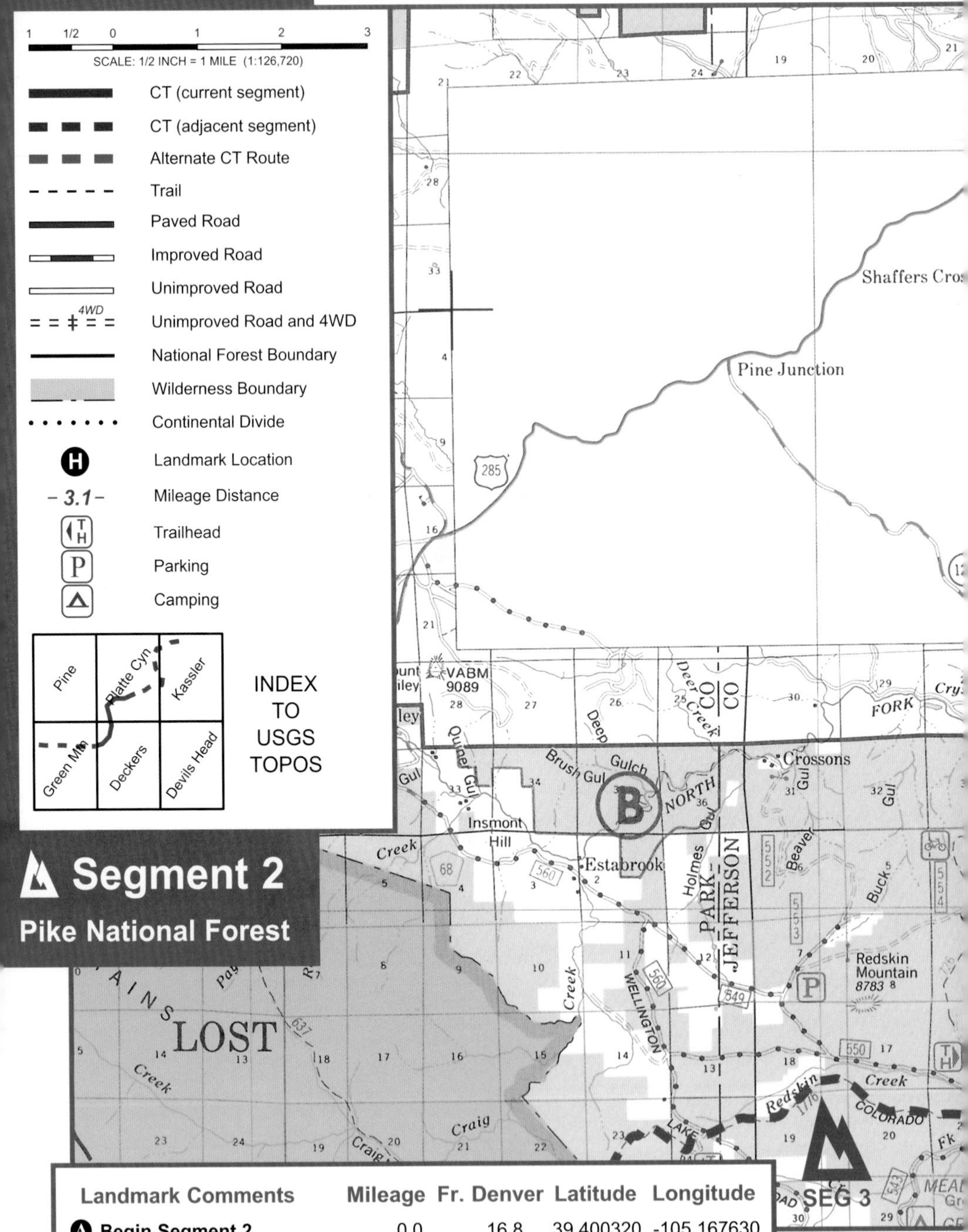

Map Legend

SCALE: 1/2 INCH = 1 MILE (1:126,720)

——	CT (current segment)
– – –	CT (adjacent segment)
– – –	Alternate CT Route
- - - -	Trail
——	Paved Road
▭▭▭	Improved Road
▭▭▭	Unimproved Road
= = ‡ = = 4WD	Unimproved Road and 4WD
——	National Forest Boundary
▬	Wilderness Boundary
• • • • • •	Continental Divide
H	Landmark Location
– *3.1* –	Mileage Distance
(T/H)	Trailhead
P	Parking
△	Camping

INDEX TO USGS TOPOS

Pine	Platte Cyn	Kassler
Green Mtn	Deckers	Devils Head

▲ Segment 2
Pike National Forest

Landmark Comments	Mileage	Fr. Denver	Latitude	Longitude
A Begin Segment 2	0.0	16.8	39.400320	-105.167630
B Old quartz mine	1.1	17.9	39.396226	-105.171860
C Good dry campsites	3.6	20.4	39.405453	-105.207819
D Join old jeep road	4.5	21.3	39.403562	-105.217478
E Cross campground road	5.8	22.6	39.400500	-105.231826
F Cross road	10.1	26.9	39.358661	-105.245121
G End of Segment 2	11.5	28.3	39.345201	-105.256812

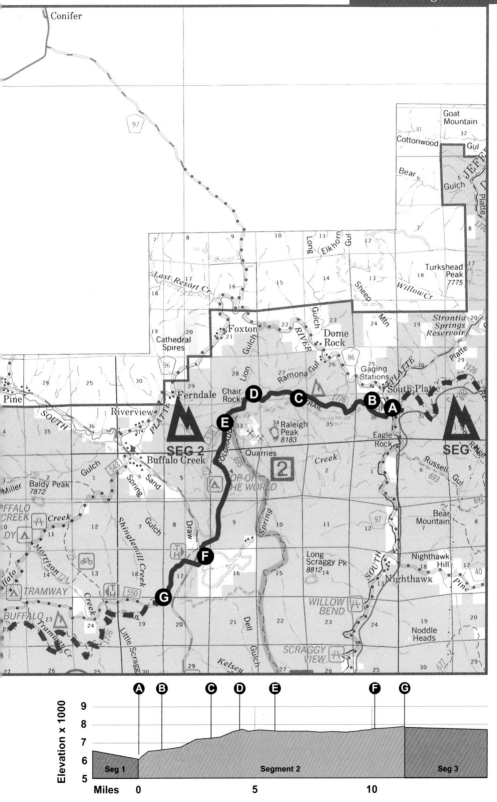

Segment 3
Colorado Trailhead FS-550 to FS-560 (Wellington Lake Road)

BELOW: *Prickly Pear Cactus are common along this portion of the CT.*

Distance: 12.7 miles
Elevation Gain: approx 1520 ft

USFS Maps: Pike National Forest, see pages 64-65.

USGS Quad Maps: Deckers, Green Mountain, Windy Peak.

Trails Illustrated map: # 105, 135.

Jurisdiction: South Platte Ranger District, Pike NF.

Access from Denver: 🚗

Access from Durango: 🚗

Availability of Water: ☕

Bicycling: 🚲

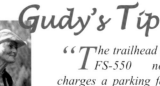

Gudy's Tip

" *The trailhead on FS-550 now charges a parking fee, so plan for that. While you may still be able park for free out along the highway, that is likely to end soon with postings of "no parking" by the county."* This has become a popular trailhead, especially on weekends and with mountain bikers. For the $4 daily use fee, a toilet and picnic tables are provided; but there's no water here.

About This Segment

When the CT first opened in 1988, the trailhead for Segment 3 was 1.5 miles north of its present location (located where the CT originally crossed Jefferson County Rd.-126.) As the traffic on the CT began to increase, it became apparent that this was not a good location since the only parking was beside the highway. There was no place to build a parking area due to private property on both sides of the road. So, the trailhead was moved to its present location. A large parking area was constructed, complete with picnic tables and a toilet — all very nice. Except, it is so popular that it has become a Forest Service Fee Use Area ($4 per day).

This whole area is extremely popular with bicyclists and day-hikers due to its proximity to Denver, its pleasant pine and fir forest, and many small streams. The area is relatively flat by Colorado Trail standards and the snow is usually gone by early spring. Therefore, the area is laced with many intersecting trails, so through-hikers should be careful to stay on the CT. The through-hiker will find this segment to be a pleasant respite from the rigors of Segments 1 and 2. They will also be relieved to find the first water available since the South Platte River.

Trailhead/Access Points

Colorado Trailhead on FS-550 🚗 : Drive southwest from Denver on US-285 for approximately 32 miles to Pine Junction (it has a stop light!). Turn left (southeast) on Jefferson Co. Rd.-126 and proceed through the hamlets of Pine and Buffalo Creek. Continue 4.3 miles past Buffalo Creek to the intersection with FS-550. Turn right (west) on FS-550 for 0.1 mile to the parking area. The Colorado Trail trailhead is at the northwest end of the parking area. To park you must pay a fee.

FS-543 Trailhead 🚗 : See Segment 4.

Supplies, Services and Accommodations

Available at **Buffalo Creek**, see Segment 2; and at **Bailey**, see Segment 4.

Trail Description

The trail begins at the interpretive sign marked "Scraggy Creek Trailhead" at the northwest end of the parking area, just off of FS-550, **mile 0.0** (7,860) ❹ . At **mile 0.4**, the trail crosses an old, abandoned jeep trail. Continue ahead to **mile 0.6** and cross FS-550 (7,855) ❸ . Another abandoned jeep trail is crossed at **mile 0.7**. Continue ahead to **mile 1.3**, where a small stream is crossed (7,820). Through-hikers will appreciate this stream; it is the first reliable water source since leaving the South Platte River at the beginning of segment 2. There is a small campsite near the stream.

At **mile 1.8** ❸ , the trail crosses the Shingle Mill Trail, which leaves to the right (7,790). Continue ahead through the well-marked intersection. Cross a small stream at **mile 2.1**, where there is a marginal camping area. Hit a abandoned jeep trail at

mile 2.8 (7,732)**Ⓓ** . Turn right and cross the stream. Ignore trails beside the stream and continue ahead. There are many good campsites in the vicinity. Cross a abandoned jeep trail at **mile 3.0**, then a stream at **mile 3.4** (7,760). At **mile 3.6**, the trail enters a lush forest of old-growth ponderosa pine, then comes a mixture of pine and fir.

Cross a stream at **mile 5.1** (7,830)**Ⓔ** , with some good campsites here. Intersect the Tramway Trail #223 at **mile 5.4** and continue in a southwesterly direction. Cross a stream at **mile 5.8** and intersect the Green Mountain Trail at **mile 6.1** (7,690)**Ⓕ** . Cross another stream at **mile 6.4**. Intersect the trail to Buffalo Creek Campground at **mile 6.8Ⓖ** and continue to the southwest. (The campground is about 0.25 mile north. It is a fee use area.)

At **mile 7.3**, reach the Green Mountain Trail #722 (7,500) and follow the Colorado Trail to the right. The intersection is well-marked. At **mile 7.5**, cross a stream. Slightly uphill and 100 feet to the left of the trail is a faucet with potable drinking water. This usually is working during the summer months. Just past the faucet, cross Meadows Campground Road at **mile 7.6** (7,420) **Ⓗ** ; and just beyond that is a gate. A trail comes in from Buffalo Campground Trailhead parking area just off of FS-550. Continue ahead to **mile 7.8**, where the trail begins following fast-flowing Buffalo Creek. There are numerous good campsites along the stream. Cross a Forest Service road at **mile 9.6** (7,950) **Ⓘ** and cross a stream at **mile 12.4** (8,240), then travel a little further to the end of the segment at **mile 12.7 Ⓚ** at FS-560 (8,290). Mountain bikers need to exit the main trail here to avoid the Lost Creek Wilderness.

RIGHT: *The CT in Segment 3 ambles through a pleasant mixed forest of aspen, pine and fir.*

Mountain Biking Etiquette on the CT

With close proximity to the major metropolitan areas of Denver and Colorado Springs, CT Segments 1, 2, & 3 are heavily used, not just by hikers but also by equestrians and mountain bicyclists, leading to potential conflicts among users. Cyclists in particular have been singled out for criticism by some for the impact they have on trails and on other users. The International Mountain Bicycling Association (IMBA) offers these etiquette guidelines for cyclists when using public trails like the CT:

Encountering Hikers: Hikers have the right-of-way, so slow down, stop or pull aside. When approaching from the rear, slow down and let them know you are there.

Encountering Equestrians: Never assume the equestrian is aware of your presence or in control of the horse. If approaching from the front, always stop and let them pass. If coming from behind, slow to their speed and ask permission to pass slowly or walk your bike around.

Ride Softly: Don't degrade the trail by your ride. Avoid riding on wet days or when the trail is fragile. Carry your bike around all soft spots and walk around puddles to avoid any widening of them.

Slow Down: Excessive speed is the single most common complaint from others. Be prepared to stop when going around corners. Don't skid or "brake slide."

Stay on Existing Trails: Never take shortcuts on tight turns or switchbacks. Stay on established trails and respect trail closures.

The Forest Service has designated a network of cycling trails on and around Segment 3 of the CT.

For more information on biking in the Pike National Forest, contact the South Platte Ranger District. For information on IMBA, visit their website at www.imba.com/ or phone (303) 545-9011.

ABOVE: *Riding through the burn area of Segment 2.*

```
1   1/2   0        1        2        3
SCALE: 1/2 INCH = 1 MILE  (1:126,720)
```

▬▬▬	CT (current segment)
▬ ▬ ▬	CT (adjacent segment)
▬ ▬ ▬	Alternate CT Route
- - - - -	Trail
▬▬▬	Paved Road
▭▭▭	Improved Road
▭▭▭	Unimproved Road
= = ‡ = = *4WD*	Unimproved Road and 4WD
▬▬▬	National Forest Boundary
▨▨▨	Wilderness Boundary
• • • • • •	Continental Divide
H	Landmark Location
– **3.1** –	Mileage Distance
(T H)	Trailhead
P	Parking
△	Camping

INDEX
TO
USGS
TOPOS

Bailey	Pine	Platte Cyn
Windy Peak	Green Mtn	Deckers

▲ Segment 3

Pike National Forest

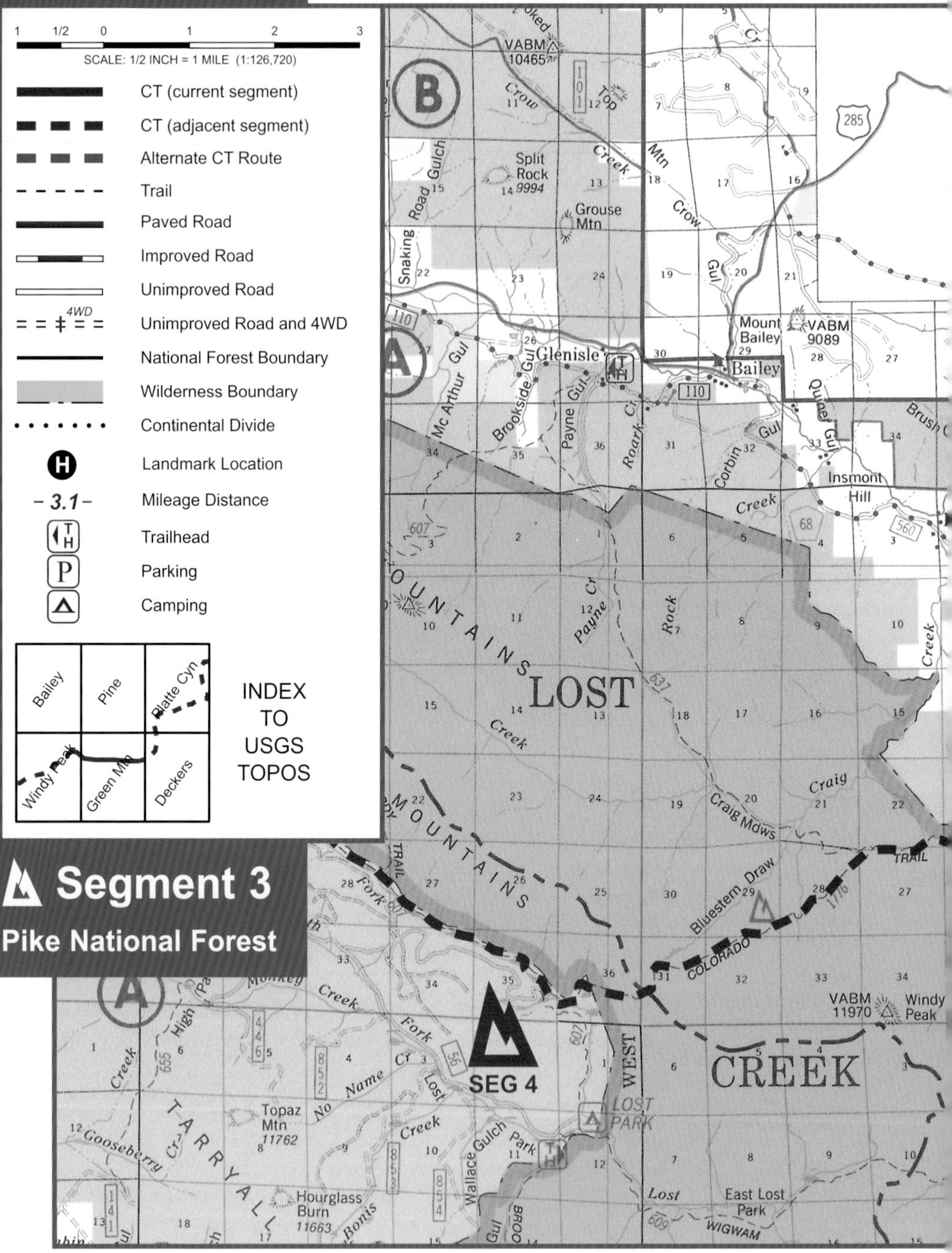

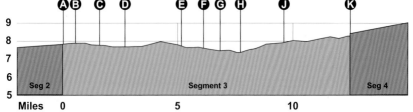

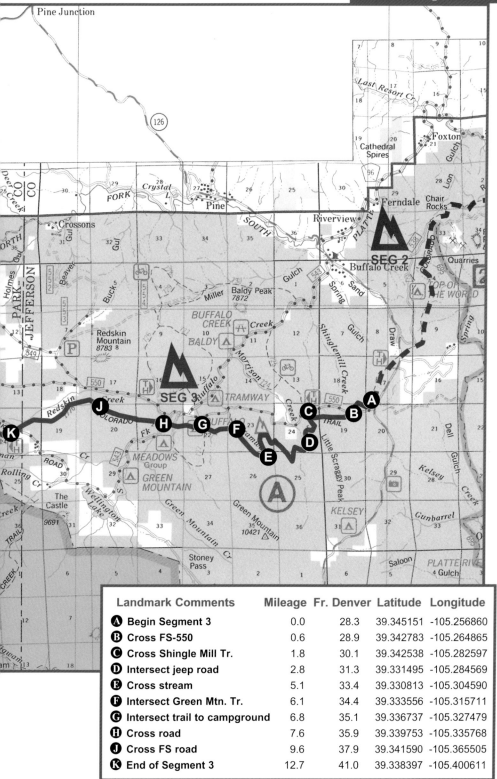

Landmark Comments	Mileage	Fr. Denver	Latitude	Longitude
Ⓐ Begin Segment 3	0.0	28.3	39.345151	-105.256860
Ⓑ Cross FS-550	0.6	28.9	39.342783	-105.264865
Ⓒ Cross Shingle Mill Tr.	1.8	30.1	39.342538	-105.282597
Ⓓ Intersect jeep road	2.8	31.3	39.331495	-105.284569
Ⓔ Cross stream	5.1	33.4	39.330813	-105.304590
Ⓕ Intersect Green Mtn. Tr.	6.1	34.4	39.333556	-105.315711
Ⓖ Intersect trail to campground	6.8	35.1	39.336737	-105.327479
Ⓗ Cross road	7.6	35.9	39.339753	-105.335768
Ⓙ Cross FS road	9.6	37.9	39.341590	-105.365505
Ⓚ End of Segment 3	12.7	41.0	39.338397	-105.400611

Segment 4
FS-560 (Wellington Lake Road) to Long Gulch

BELOW: *Open meadows punctuate the Lost Creek Wilderness Area.*

Distance: 16.6 miles
Elevation Gain: approx 2840 ft

USFS Maps: Pike National Forest, see pages 72-73.

USGS Quad Maps: Windy Peak, Topaz Mountain.

Trails Illustrated map: # 105.

Jurisdiction: South Park and South Platte Ranger Districts.

Access from Denver:

Access from Durango:

Availability of Water:

Bicycling: ❌ see pg. 70-71.

Gudy's Tip

"Segments 1 through 3, and then again in Segment 5, see heavy use by day-hikers and cyclists. You'll find peace and solitude in the Lost Creek Wilderness." This is the first of six designated wilderness areas that the CT passes through on its 483-mile route. Review the wilderness regulations on page 25; especially, note that bicycles are prohibited and dogs should be leashed.

About This Segment

This start of this segment has essentially two trailheads; one at FS-560, and another 0.25 mile up a small dirt road. This segment begins at FS-560, but parking is available at both locations. Segment 4 is highlighted by entry into the Lost Creek Wilderness Area. Bicyclists need to leave the Colorado Trail at FS-560 and begin the long detour to Rock Creek.

Trailhead/Access Points

FS-560/Rolling Creek Trailhead : Drive west from Denver on US-285 for about 39 miles to Bailey. Turn left on Park Co Rd-68 (the main intersection in town, heading southeast) which eventually turns into FS-560 (Wellington Lake Road) without fanfair. After about 5 miles, come to a "Y" in the road. Take the right branch, which continues to be FS-560. Continue another 3 miles to a small parking area on the right with a very small road heading a short distance southwest to another small parking area. Drive slow, it is easy to miss.

North Fork Trailhead : This trailhead is remote and the last 4 miles of the road are seldom used (except perhaps during hunting season). It is suitable only for 4WD vehicles with high clearance. Drive southwest from Denver on US-285 for 58 miles to Kenosha Pass. Continue another 3.2 miles to a gravel side road on the left marked "Lost Park Road" (Jefferson Co Rd-56 and later FS-56). Proceed a little over 16 miles to a side road (FS-134) that branches off to the left and starts to climb. Follow it about 4 miles to its end. The CT is just a short walk across the valley on the other side of the stream. The Brookside-McCurdy Trail comes into the trailhead from the southeast and joins the CT, going northwest for a couple of miles, then exiting to the north.

Lost Park Campground Access : An alternative way to get to the North Fork Trailhead in a 2WD vehicle is to continue on FS-56 for a total of 20 miles to its end at Lost Park Campground and walk north on the Brookside-McCurdy Trail for 1.7 miles to join the CT at the North Fork Trailhead.

Long Gulch Trailhead : See Segment 5.

Trail Description

From FS-560, **mile 0.0** (8,280) **A**, hike up a small Forest Service road to the west. The road ends at **mile 0.3** (8,360), where there is a trail register and parking area. Follow the well-marked trail as it heads uphill to the southwest. Join a former logging road at **mile 0.9** (8,530). This road was originally built by W. H. Hooper between 1885 and 1887, who operated a sawmill in the area. Pass a spring at **mile 1.2 B** on the left side of the trail. Pass a dry campsite at a fence at **mile 1.3**, then continue on to the Lost Creek Wilderness boundary at **mile 1.8 C**. Pass a dry campsite at **mile 2.3**, then cross a small stream at **mile 2.6**. There is a fairly good , but dry campsite at **mile 2.7**. Cross seasonal streams at **mile 2.8** and **mile 2.9**. Intersect the Payne Creek Trail at **mile 3.0 D**. Hike southwest and cross seasonal streams at **miles 3.4, 3.8, 3.9, 4.0** and **4.2**. Cross the headwaters of Craig Creek, a

The town of **Bailey**, located on busy US-285 approximately 8 miles west of the Rolling Creek Trailhead using FS-560 and Park Co Rd-68, has a small business center supported by dispersed mountain residences west of Denver.

Bailey Services

Distance From CT:	
	8 miles
Elevation:	7,750
Zip Code:	80421
Area Code:	303

Supplies, Services and Accommodations

Dining	Crow's Foot	60629 Hwy 285	(303) 838-5298
	El Rio	PO Box 550	(303) 838-9345
Gear	Knotty Pine	60641 Hwy 285	(303) 838-5679
Groceries	Bailey Country Store	149 Main	(303) 838-2505
Info	Chamber of Commerce	PO Box 477	(303) 838-9080
Laundry	Bailey Laundromat	Hwy 285	(303) 838-2768
Lodging	Glen Isle Resort	Hwy 285	(303) 838-5461
	Bailey Lodge	Hwy 285	(303) 838-2850
Medical	Platte Canyon Med. Ctr.	460 CR43A	(303) 838-1166
Post Office	Bailey Post Office	24 River Rd	(800) 275-8777

strong running stream with good campsites at **mile 4.5** (9,380). Cross another stream at **mile 5.0**. The trail exits the old logging road to the left at **mile 5.4** (9,893) ❸, then ascends quickly through a mature forest of mixed fir and aspen. Top out at **mile 6.7** (10,650) and drop back down to the old logging road at **mile 7.2** (10,480) ❻. Resume following the logging road and pass by a spring at **mile 7.8**, then exit the wilderness area at **mile 8.0** (10,310).

Soon, you will enter a large, grassy valley and follow the North Fork of Lost Creek. There are numerous camping spots along the way. Pass an old sawmill site at **mile 8.5**, then reach a trailhead and register at **mile 8.7** ❼. The Brookside-McCurdy Trail joins the CT at this point. Continue up the valley, crossing streams frequently. The Brookside-McCurdy Trail exits to the right at **mile 11.0** ❽. Continue ahead, crossing several more small streams. At **mile 13.0**, enter a boggy area . This section of trail was one of the most problematic for trail crews, who have spent years building bridges and

LEFT: *Trail register near Lost Park..*

ABOVE: *Panorama of South Park and the Continental Divide.*

filling in wet areas. Thanks to their efforts, the section is much easier to navigate today than in the past.

Pass a rock face at **mile 14.1**, then leave the valley and enter the forest at **mile 14.4** (10,920) ❶. The trail leaves the old Hooper road and begins a sharp descent towards the trailhead on FS-817, just off of Lost Park Road. The trail descends through a beautiful spruce-fir forest of mature trees. At **mile 16.3** (10,170), intersect the Long Gulch Trail, leading down to the parking area and trailhead on FS-817. There is a good campsite about 200 feet past the intersection on the Colorado Trail, with water and eliminating the need for through-hikers to walk the 0.25 mile down to the trailhead. There are more good campsites at the trailhead area at **mile 16.6** (10,105) ❶.

Hayman Fire

Beginning in a campfire circle on the morning of June 8, 2002, the Hayman Fire quickly escaped to become the largest wildfire in Colorado's recorded history. Drought conditions, high winds and record hot weather caused the blaze to burn nearly 138,000 acres over the course of three weeks. The fire destroyed 132 homes and cost nearly $40 million. Spurred on by the weather, the fire leapt highways, clear cuts and prescribed burn areas; pushing on into the heavy underbrush and timber of the southern portion of the Lost Creek Wilderness, stopping only a few miles short of the CT. Thus, CT hikers will see little evidence of this catastrophe. However, mountain bikers, who have to bypass to the south of the wilderness on Forest Service roads, will see firsthand nature's fury. Campers in the wilderness are reminded to use a stove and forego building fires.

Mountain Bicycle Detour

Lost Creek Wilderness Detour — *Segments 3, 4 and 5 (Pike National Forest):* This long, mandatory detour avoids the Lost Creek Wilderness Area. It follows several dirt roads, skirting the wilderness to the south and rejoining the CT at the Rock Creek Trailhead at mile 8.0 of Segment 5. The detour passes through the area devastated by the Hayman Fire, the largest wildfire in Colorado history. This lengthy detour skips 24.4 miles of the CT.

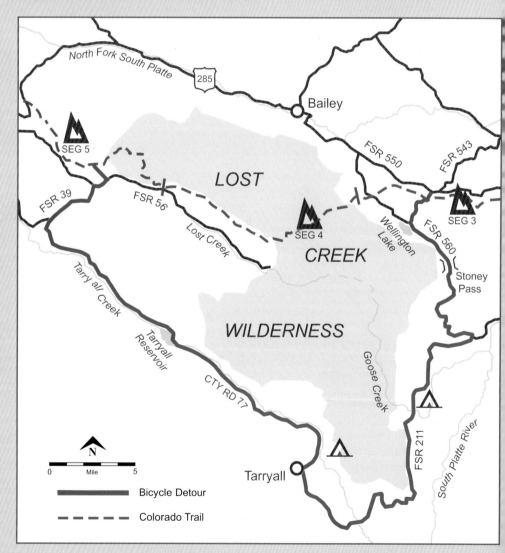

RIGHT:
Fall riding.

Detour Description: The detour begins at the end of Segment 3 at FS-560 (Wellington Lake Road). Turn left and follow the road southeast for 2.8 miles to an intersection located next to Wellington Lake (8,040). Continue straight ahead here and cross a stream at **mile 3.8**. Continue uphill to **mile 5.2** and cross Stoney Pass (8,562). Continue ahead and cross streams at **mile 8.1** and **mile 8.6** (7,920). Ignore a fork to the right at **mile 9.7** and continue ahead to another intersection with FS-51 at **mile 12.0** (7,495). Stay on FS-560 to the left here. Hit FS-211 at **mile 13.6** and follow it to the right (west) (7,475). Cross a creek at **mile 18.8** (7,555) and reach an intersection just beyond at **mile 19.0**. Take the right fork here, continuing on FS-211. Pass by the Goose Creek Campground at **mile 21.8** (7,720). (This campground was closed after the Hayman Fire, but water can be filtered from the creek.)

Continue to follow FS-211. Pass a private campground at **mile 35.4** and hit Park County Road #77 at **mile 35.9** (8,230). Follow the paved road to the right (northwest). Pass through the small community of Tarryall at **mile 41.0** (8,700). Pass by a summer camp called "Outpost Wilderness Adventures" at **mile 49.4**. This is a summer camp that trains adventure racers, mountain bikers and mountaineers. The camp has offered to provide low cost, bunkhouse-style lodging and cafeteria meals to through-bikers; but you should probably contact them first to be sure of space. They may be contacted via the internet at *www.owa.com*.

Continue on RD-77 to **mile 63** at an intersection with Park County Road #39. Turn right on RD-39 to **mile 68.6** at an intersection with Lost Park Road (FS-56). Turn right (east) on Lost Park Road to **mile 70.7**. Turn left on FS-133 at the sign pointing out "Colorado Trail, Rock Creek Trailhead". Turn left and petal for a little over a mile to rejoin The Colorado Trail.

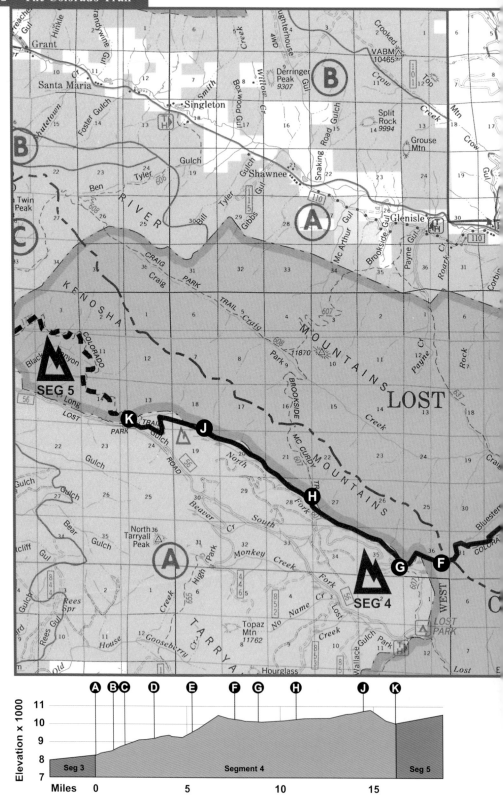

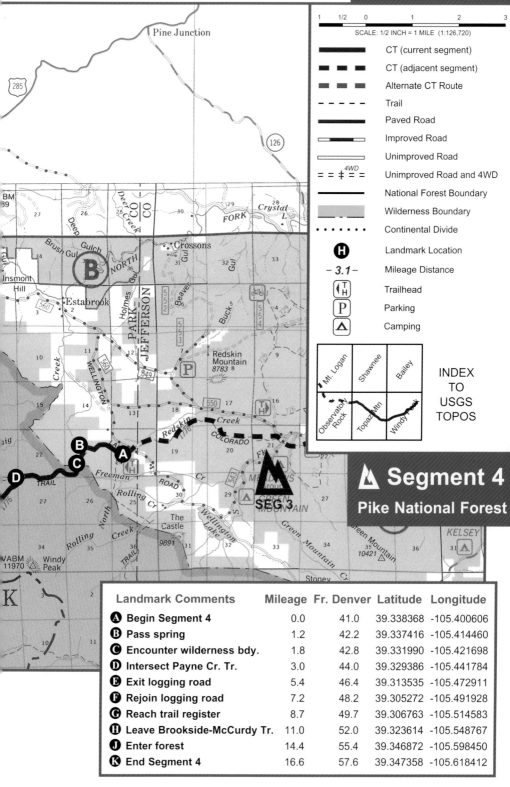

SCALE: 1/2 INCH = 1 MILE (1:126,720)

▬▬▬	CT (current segment)
▬ ▬ ▬	CT (adjacent segment)
▬ ▬ ▬	Alternate CT Route
- - - - -	Trail
▬▬▬	Paved Road
▭▬▭	Improved Road
▭▭▭	Unimproved Road
= = ‡ = =	Unimproved Road and 4WD
▬▬▬	National Forest Boundary
	Wilderness Boundary
• • • • • •	Continental Divide
Ⓗ	Landmark Location
– 3.1 –	Mileage Distance
🚹	Trailhead
🅿	Parking
⛺	Camping

INDEX TO USGS TOPOS

▲ **Segment 4**

Pike National Forest

Landmark Comments	Mileage	Fr. Denver	Latitude	Longitude
Ⓐ Begin Segment 4	0.0	41.0	39.338368	-105.400606
Ⓑ Pass spring	1.2	42.2	39.337416	-105.414460
Ⓒ Encounter wilderness bdy.	1.8	42.8	39.331990	-105.421698
Ⓓ Intersect Payne Cr. Tr.	3.0	44.0	39.329386	-105.441784
Ⓔ Exit logging road	5.4	46.4	39.313535	-105.472911
Ⓕ Rejoin logging road	7.2	48.2	39.305272	-105.491928
Ⓖ Reach trail register	8.7	49.7	39.306763	-105.514583
Ⓗ Leave Brookside-McCurdy Tr.	11.0	52.0	39.323614	-105.548767
Ⓙ Enter forest	14.4	55.4	39.346872	-105.598450
Ⓚ End Segment 4	16.6	57.6	39.347358	-105.618412

Segment 5
Long Gulch to Kenosha Pass

BELOW: *The Continental Divide looms ahead for a hiker near Long Gulch.*

Distance: 14.4 miles
Elevation Gain: approx 1540 ft

USFS Maps: Pike National Forest, see pages 78-79.

USGS Quad Maps: Topaz Mtn., Observatory Rock, Mount Logan, Jefferson.

Trails Illustrated map: # 105.

Jurisdiction: South Platte and South Park Ranger Districts.

Access from Denver: 🚗

Access from Durango: 🚗

Availability of Water: ☕

Bicycling: 🚲 see page 71.

Gudy's Tip

"*B etween Black Canyon and Kenosha Pass, stop to take in the incredible vistas of South Park and the mountainous backdrop.*" You get your first look at the Continental Divide, dominated in this area by Mount Guyot's lofty pyramid. Note Georgia Pass, the low point to the right of Mt. Guyot, where the CT first enters the alpine and crosses the "Great Divide" in Segment 6.

About This Segment

The first 12 miles of this segment roughly parallel the Lost Park Road, which can frequently be seen in the valley below. Then, towards the end, spectacular views of South Park start come into view. At the terminus of this segment, there is an interpretive display describing the old Denver and South Park Railroad switchyard, which graced Kenosha Pass until the early 1930s.

> **!** The last reliable water source in Segment 5 is at mile 8.3! There is a stream at mile 2.8 of Segment 6 that has water.

There are Forest Service facilities (a campground and a picnic area) on either side of the highway at Kenosha Pass. They are fee use areas, so the CT now goes around them.

Trailhead/Access Points

Long Gulch Trail Access 🚗 : Drive west from Denver on US-285 for about 60 miles to Kenosha Pass. Continue another 3.2 miles to a turn off on the left side of the road marked "Lost Park Road." Follow this road for 10.8 miles. Look for a gully on the left side marked as FS-817. Drive or walk up this road for 0.2 mile to its end. Walk a short distance up the gully to the FS sign in box. Angle slightly to the right and follow the access trail to its intersection with the CT.

Rock Creek Trailhead (FS-133) 🚗 : Follow the instructions above to the Lost Park Road. Drive 7.5 miles down the Lost Park Road to a primitive road that branches off to the left. Proceed up this primitive road for 1.2 miles to the intersection with the CT. There is limited parking here.

Kenosha Pass Trailhead 🚗 : See Segment 6.

Supplies, Services and Accommodations

The town of **Jefferson** is approximately 4.5 miles southwest from Kenosha Pass on US-285. The Jefferson Market (719) 836-2389, an old general store, provides basics and has a very small post office within (719) 836-2238.

Trail Description

This description begins at the trailhead parking area and sign just off of Lost Creek Road. A side trail from this location goes 0.2 mile up the hillside to intersect the Colorado Trail. This trail is marked as the Long Gulch Trail. Through-hikers who do not follow the trail to the trailhead may continue along the CT without visiting this location.

From the trailhead, **mile 0.0** (10,100) **A** , cross the creek on a small bridge and go uphill 0.2 mile to the CT. Westbound hikers will turn left at this well-marked intersection. There is a good campsite near here, with water available from a fast moving creek. Cross the creek at about 300 feet past the intersection. At **mile 0.3**, enter the Lost Creek Wilderness Area (10,260). Cross a seasonal stream at **mile 0.6**. The trail passes through a mixed aspen-fir forest, then by some bristlecone pines at **mile 1.6**. Pass a good campsite next to a stream at **mile 2.8**. Cross the stream in a willows thicket, then re-enter the forest. Enter another thicket at **mile 3.0** (10,380) where the trail is usually marshy. Cross another stream at **mile 4.3 Ⓑ**. Camping here would be difficult.   Another stream at **mile 5.1** (10,180) Ⓒ has several small campsites. At about **mile 6.2**, the forest gives way to an area of open meadows and aspen stands. Head downhill, then leave the wilderness area at **mile 6.4**. A trail register is passed at **mile 7.1** (9,550), just before crossing Rock Creek on a bridge. After crossing the creek, the trail "T"s into the Ben Tyler Trail at a well-marked intersection. This is an old jeep trail.

Turn left and follow the trail along the stream past some beaver ponds. An old ranch is visible ahead.   At **mile 7.3 Ⓓ**, the Colorado Trail veers off the jeep trail and climbs up out of the valley. Pass through a Forest Service gate and continue to the Rock Creek Trailhead at **mile 7.8** (9,740). Cross the road and pass a sign identifying the Colorado Trail.   Cross Johnson Gulch and a stream at **mile 8.3** (9,510) Ⓔ . Camping is possible here at the last reliable water source until Kenosha Pass.

Cross a jeep trail, just past the stream. The trail is identified ahead with a post and confidence mark. At **mile 9.4**, the trail passes through a stand of large aspen. Notice how the bark has been eaten by elk in the winter time. Follow the trail past several nice panoramas of mountains to the south and west. Cross another jeep trail at **mile 10.7** (9,940) Ⓕ and at **mile 11.3**, the trail joins a track that is actually an old stock driveway. Nice views of Jefferson and the valley open up at **mile 11.6**.

Cross an abandoned irrigation canal at **mile 12.6** (10,250) Ⓖ and pass by a Forest Service interpretive sign about old railroads at mile 13.8, then through a Forest Service gate. Cross the dry, irrigation canal again, then enter a parking and trailhead area at **mile 14.1** (10,010). Turn left along the road and walk to US-285. Follow the highway for 300 feet to the north, then cross through a campground gate to the end of the segment at the trail register at **mile 14.4** (10,000) Ⓗ .

BELOW: *South Park in the fall.*

Lost Creek Wilderness

claim it is hidden among the strange granite outcrops that dot the hills above Lost Park, a frequent hideout for the gang.

Dreamers often vanished into the recesses of Lost Creek looking for riches. Both the Lost Jackman Mine and the Indian Mine were supposed to be fabulously rich in gold; but if they ever existed at all, they are lost forever to time.

Perhaps the most ambitious scheme was an early 20th-century attempt to build an unusual subterranean dam on Goose Creek that would have flooded a major valley to meet the water needs of Denver.

Fortunately this effort failed, and Denver citizens have benefited more by having this magnificent wilderness preserved at their doorstep. Lost Creek Wilderness was established in 1980. Despite heavy use by recreationalists, there are still some unexplored corners and hidden places in the Lost Creek. In the early 1990s, prolific peakbagger Bob Martin frequently visited the area in his quest to climb every peak in Colorado over 11,000 feet. He discovered half-a-dozen remote "eleveners" tucked away in the wilderness area without signs of a previous ascent. He reports that most were difficult scrambles, some requiring the assistance of a rope.

ABOVE: *Granite pillars, Lost Creek Wilderness.*

BELOW: *Boundary sign, Lost Creek Wilderness.*

 The name "Lost Creek" conjures up an image of an enigmatic place. And indeed, this 119,790-acre designated wilderness has a fascinating history of lost gold, vanished dreams, and hidden places.

Lost Creek begins in the open meadows of Lost Park, sandwiched between the granite knobs of the Kenosha and Tarryall Mountains. Lost Park was the scene of the last native bison killed in Colorado in 1897. From here the creek descends into a deeply etched canyon, vanishing among tumbled boulders and through underground tunnels, and reappearing nine times. The "lost" stream eventually re-emerges for good as Goose Creek at the southeast end of the wilderness.

Over a century ago, the notorious Reynolds gang terrorized nearby South Park, holding up stagecoaches and lone riders for their gold. The stories vary, but some say that the gang stashed their lost cache in Handcart Gulch, north of Kenosha Pass, while others

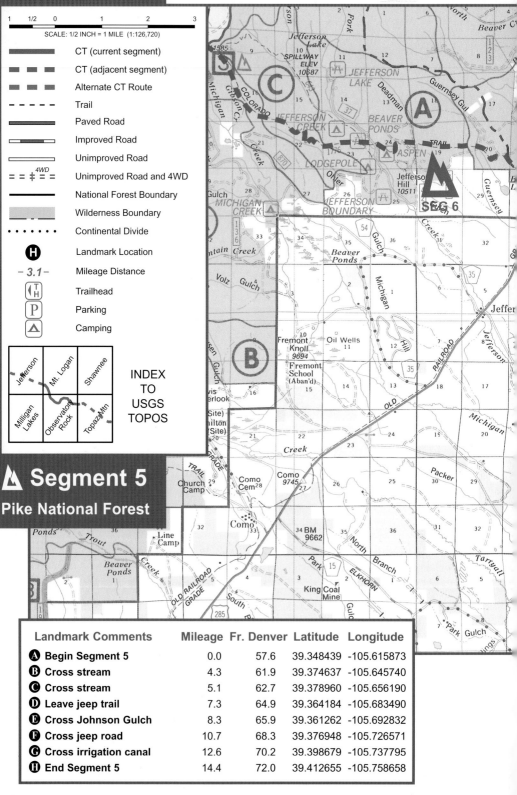

	SCALE: 1/2 INCH = 1 MILE (1:126,720)
———	CT (current segment)
– – –	CT (adjacent segment)
▬ ▬ ▬	Alternate CT Route
- - - - -	Trail
▬▬▬	Paved Road
▭▬▭	Improved Road
▭▭▭	Unimproved Road
= = ‡ = =	Unimproved Road and 4WD
———	National Forest Boundary
▬▬▬	Wilderness Boundary
• • • • • • •	Continental Divide
H	Landmark Location
– 3.1 –	Mileage Distance
TH	Trailhead
P	Parking
△	Camping

INDEX
TO
USGS
TOPOS

▲ Segment 5
Pike National Forest

Landmark Comments	Mileage	Fr. Denver	Latitude	Longitude
Ⓐ Begin Segment 5	0.0	57.6	39.348439	-105.615873
Ⓑ Cross stream	4.3	61.9	39.374637	-105.645740
Ⓒ Cross stream	5.1	62.7	39.378960	-105.656190
Ⓓ Leave jeep trail	7.3	64.9	39.364184	-105.683490
Ⓔ Cross Johnson Gulch	8.3	65.9	39.361262	-105.692832
Ⓕ Cross jeep road	10.7	68.3	39.376948	-105.726571
Ⓖ Cross irrigation canal	12.6	70.2	39.398679	-105.737795
Ⓗ End Segment 5	14.4	72.0	39.412655	-105.758658

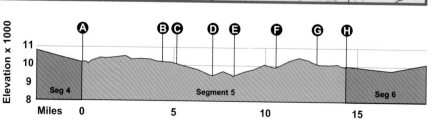

Segment 6
Kenosha Pass to Goldhill Trailhead

BELOW: *Dawn on Georgia Pass.*

Distance: 32.9 miles
Elevation Gain: approx 4520 ft

USFS Maps: Pike and White River NF, see pages 86-87.

USGS Quad Maps: Jefferson, Boreas Pass, Keystone, Frisco.

Trails Illustrated map: # 105, 108, and 109.

Jurisdiction: South Park Ranger District and Dillon Ranger District.

Access from Denver:

Access from Durango:

Availability of Water: 🍵

Bicycling: 🚲

Gudy's Tip

"*If you decide to take the old, shorter CT route down the Swan River Road be forewarned that it is very dusty and unpleasant for hiking. The new official CT route is a much more enjoyable experience.*" Unless you're in a big hurry, stay on the new CT route which offers water, camp sites and a secluded walk through the woods. The original CT route is via a dirt road with traffic, noise and dust.

About This Segment

This segment originally started at the Kenosha Pass Campground driveway and proceeded through the campground and out the back gate. (There was even a small parking area off of the driveway for CT users.) While passing through the campground, the backpacker or bicyclist could refill water bottles at the hand pump, empty trash in the dumpster and enjoy the luxury of a sit-down toilet. However, now that the campground is under commercial management, any use requires payment of a fee. The CT is now routed south around the campground and the CT parking area has been eliminated. A similar situation exists at the Jefferson Lake access point, as several miles along Jefferson Creek have been declared a fee area.

When the CT first opened in 1988, it went directly over Georgia Pass and down a jeep road to join the Tiger Road, following it all the way to CO-9. It was a miserable hike down the road with every passing car kicking up clouds of choking dust. A plan was immediately set in motion to re-route the CT off the Tiger Road. The re-route was not completed until 2003, when the final bridge was put in place over Swan Creek by Summit County.

The re-routed trail curves to the north about 0.25 mile before reaching Georgia Pass. This point is the CT's first crossing of the Continental Divide. In another 0.25 mile, the CT crosses a jeep road and descends into the forest. After crossing the Middle Fork of the Swan and the North Fork of the Swan (both of which offer some fairly good camp sites), the CT climbs to the high ground again with views of the Keystone and Breckenridge ski resorts. Finally, the trail descends down to the Swan, near its intersection with CO-9. There is a bus stop where the CT crosses the highway for the Summit County Stage, which offers free bus service around Summit County. The Goldhill Trailhead, the end of this segment, lies across CO-9 and is 0.25 mile north.

Trailhead/Access Points

Kenosha Pass Trailhead : From Denver, drive southwest on US-285 for about 58 miles to Kenosha Pass. The Kenosha Pass Campground is on the right and the Kenosha Pass Picnic Area can be seen on the left side of the highway, back in the trees. Both of these are fee areas, meaning that the use of any facility required a minimum payment of $4 in 2005. One may park alongside the highway without the payment of a fee. The beginning of Segment 6 is on the northwest (right-hand) side of the highway, just past the turn-in to the campground. The CT is visible from the highway, proceeding into the forest in a northwesterly direction. Note that the Colorado Trail no longer goes through the campground. Water is only available in the campground from a hand pump, after payment of the fee. As of 2005, there was no fee charged for parking on the short access road to the Picnic Area. If one proceeds through the picnic area and a short way into the forest, there is a meadow suitable for camping without fee payment.

Jefferson Lake Road Access : This access requires a fee payment. From Kenosha Pass, continue southwest on US-285 for 4.5 miles to Jefferson. Turn right on the Jefferson Lake Road. Drive 2.1 miles to an intersection. Turn right and

82 The Colorado Trail

proceed approximately 1.0 mile to the fee collection point. Continue 2.1 miles to where the CT crosses the road. A small parking area is 0.1 mile further on the left. Another, larger parking area is 0.6 mile down the road, near the Jefferson Lake Campground.

Georgia Pass Trail Access 🚗 : Using the driving instructions above for the Jefferson Lake Road access, turn right on the Jefferson Lake Road, which is also known as the Michigan Creek Road. After 2.1 miles, the Jefferson Lake Road turns right while the Michigan Creek Road continues straight ahead for 10 additional miles to Georgia Pass. The last 2 miles are a little rough, but most 2WD vehicles with reasonable ground clearance can make it. From the pass, the CT crosses the jeep trail 0.2 mile to the right. There is a parking area at the pass, but none at the CT crossing. The last 0.2 of a mile to the CT crossing is very rough.

North Fork of the Swan River Access 🚗 : From Denver, travel west on I-70 for about 75 miles to exit-203 (Frisco). Proceed south on CO-9 for 7.0 miles to a stoplight at the Tiger Road. Turn left on Tiger Road and drive 7.0 miles to an intersection with the drainage of the North Fork of the Swan River. Turn left on a small single-lane road for 0.5 mile to a nice open area, suitable for camping, just before the road enters the forest. The CT comes out of the forest about 100 yards up a drainage on the left side of the road and proceeds north out of the valley up a closed logging road.

Middle Fork of the Swan River Access 🚗 : Follow the instructions above for the North Fork until the point where one turns left onto a small single-lane road. Don't turn left. Continue straight ahead for a little over a mile, then turn left up the Middle Fork of the Swan. Continue up the Middle Fork for 1.5 miles to the CT crossing. Stay alert, the CT crossing is not very obvious.

Goldhill Trailhead: 🚗 : See Segment 7.

Supplies, Services and Accommodations

The town of **Jefferson** is approximately 4.5 miles southwest from Kenosha Pass on US-285. The Jefferson Market (719) 836-2389, an old general store, provides basics and has a very small post office within (719) 836-2238.

Trail Description

This segment begins at Kenosha Pass on the south side of the campground driveway. There is a large parking area on both sides of the highway. Parking is not allowed on the driveway to the campground or in the campground itself without the payment of a daily fee. (The CT no longer goes through the campground.) Just to the left of the campground driveway is a trail register and the beginning of the trail, **mile 0.0 (10,000) Ⓐ**. Continue ahead, passing under a power line at **mile 0.4**. Head out on a forested ridge at **mile 1.0 (10,400)**, to be rewarded with spectacular views to the west. Cross an old, unused jeep trail at **mile 1.5 (10,290) Ⓑ**. Begin heading downhill at **mile 2.2**, then pass through a beautiful aspen grove. The trees give way to open meadows along the side of the mountain. Cross an irrigation ditch at **mile 2.8**, then cross a road. The trail resumes across the road and to the left. Just past the road, cross a stream (9,850). There are some good campsites here. Continue ahead on the well-marked trail. At **mile 4.3**, cross a road, then cross Deadman Creek on a bridge (10,170). At **mile 4.6 ⓒ**, turn right and follow an old abandoned jeep trail. The road becomes a single-track trail again at mile 4.8, making a sharp turn as it leaves the road. Pass through a Forest Service gate at **mile 5.2**. Cross another abandoned jeep road at **mile 5.9**, then pass the Jefferson Creek Road at **mile 6.0** (10,130) **ⓓ**. Cross a sidetrail following the creek, then pass over Jefferson Creek on a bridge at **mile 6.1** (9,980). Hit the West Jefferson Trail at **mile 6.2** and follow it to the right to **mile 6.3**, where the CT leaves the trail in a sharp turn to the left. Cross a small stream at **mile 7.0 ⓔ**, then an abandoned logging trail at **mile 7.4**. An

ABOVE: *Riding on a foggy morning near Kenosha Pass.*

The Legacy of Two Passes

The CT wanders through two historic mountain passes in Segment 6. Kenosha Pass isn't especially high by Colorado standards, never reaching treeline, but it's been an important crossing of the Front Range for centuries. The pass was used by Ute bands, then white trappers to reach hunting grounds in South Park. Explorer John C. Fremont crossed over the pass in the 1840s. During the gold rush, prospectors heavily used the pass to reach placer diggings around Fairplay. With the discovery of gold near present-day Breckenridge in 1860, southern miners poured over the Continental Divide at a low point, christening it Georgia Pass. A toll road was built to the new diggings, and it was stage driver Clark Herbert who named Kenosha Pass for his hometown. The silver boom of the 1870s brought the narrow gauge tracks of the Denver, South Park and Pacific Railroad through Kenosha Pass. A switchyard was built on its flat meadows. With the coming of the railroad, the wagon road over Georgia Pass fell into disuse, becoming the obscure jeep track that it is today. However, when tracks were removed in 1937, a modern highway, essentially following the old rail route, was built and continues to this day to bring visitors and commerce over Kenosha Pass to South Park.

ABOVE: *A hiker does some early season "postholing" beneath the pass.*

old, abandoned log cabin is visible about 250 feet off the trail at **mile 7.6**. Intersect the Michigan Creek Trail at **mile 7.8** (10,680') **F**, staying on the CT to the right. There is a dry campsite at **mile 9.1**, but it's a bit too close to the trail. Begin entering a sub-alpine forest at **mile 11.0** (11,580), then intersect the Jefferson Creek Trail at **mile 11.7**. Cross a road at **mile 12.1**, reaching the top of Georgia Pass and the Continental Divide at **mile 12.3** (11,880) **G**.

Cross a road at **mile 12.5**. The trail heads out in a northerly direction that is roughly parallel to the Divide. At **mile 14.2**, the CT turns to the west, then descends into a mature spruce-fir forest. Cross an ATV trail at **mile 15.4** **H**, then another trail at a well-marked intersection at **mile 15.8**. Pass a pond with a good campsite at **mile 16.3**. Cross a small stream, then the Middle Fork of the Swan River at **mile 17.1** **J** on a good bridge. Just past the rive, hit a road and go right 50 feet. Here, the Colorado Trail resumes to the left. There are many places to camp along the river. This crossing is also accessible to vehicles, so it is possible to re-supply here with some help.

After crossing the road, the trail begins to climb out of the valley. A stream is crossed at **mile 19.3**, then the North Fork of the Swan River at **mile 19.5** (9,915) **K**. There are many good campsites along the river. This area is also accessible by automobile. At **mile 19.7**, intersect a trail and continue ahead. Cross road FS-221 at just past the trail at a well-marked intersection. Cross a small stream at **mile 20.0** with good camping spots in the vicinity. After crossing the stream, head to an old log fence. The trail resumes uphill at the fence. Head up the hill and cross the stream again on a bridge. Enter an old clear-cut area at **mile 20.5**. Pass through the area into another area of young trees. At **mile 21.5**, the trail parallels an old logging trail. Keystone Ski Resort becomes visible to the north, as you reach the highpoint along the ridge (11,150). At **mile 22.8** **L**, an intersection is encountered. Take the left fork. At **mile 23.1**, there are several good, dry campsites. At **mile 24.0**, there is another intersection. Take the left fork again. Pass through a gate at **mile 26.1** (10,100) and continue 0.1 mile further to **mile 26.2** **M**, where once again you must take the left fork at an intersection. Enter a forest of rather scraggly fir trees. At **mile 27.4**, there is a spring in a gully at 100 feet below the trail. Just past this point, there is yet another intersection. This time take the right fork. Drop into a small valley at **mile 28.7** and pass under a power line. Cross the road (FS-231) under the power line, then cross the stream running down Horseshoe Gulch. There are campsites here, if one doesn't mind camping near power lines. At **mile 29.5**, an intersecting trail goes off to the right. Continue straight ahead. Another trail leaves to the right at **mile 29.8** (9,725)  , and again, continue ahead. Pass through a gap in a fence at **mile 30.0**. A trail leaves to the left at **mile 31.4**. Continue ahead and begin to descend switchbacks into the Tiger Run Resort.

At **mile 31.9**, there is an intersection at a switchback. Go to the left and down. Do not continue straight ahead. This point is well-marked. The trail drops down into the back of a subdivision, then crosses a bridge at **mile 32.1**, near a small pond (9,190). The CT then hits a paved road at **mile 32.2**. Cross the road and go right for 50 feet to where the trail continues across a stream on a footbridge. After crossing the bridge, the trail parallels the paved road to a road intersection with busy CO-91 at **mile 32.6**. Cross the highway and turn right at 100 feet further on a paved bike path. Follow the bike path to the right to the end of the segment ❶ at **mile 32.9** (9,200). There is a trailhead parking area here.

BELOW: *CT hikers walking through a meadow take in views of the Tenmile Range.*

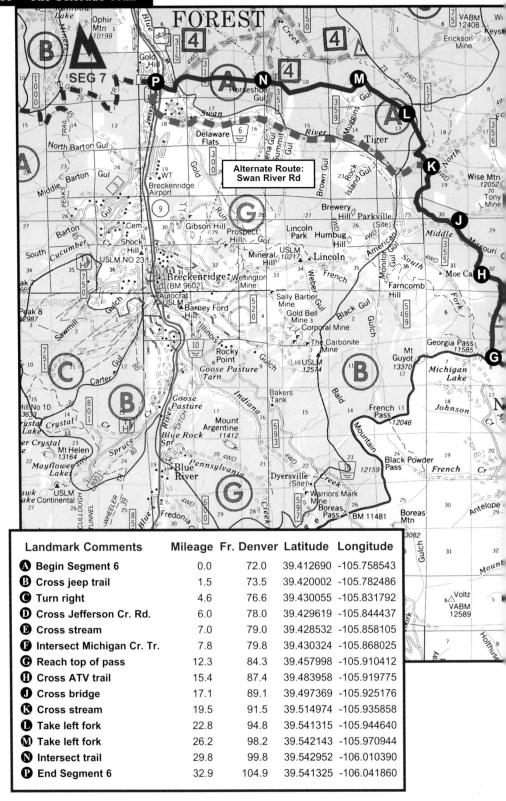

Landmark Comments	Mileage	Fr. Denver	Latitude	Longitude
Ⓐ Begin Segment 6	0.0	72.0	39.412690	-105.758543
Ⓑ Cross jeep trail	1.5	73.5	39.420002	-105.782486
Ⓒ Turn right	4.6	76.6	39.430055	-105.831792
Ⓓ Cross Jefferson Cr. Rd.	6.0	78.0	39.429619	-105.844437
Ⓔ Cross stream	7.0	79.0	39.428532	-105.858105
Ⓕ Intersect Michigan Cr. Tr.	7.8	79.8	39.430324	-105.868025
Ⓖ Reach top of pass	12.3	84.3	39.457998	-105.910412
Ⓗ Cross ATV trail	15.4	87.4	39.483958	-105.919775
Ⓙ Cross bridge	17.1	89.1	39.497369	-105.925176
Ⓚ Cross stream	19.5	91.5	39.514974	-105.935858
Ⓛ Take left fork	22.8	94.8	39.541315	-105.944640
Ⓜ Take left fork	26.2	98.2	39.542143	-105.970944
Ⓝ Intersect trail	29.8	99.8	39.542952	-106.010390
Ⓟ End Segment 6	32.9	104.9	39.541325	-106.041860

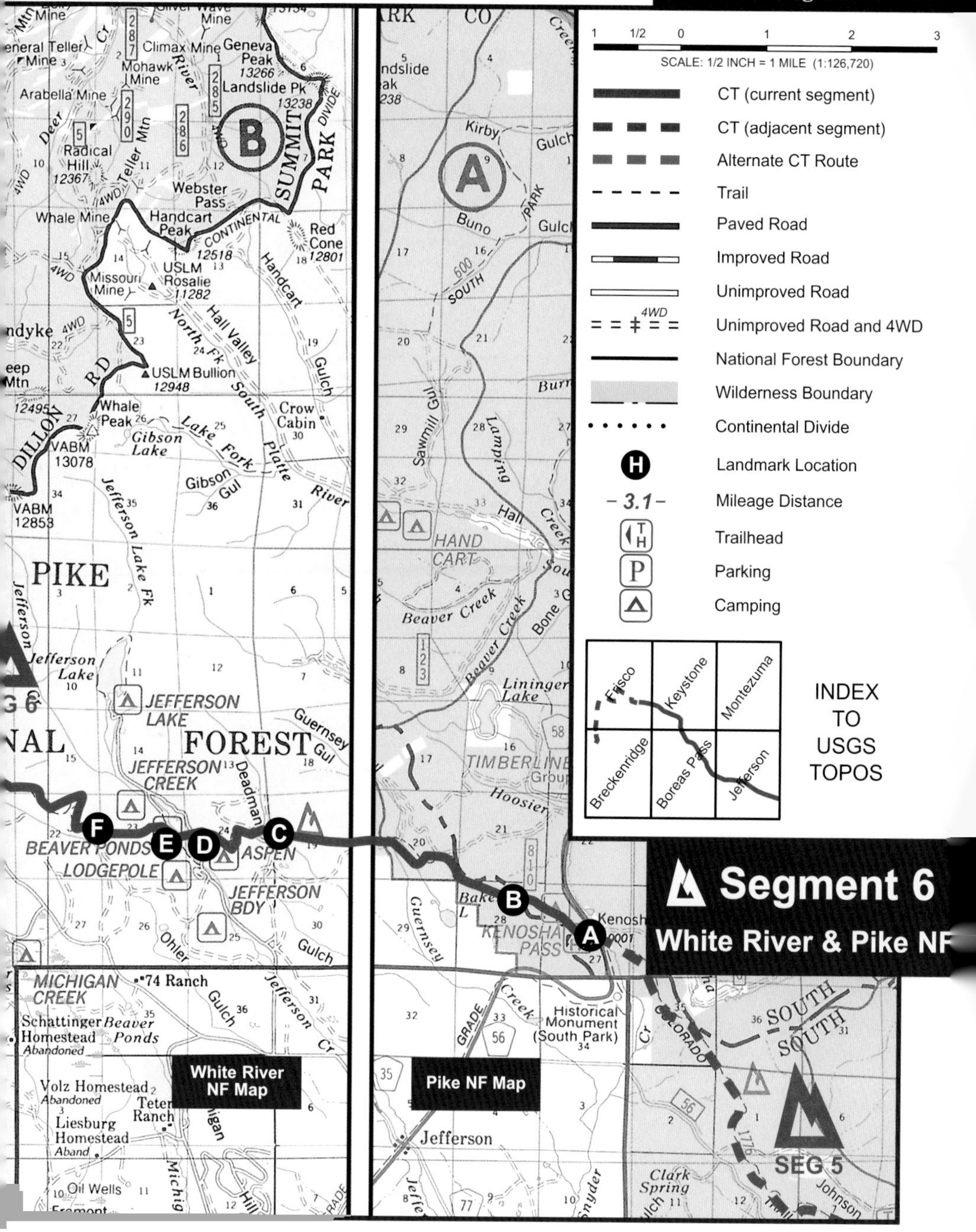

Segment 6

White River & Pike NF

Legend:

	CT (current segment)
	CT (adjacent segment)
	Alternate CT Route
	Trail
	Paved Road
	Improved Road
	Unimproved Road
4WD	Unimproved Road and 4WD
	National Forest Boundary
	Wilderness Boundary
	Continental Divide
H	Landmark Location
– 3.1 –	Mileage Distance
TH	Trailhead
P	Parking
△	Camping

SCALE: 1/2 INCH = 1 MILE (1:126,720)

INDEX TO USGS TOPOS

| Frisco | Keystone | Montezuma |
| Breckenridge | Boreas Pass | Jefferson |

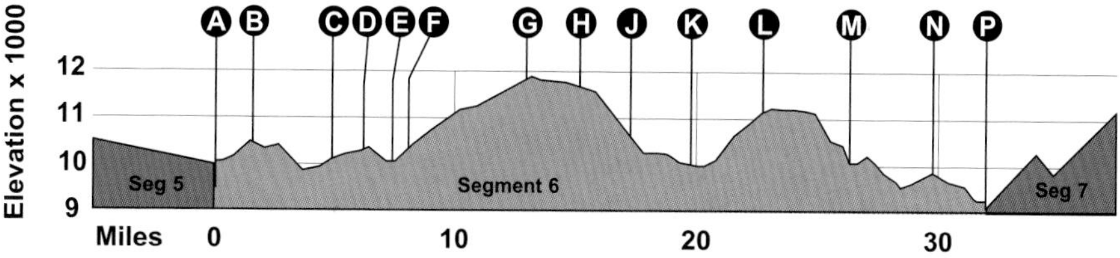

Segment 7
Goldhill Trailhead to Copper Mountain

BELOW: *Cresting out among spring flowers in the Tenmile Range.*

Distance: 12.8 miles
Elevation Gain: approx 3600 ft

USFS Maps: White River National Forest, see pages 94-95.

USGS Quad Maps: Frisco, Copper Mountain, Vail Pass.

Trails Illustrated map: # 108, 109.

Jurisdiction: Dillon Ranger District, White River NF.

Access from Denver:

Access from Durango:

Availability of Water:

Bicycling: see page 92.

Gudy's Tip

"The hanging glacial valley at 11,000 feet in the Tenmile Range supports a huge colony of pikas." You are more likely to hear first, then see, these tiny creatures of the rock slides. The uninitiated may confuse their alarm calls with marmots, who are also numerous in these high cirques. Marmots make a high pitched whistle, whereas the pika call is shrill bark - *"eeek"*

About This Segment

This segment of the CT crosses the Tenmile Range. It is a steady, 6-mile, 3600-foot ascent of the east side, crossing the ridge between Peaks 5 and 6 at nearly 12,500 feet, then a descent of 3,000 feet on the west side in about 6 miles. However, while you are up on the tundra, you are rewarded with some spectacular views! The snow fields tend to linger until mid-July and might present a problem before the end of June. If snow is a problem, optionally you may take the bike path to Frisco and up Tenmile Canyon, rejoining the CT at Copper Mountain. But you'll miss the great views.

There is a fairly good camping area at about 0.25 mile up the CT from the trailhead on the south side of the trail. You can get water from the Blue River on the south side of the hill. Once you pass Miners Creek, there are not any good camping spots until near the end of this segment.

Trailhead/Access Points

Goldhill Trailhead   : Drive west from Denver on I-70 for about 75 miles to exit-203 (Frisco/Breckenridge). Proceed south on CO-9 for about 6 miles. The trailhead is beside the highway on your right at the intersection with Gateway Drive. (If you cross the bridge over the Blue River, you have gone 0.25 mile too far.)

Miners Creek Access Point   : The CT can be accessed via the Miners Creek 4WD road at about mile point 4.8. Miners Creek Road departs south of Peak One Blvd. at the south edge of Frisco (just west of the Summit County Government offices).

Wheeler Flats Trailhead   : See Segment 8.

Trail Description

Begin this segment at the Goldhill Trailhead on the west side of CO-9, where there is a gravel parking area. This segment is poorly marked in places. For the most part, markings consist of blue, ski-trail markers.

From the parking area, cross the gravel road to the west at a well-marked intersection., **mile 0.0** (9,200) **Ⓐ**. Follow the trail to **mile 0.9** (9,640) **Ⓑ** and another trail intersection. Follow the CT to the left (south). The intersection is marked and easy to understand. Cross a fire trail at **mile 1.6** (9,995), passing an old clear-cut forest that is now planted with small trees. Ignore another side trail to the right at **mile 2.0** (10,160)**Ⓒ** , staying left. This intersection is marked. Cross a road at **mile 2.6** (10,170), heading straight ahead. Turn left on the Peaks Trail at **mile 3.1** (9,960), near some beaver ponds. This intersection is poorly marked and confusing. There is water here and possible campsites. At **mile 3.4 Ⓓ** , turn right on the Miners Creek Trail (10,020). The trail sign here does not identify the Colorado Trail, but there are confidence markers on trees on both sides of the intersection.   At **mile 3.5** (10,030), cross a stream on a good bridge, with an excellent campsite nearby. Cross the stream two more times at **mile 3.9** and **mile 4.0**. Cross again at **mile 4.6** (10,550) **Ⓔ** on an aging bridge. There is a good campsite here.

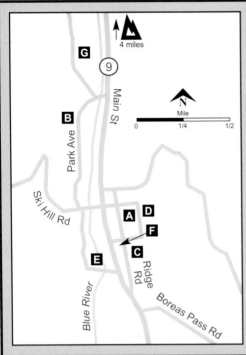

Breckenridge Services

Distance From CT:	
	4 miles
Elevation:	9,605
Zip Code:	80424
Area Code:	970

Breckenridge is approximately 4 miles south of Goldhill Trailhead on Colorado Hwy-9. Frisco has comparable services and is located approximately 5 miles northwest of the trailhead. Summit Stage provides free bus service between towns with a bus stop 100 meters south of the trailhead. Both towns are restored mining/railroad towns serving the popular Summit County resorts; so lodging and restaurants may be pricey.

Supplies, Services and Accommodations

Bus		Summit Stage	(970) 668-0999
Gear	A	Mountain Outfitters	112 S Ridge	(970) 453-2201
Groceries	B	City Market	400 N Park Ave	(970) 453-0818
Information	C	Chamber of Commerce	311 S Ridge	(970) 453-2913
Laundry	D	Village Norge	105 S French	(970) 453-2426
Lodging		Breckenridge Central Reservations	(800) 221-1091
Medical	E	Breckenridge Med. Ctr	555 S Park Ave	(970) 453-9000
Post Office	F	Breckenridge Post Office	311 S Ridge Rd	(970) 453-5467
Showers	G	Breckenridge Rec. Ctr	880 Airport Rd	(970) 453-1734

A few hundred feet past the stream, hit an old jeep trail at an unmarked intersection and turn left on the Miners Creek Trail (10,560). Eastbound hikers should be careful to turn right here, instead of continuing ahead on the jeep trail. Cross Miners Creek at **mile 4.7** (10,575). There are several more stream crossings in the next mile, most with potential campsites. The last crossing before entering the tundra is at **mile 5.9** (11,180) .

At **mile 7.9** (12,495) **F**, top out and begin following the long ridge to the southwest, passing just to the west of Peak 6. The trail begins descending, crossing small seasonal streams at **mile 10.1** and **mile 10.2**. Hit the Wheeler Trail at **mile 10.3** (11,240) **G** and turn right. The intersection is identified with a post. Cross a stream at **mile 10.5**. There is no good camping here. Cross several more seasonal streams, then cross a creek on a wooden bridge at **mile 11.8** (10,105)●. There are some campsites possible here. Cross another smaller creek on a bridge at **mile 12.0**, then begin crossing a large wetland area on a series of wooden bridges. Reach the bottom of the descent at **mile 12.4** and cross over Tenmile Creek on a good bridge (9,765). Immediately past the bridge, turn left on a small jeep road into an informal, but heavily-used camping area. A post marks this intersection. Continue walking to the south through the camping area until you pass under a power line, then bear west towards the highway on a well-defined trail. Through-hikers should consider camping here since camping is not permitted inside the boundary of the Copper Mountain Resort. (The CT lies inside the resort for the next four miles.) This segment ends at the road at **mile 12.8   ●** , just across from the southern limit of the Copper Mountain Golf Course (9,800). There are large shoulder areas along CO-91, but they are posted "No Parking".

ABOVE: *Single-file through the quiet forest.*

BELOW: *Hikers on the CT near treeline of the Tenmile Range.*

Mountain Bicycle Detour

Tenmile Range Detour: This optional detour is suggested to avoid an arduous, high-altitude crossing of the Tenmile Range. Approaches from both sides of the range are steep and difficult, requiring excellent single-track technique. The detour takes advantage of an well-maintained (and popular), paved bike path running between the towns of Breckenridge, Frisco and Copper Mountain Resort (with a connecting path on to Vail.) There is little elevation gain or loss; but be aware of side roads with heavy cross traffic, especially near Frisco. Total riding distance is about 11.5 miles.

Detour Description: This optional detour starts at the Goldhill Trailhead at the start of Segment 7. Go north, paralleling CO-9 to Frisco, then pedal west through the edge of town, finally turning south through Tenmile Canyon to the Wheeler Flats Trailhead near Copper Mountain. Continue south on CO-9 for about 1 mile to where the trail crosses the highway at the start of Segment 8.

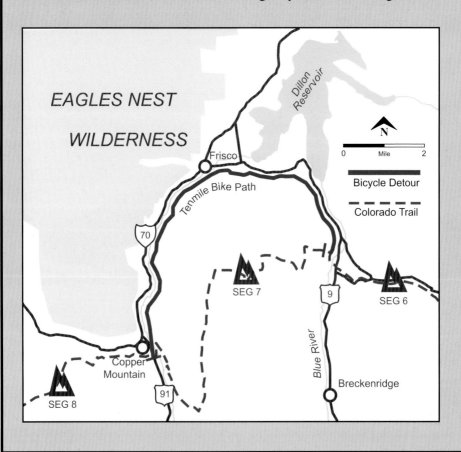

Tundra Plants

In portions of Segments 6 & 7, the CT passes into the open realm of the tundra for the first time. In Colorado, this alpine zone varies from above an altitude of 10,500 feet in the northern part of the state to more than 12,000 feet near the border with New Mexico. Above the treeline, a harsh environment exists — one where summer lasts a fleeting 30 to 40 frost-free days; and in winter, temperatures can fall to well below zero.   In essence, the tundra is a cold desert offering precipitation levels of 20 inches per year or less, with moisture falling mainly as snow. How this snow is distributed by the wind dictates distribution of the hardy alpine plants.

The alpine tundra in Colorado, compared to other alpine regions in the lower 48 states, is particularly rich in numbers and species, putting on a spectacular display beginning with the first alpine forget-me-nots (*Eritrichium elongatum*) in June, until arctic gentians (*Gentiana algida*) in early September signal the rapid approach of fall. Most of these species are "cushion" plants or miniature versions of species common at lower altitudes — a concession to a severe environment. The growth rate is slow, with some plants taking up to a century to produce a mat only a foot or so in diameter. All the more reason to stay on the trail, avoiding damage from lug soles.

As you progress westward on the CT, this summer display of wildflowers becomes even more striking with the deeper soils and more abundant moisture of the western ranges, reaching a climax in the high alpine basins of the San Juan Mountains.

BELOW: *Alpine forget-me-nots, June in the Tenmile Range.*

RIGHT: *Arctic gentian, September in the Tenmile Range.*

SCALE: 1/2 INCH = 1 MILE (1:126,720)

CT (current segment)	
CT (adjacent segment)	
Alternate CT Route	
Trail	
Paved Road	
Improved Road	
Unimproved Road	
Unimproved Road and 4WD	
National Forest Boundary	
Wilderness Boundary	
Continental Divide	
Landmark Location	H
Mileage Distance	– 3.1 –
Trailhead	TH
Parking	P
Camping	△

INDEX TO USGS TOPOS

Red Cliff	Vail Pass	Frisco
Pando	Copper Mtn	Breckenridge

▲ Segment 7
White River NF

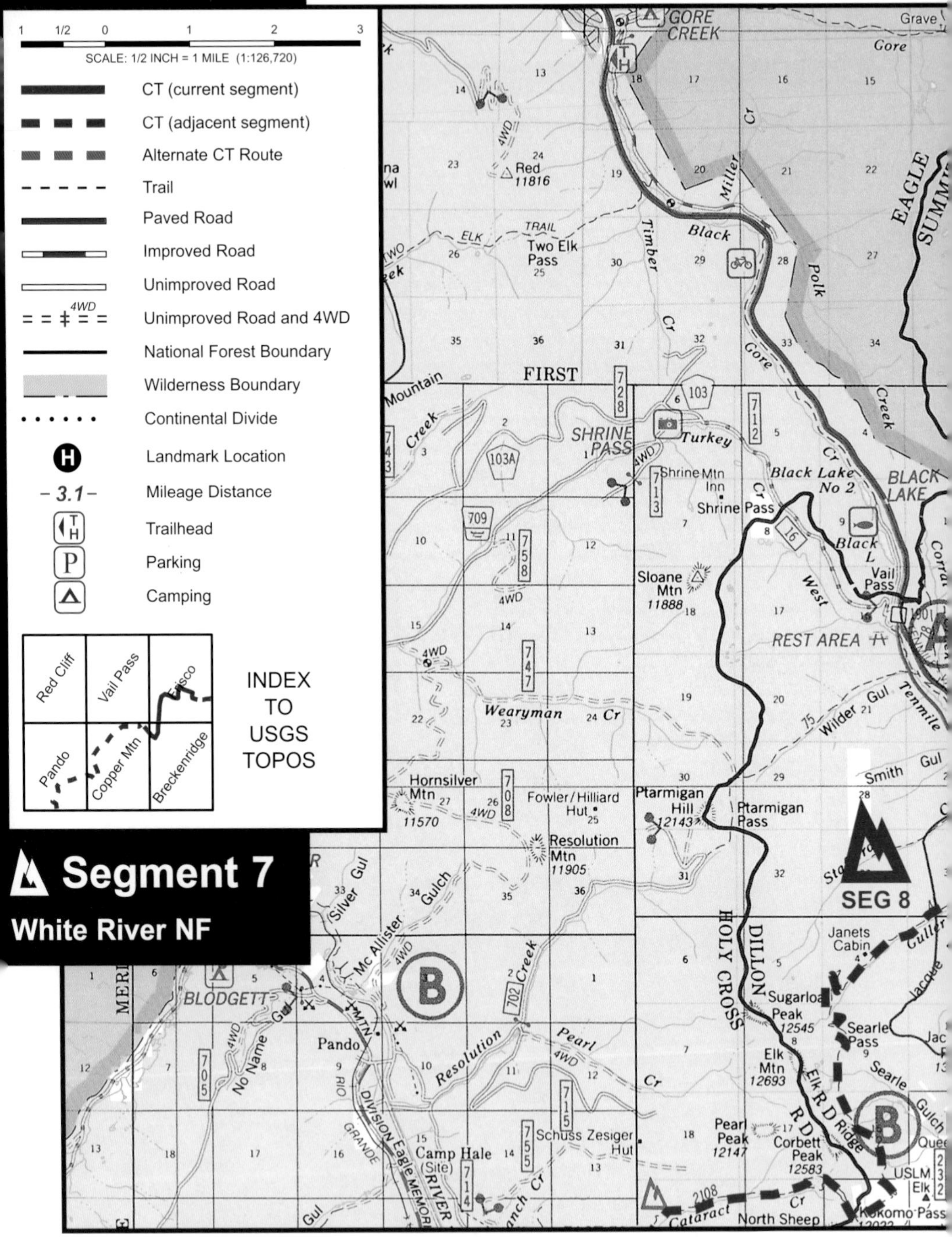

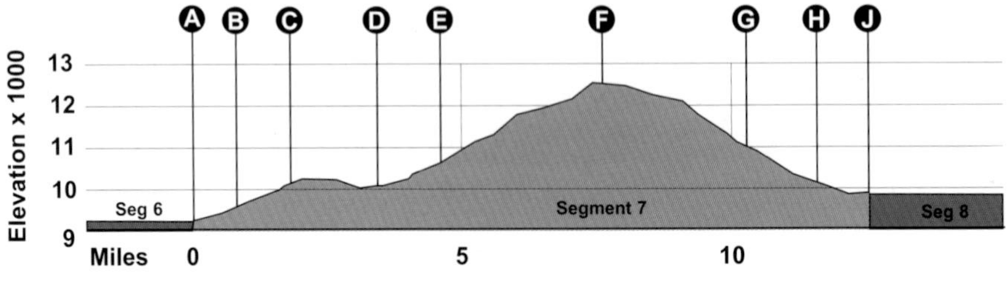

Elevation profile: Elevation x 1000 (9–13), Miles 0 to ~12, with points A B C D E F G H J; Seg 6, Segment 7, Seg 8.

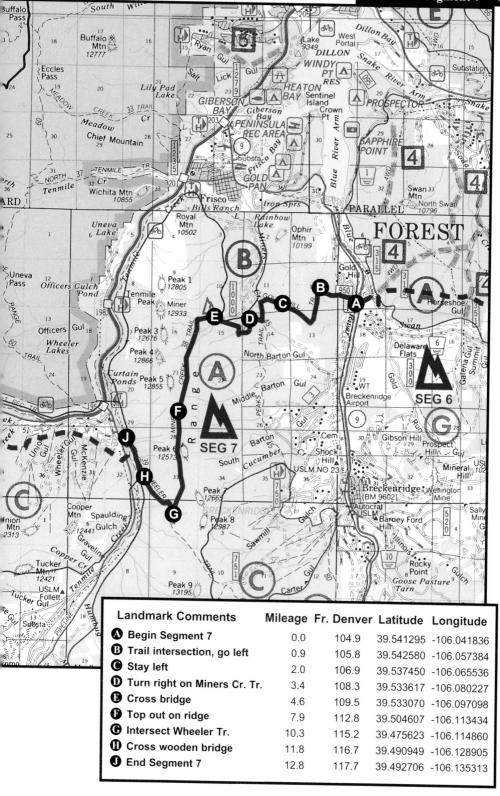

Landmark Comments

	Landmark Comments	Mileage	Fr. Denver	Latitude	Longitude
Ⓐ	Begin Segment 7	0.0	104.9	39.541295	-106.041836
Ⓑ	Trail intersection, go left	0.9	105.8	39.542580	-106.057384
Ⓒ	Stay left	2.0	106.9	39.537450	-106.065536
Ⓓ	Turn right on Miners Cr. Tr.	3.4	108.3	39.533617	-106.080227
Ⓔ	Cross bridge	4.6	109.5	39.533070	-106.097098
Ⓕ	Top out on ridge	7.9	112.8	39.504607	-106.113434
Ⓖ	Intersect Wheeler Tr.	10.3	115.2	39.475623	-106.114860
Ⓗ	Cross wooden bridge	11.8	116.7	39.490949	-106.128905
Ⓙ	End Segment 7	12.8	117.7	39.492706	-106.135313

Segment 8
Copper Mountain to Tennessee Pass

BELOW: *Checking the CT Databook near Kokomo Pass.*

Distance: 25.4 miles
Elevation Gain: approx 4020 ft

USFS Maps: White River National Forest, see pages 102-103

USGS Quad Maps: Vail Pass, Copper Mountain, Pando, Leadville North.

Trails Illustrated map: # 109.

Jurisdiction: Holy Cross and Dillon Ranger Districts.

Access from Denver:

Access from Durango:

Availability of Water:

Bicycling:

Gudy's Tip

"*B*e sure to stop for a quick shower under the falls along Cataract Creek near Camp Hale. There's even a resting bench. But take note of all the shell holes made during World War II training at Camp Hale in the Tennessee Pass area. They become "pitfalls" with night walking or with engrossing daytime conversation.*"

About This Segment

This segment begins off of CO-91 at the south edge of the Copper Mountain Resort Golf Course. The CT continues generally westward, staying south of the built-up areas while passing under the lower ends of several ski lifts. It passes close to the Copper Mountain Village Center at one point (mile 1.7), where there are restaurants and limited grocery shopping.

At about mile 2.2, the CT joins the Copper Mountain horse trail and shares this trail for about 1.2 miles. It gently climbs the mountain, passes through several ski runs and leaves the developed ski area at about mile 4.4. At around mile 5.4, the CT crosses Guller Creek and continues up the gulch to Searle Pass. From Searle Pass to Kokomo Pass, the CT contours across the tundra on the east side of Elk Ridge at the 12,000-foot level, providing some nice views. It then curves around the south end of Elk Ridge and descends into the valley containing old Camp Hale. It then parallels south-bound CO-24, first on the east side, then on the west side to Tennessee Pass.

Trailhead/Access Points

Trailhead access to the Colorado Trail in this area is a bit unusual. The CT was re-routed from the main street running through Copper Mountain Resort to the forested area south of the built-up portion of the resort. Parking is prohibited on the wide shoulders of CO-91 where the CT crosses. As of 2005, the official parking areas are the Wheeler Flats Trailhead or Copper Mountain's Chapel Parking Lot.

Wheeler Flats Trailhead ☎ : Drive west from Denver on I-70 for about 80 miles to exit-195 (Copper Mountain/Leadville/CO-91). Immediately after crossing over I-70 and exiting the interchange, take the first left-hand road. Continue down the side road 0.4 mile to where it dead-ends at the Wheeler Flats Trailhead parking area. To get to the trail, hike down the power line access road going south from the trailhead on the east side of Tenmile Creek for approximately 1 mile, joining the CT at a bridge that crosses Tenmile Creek. After crossing the creek, follow the CT south to a crossing of CO-91. Segment 8 begins on the west side of the highway. Use extra caution crossing the highway; sometimes the traffic comes very fast from both directions.

Chapel Parking Lot Access ☎ : From Denver, follow the instructions above until after exiting the I-70 interchange, then take the first right turn into the Copper Mountain Resort. Continue approximately 1.0 mile, then turn left into the Chapel parking area. Walk south and west to the Village Center Plaza in the area of .the American Eagle chair lift. To intersect the CT, go about 150 yards diagonally southeast between the condos on the left and the American Eagle lift on the right. To go toward Searle Pass and Camp Hale, turn right and climb diagonally west-southwest under the American Eagle ski lift. (Turn left (east) for about 1.6 miles to get to the start of this segment at CO-91.)

Union Creek Ski Area Access ☎ : Instead of parking at the Chapel lot as above, continue through Copper Mountain Village to the Union Creek area drop-off parking area. (Parking is permitted here in off-ski-season months.) Cross over the covered bridge, go past the ticket office and under the elevated walkway, turn right on a gravel road, pass under a ski lift and go about 200 yards on the road. Turn left up the road, around a green security gate, and follow the road uphill east about 400 yards to a wide area in the road. Pick up the single track of the CT to the right, by a painted white rock.

Tennessee Pass Trailhead Access 🚗 : See Segment 9.

Trail Description

This segment begins at CO-91, at the south edge of the Copper Mountain Golf Course. After leaving the highway, **mile 0.0** (9,820) **Ⓐ** , enter the forest and follow a well-marked trail that heads generally southwest, avoiding the golf course. A few switchbacks bring you up above the valley. Cross a bridge and pass under a power line and, at **mile 0.2**, bear northwest along the base of the ski mountain, above the golf course, and traverse across several ski runs and under two ski lifts. Pass over a bridge at **mile 0.6**, then go down four switchbacks and over another bridge at **mile 1.2**. At **mile 1.3** (9,840) **Ⓑ**, cross a faint jeep trail heading up a ski slope. Pass behind a large, brown pumphouse and head straight towards the top of a small ski lift, past a golf tee-off. This route is marked with a post, with another at 200 feet beyond.

At **mile 1.4**, pass in front of a green, natural gas line shed, then enter a road. When you reach the road, turn left at the well-identified intersection, near some condos, and follow the road west to the Copper Mountain Village Center and the American Eagle Ski Lift (**mile 1.6**). There are restaurants, sporting goods shops and limited grocery shopping in this area. To continue on the CT, follow the well-marked trail, identified by confidence signs and Forest Service arrows, southwest across the ski slope and under the American Eagle chairlift, directly ahead. Pass under the ski lift, then hit another road at **mile1.7**. Follow the road straight ahead and uphill. There is a post ahead at the edge of the trees marking the trail. Pass under another chairlift

Mount of the Holy Cross

From vantage points on Segment 8 of the CT, hikers have excellent views to the west of the photogenic 14er, Mount of the Holy Cross. Nearly a century ago, this was perhaps the most famous and revered mountain in America.

For decades in the early 1800s, explorers had brought back rumors of a great mountain in the west that displayed a giant cross on its side, yet the exact location was shrouded in mystery. The search for the peak became one of the most intriguing in the history of the west. F.V. Hayden set this as a top priority in the 1873 field session of his topographic survey. Hayden's team determined that the peak lay somewhere north and west of Tennessee Pass. After several arduous days of trail-less travel, Hayden reached the summit on August 22nd. Across the valley, on nearby Notch Mountain, famed western photographer W. H. Jackson captured an image of the immense snowy cross.

It's hard to imagine in today's age the impact, but in another generation, steeped in religious symbolism, Jackson's photo created a sensation in the country. Longfellow was moved to write a poem after viewing the image and well-known artists, such as Thomas Moran, made the arduous journey to Colorado to paint the peak. Hundreds of people made pilgrimages up Notch Mountain to view the cross, faith healings were reported, and Congress established a national monument in 1929.

The mountain was used for

			Copper Mountain Services
Bus	Summit Stage	(970) 668-0999	
Groceries	McCoy's Mountain Market		
	Village Square Bldg	(970) 968-2182	
Info	Copper Mountain Chamber of Commerce		**Distance From CT:** 0 miles
	Snow Bridge Square Bldg	(970) 968-6477	
Lodging	Copper Lodging Services	(800) 458-8386	**Elevation:** 9,600
Medical	closest in Vail	(970) 476-2451	**Zip Code:** 80443
Post Office	West Lake Lodge Bldg	self-service only	**Area Code:** 970
	Full-service in Frisco at	(970) 668-0610	

Supplies, Services and Accommodations

The CT passes close to **Copper Mountain** resort at the start of this segment. Copper Mountain is not a town, but rather, a large ski resort developed since the 1970s. Overnight accommodations and restaurants may be pricey. There is a convenience store/gas station near Wheeler the Flats Trailhead.

at **mile 1.8**. At **mile 1.9**, cross the bottom of a ski slope where lingering snow from a snowboard park may remain late into the summer. Pass by an emergency telephone; confidence signs and arrows are on a nearby tree.

At **mile 2.0**, cross the road west to where the single-track trail begins. A painted confidence sign is on a rock where the trail starts. Cross two ski runs and under a ski lift. At **mile 2.2 ☮** , turn left and join a horse trail coming up from Copper Mountain Stables.   This intersection is well-marked with a post and a confidence sign on a tree at 75 feet

mountaineering training by nearby Camp Hale troops during WWII, including a first-ever winter ascent of the 1,200-foot-high cross in December of 1943. But as time passed, religious interest faded and the monument status was rescinded shortly after the war.

A USGS survey determined that the 14,005-foot peak just barely qualified as a 14er (Hayden had listed it at 13,999 feet) and today, Mount of the Holy Cross is a favorite with peakbaggers.

ABOVE: *Jackson's famous image.*

mile 2.6, cross a stream on a log bridge, then cross a seasonal stream on another bridge at a few hundred feet further. About 300 hundred feet further, turn sharply to the left on well-used horse trail. This intersection is clearly marked with a post and confidence marker at 200 feet past the intersection. (This corner provides a good view back toward the Tenmile Range to the east.) At **mile 2.8**, hit a "Y" intersection where the horse trail splits (10,180). Take the right fork which is marked with a post and a confidence mark on a tree at 250 feet ahead. Pass by a closed trail and continue ahead following the switchbacks uphill. At **mile 3.4** (10,350)**D**, bear sharply to the right and leave the horse trail. This is clearly marked with another post and a confidence marker at 50 feet ahead. Cross a small bridge at **mile 3.9**, then cross a boardwalk and narrow ski run. At **mile 4.3**, pass under a ski lift and cross a boardwalk , then a third ski run and boardwalk at **mile 4.4** where you leave the developed ski area. At **mile 5.0 E**, the cross-country ski trail to Janet's Cabin comes down from the left and joins the Colorado Trail. Continue straight ahead.

The trail crosses Jacque Creek at **mile 5.3** (10,480) on a sturdy bridge. There is a good hard-packed campsite near the bridge. Cross Guller Creek in another 100 yards ,then turn left and up the valley. This is a beautiful valley with a heavy spruce-fir forest. There are many good campsites along the valley floor.

Pass by the ruins of an old cabin at **mile 6.7**, as the trail steadily ascends the valley. At **mile 7.9** (11,380) **F** , cross a stream with a possible small campsite. Cross a seasonal stream at **mile 8.4** and begin leaving the forest.

At **mile 9.0**, pass directly above Janet's Cabin, a popular ski hut. Finally, reach Searle Pass at **mile 9.7** (12,040) **G** and continue in a southerly direction, following the trail marked by wood posts along the tundra.

Cross a stream at **mile 10.2**. Continue following the posts to the south and climb to the top of Elk Ridge at **mile 12.4** (12,280). This is the highest point on this segment. Descend from the ridge to Kokomo Pass at **mile 12.9** (12,022) **H** . The trail turns to the right here and heads in a northwesterly direction. This intersection is marked by a large "Colorado Trail" sign and a confidence marker at 200 feet further. At **mile13.5**, re-enter the forest. There is a nice campsite with water, just as the trees begin. At **mile 13.6 J**, cross a small stream on a log bridge. Cross another small stream at **mile 14.2**, then begin following Cataract Creek. There are numerous good camping spots along the creek. Pass the ruins of a old log house at **mile 14.4**, then cross another stream at **mile 14.5** (10,920) **K** and another at **mile 16.1**. A old mining trail leaves to the right near here. Continue ahead on the main trail, then intersect another old road at **mile 16.4** (10,180). Turn left and follow the road downhill to a log bridge, crossing the stream at **mile 16.5**. Continue to a "Y" intersection at **mile 16.6 L** and turn to the right. There is a good campsite nearby, the last good spot to camp before entering Camp Hale in Eagle Park.

Camping is NOT allowed between Cataract Creek and the South Fork of the Eagle River (due to undiscovered munitions.) White arrows sign the travel corridor.

Pass by the ruins of old cabin at **mile 16.7**, then under a power line at **mile 17.0**. Hit a intersection just above a road at **mile 17.1**. Turn right at the intersection and cross a bridge at **mile 17.2**. There is a waterfall to the right and a bench built here, with a possible small campsite above the bench. Camping is no longer allowed until reaching campgrounds on the other side of Camp Hale.

At **mile 17.7**, pass under a power line. There is a seasonal spring here. Hit a road at **mile 18.0** and turn to the right and follow the road. At **mile 18.1** (9,415) **Ⓜ** , leave the road on the trail to the right. The intersection is well-marked. The trail begins following parallel to the road through sagebrush meadows. At **mile 18.7**, the trail turns sharply to the left and goes for 300 feet to FS-714. Turn right and follow the road for approximately 650 feet to the intersection with FS-714.C at **mile 18.9**. Turn left and walk through the remains of Camp Hale. Pass by some old concrete bunkers at **mile 19.2**, then leave the road, crossing a bridge (9,330). Pass through a area with old cement pier blocks, the foundations of former buildings. After about 0.2 mile, re-enter the forest and move out of the Camp Hale area.

At **mile 20.1**, cross a dirt road at a FS gate, passing diagonally through the gate, then continue ahead on the other side (9,670). At **mile 20.4** (9,750), reach a wooden bench overlooking the valley and Camp Hale. At **mile 20.8**, cross a small seasonal stream and cross another, more reliable stream at **mile 21.7**, with campsites nearby.

At **mile 21.8**, cross a jeep road. Reach US-24 at **mile 22.1** (9,970) **Ⓝ** and cross the highway, then cross the railroad at **mile 22.2** in the valley ahead. Cross a creek in a series of three, small bridges at **mile 22.3**. The trail leaves the swampy area, then turns to the southwest and follows Mitchell Creek in a wide grassy meadow. There are good places to camp along the meadow. At **mile 23.6** (10,190), the trail begins following a old railroad grade and leaves the valley to the left. Cross a foot bridge in a seasonally wet area at **mile 24.3**, then cross an old railroad bridge at **mile 24.5**. Pass by some old charcoal/coke ovens at **mile 24.9**, then reach the end of the segment at **mile 25.4** **Ⓟ** at the Tennessee Pass Trailhead parking area (10,424).

The Legacy of Camp Hale

Begun in 1942, Camp Hale was built as a unique military base to train troops for mountain and winter warfare during World War II. The famed 10th Mountain Division learned techniques in winter survival, skiing, rock climbing and campcraft, in addition to normal basic military training, before embarking for the European theater to fight the Nazis. Attached to the 5th Army, the 10th fought bloody battles up the spine of Italy's Apennine Mountains, taking heavy casualties, and culminating in the strategic taking of Riva Ridge and Mt. Belvedere. The division suffered nearly 25% casualties, one of the highest of any unit in the war. After the war, many 10th veterans, intrigued by the powder snow that they encountered in Colorado,

returned to the state and were instrumental in developing the ski industry. Camp Hale itself was largely abandoned, until completely dismantled in 1963. Not much remains to be seen at the site (although ordinance continues to be found at times.) A plaque on Tennessee Pass commemorates the sacrifice of the 10th.

Historic remnants of the old narrow gauge, Denver & Rio Grande railroad also lie around the pass, including bridges and charcoal/coke ovens.

RIGHT: *Bunkers at Camp Hale.*

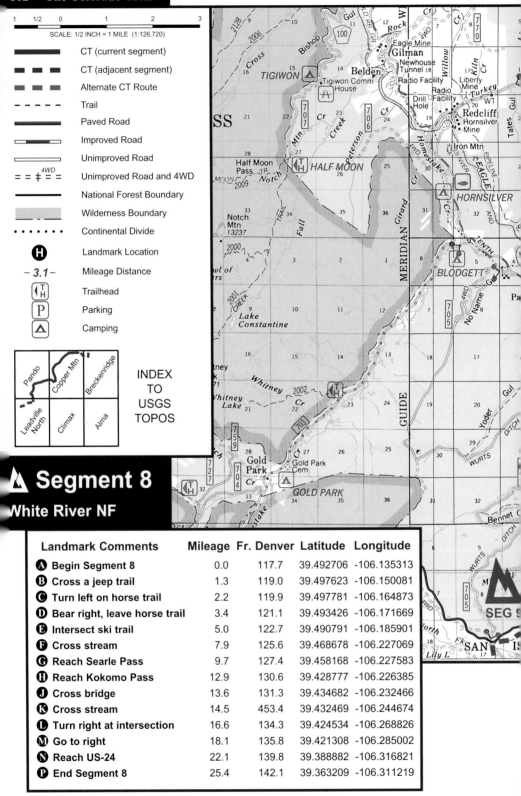

SCALE: 1/2 INCH = 1 MILE (1:126,720)

	CT (current segment)
	CT (adjacent segment)
	Alternate CT Route
	Trail
	Paved Road
	Improved Road
	Unimproved Road
	Unimproved Road and 4WD
	National Forest Boundary
	Wilderness Boundary
	Continental Divide
H	Landmark Location
– 3.1 –	Mileage Distance
TH	Trailhead
P	Parking
△	Camping

INDEX TO USGS TOPOS

Segment 8

White River NF

Landmark Comments	Mileage	Fr. Denver	Latitude	Longitude
Ⓐ Begin Segment 8	0.0	117.7	39.492706	-106.135313
Ⓑ Cross a jeep trail	1.3	119.0	39.497623	-106.150081
Ⓒ Turn left on horse trail	2.2	119.9	39.497781	-106.164873
Ⓓ Bear right, leave horse trail	3.4	121.1	39.493426	-106.171669
Ⓔ Intersect ski trail	5.0	122.7	39.490791	-106.185901
Ⓕ Cross stream	7.9	125.6	39.468678	-106.227069
Ⓖ Reach Searle Pass	9.7	127.4	39.458168	-106.227583
Ⓗ Reach Kokomo Pass	12.9	130.6	39.428777	-106.226385
Ⓙ Cross bridge	13.6	131.3	39.434682	-106.232466
Ⓚ Cross stream	14.5	453.4	39.432469	-106.244674
Ⓛ Turn right at intersection	16.6	134.3	39.424534	-106.268826
Ⓜ Go to right	18.1	135.8	39.421308	-106.285002
Ⓝ Reach US-24	22.1	139.8	39.388882	-106.316821
Ⓟ End Segment 8	25.4	142.1	39.363209	-106.311219

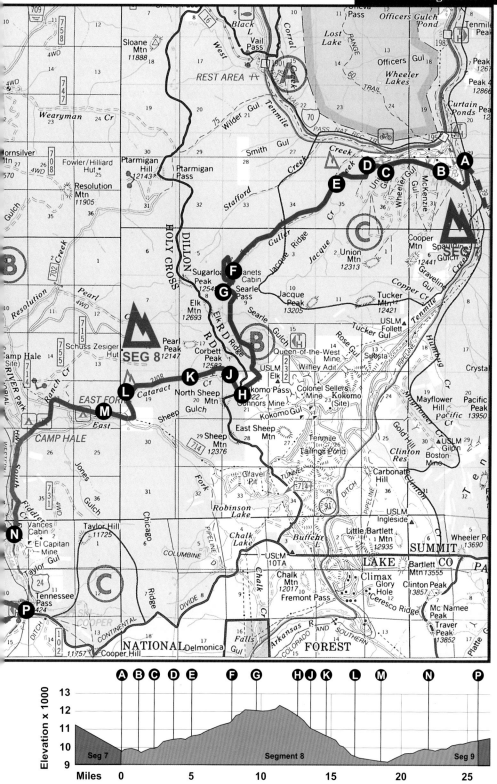

Segment 9
Tennessee Pass to
Timberline Lake & CT Trailhead

BELOW: *Hikers near treeline in the Holy Cross Wilderness Area.*

Distance: 13.6 miles
Elevation Gain: approx 2120 ft

USFS Maps: San Isabel National Forest, see pages 108-109.

USGS Quad Maps: Leadville North, Homestake Reservoir.

Trails Illustrated map: # 126, 127.

Jurisdiction: Leadville Ranger District, San Isabel NF.

Access from Denver:

Access from Durango:

Availability of Water:

Bicycling: ✕ see page 115.

Gudy's Tip

"*I*n *the Holy Cross Wilderness, there is a fascinating tundra walk between Longs Gulch and the St. Kevins Lake Trail.*" There are several lakes and ponds, ideal for camping, situated just off the trail and beneath the glaciated headwalls of the Continental Divide, exemplified by Porcupine Lakes (mile 7.7), a beautiful spot for high-altitude camping.

About This Segment

This segment has had several changes since our last guidebook (sixth edition) was published. Two of the changes are re-routes in order to avoid wetlands, and the third involves a different terminus location.

The first re-routed section begins at about mile 2.5 and rejoins the old trail at mile 3.7. The second begins at mile 9.0 and rejoins the old trail at mile 10.0. In both re-routes, the trail was moved to the west of the old trail. The second re-route also bypasses the St. Kevin Trailhead. The third change to this segment is at its end point. Previously, the end point was the Hagerman Pass Road, but no parking is permitted there. So the new end point is an unnamed trailhead beside the Lake Fork of the Arkansas River, referred to by the Forest Service as the Timberline Lake and Colorado Trail Trailhead. The Lake Fork is the stream that feeds the western end of Turquoise Lake. The trailhead is about 1 mile west of the western end of the lake.

In this segment, the CT turns south and stays on a southerly heading for the next 120 miles, all the way to Marshall Pass. It skirts along the eastern flank of the Sawatch Range between the 9,000 and 12,000-foot levels, following much of the path of the old Main Range Trail that was constructed by the Civilian Conservation Corp in the 1930s. It was built both for recreation and fire protection. There are many high points along this route that provide spectacular views of the Arkansas River Valley. Toward the end of this segment, the CT passes through the southeast corner of the Holy Cross Wilderness Area with some great views of Mt. Massive to the south. It is the second highest mountain in Colorado at 14,421 feet. Shortly after leaving the Wilderness Area, this segment terminates at a trailhead by the Lake Fork of the Arkansas River.

Trailhead/Access Points

Tennessee Pass Trailhead 🚗 *:* Travel north from Leadville on US-24 for approximately 9 miles to the top of Tennessee Pass. A parking area on the west side of the highway is the beginning for this segment.

Wurtz Ditch Road (FS-705) Trail Access 🚗 *:* Drive north from Leadville on US-24 for about 7.5 miles to the Wurtz Ditch Road (FS-705). It's easy to identify by an old-fashioned yellow road grader parked beside the road. Proceed about 1 mile on the gravel road to an intersection. Turn right. Proceed 0.3 mile to the CT crossing. Parking space is very limited.

Timberline Lake and Colorado Trail Trailhead 🚗 *:* See Segment 10.

Supplies, Services and Accommodations

Available in Leadville (see Segment 10, see page 113).

Trail Description

This segment begins at the parking area atop Tennessee Pass west of US-24, **mile 0.0** (10,424) **Ⓐ** . From the large display sign, follow the trail to the south. At **mile 1.1 Ⓑ**, the trail merges with the Treeline Ski Trail at a well-marked intersection.

Intersect another old, faint trail at **mile 1.5**, continuing ahead and to the left on the Colorado Trail. Cross the Wurtz Ditch at **mile 2.5** (10,420) **C** on a footbridge. This is an irrigation diversion, but it is usually a fast moving stream. There are good campsites in the vicinity. Cross the Wurtz Ditch Road at **mile 2.7** (10,490). Mountain bikers should leave the trail at this intersection to avoid the wilderness area ahead. The trail continues straight across the road. Hikers should be careful as they begin to navigate a somewhat confusing section of trail for the next three miles.

At **mile 3.4**, cross a jeep trail. Then at **mile 3.5 D**, cross the North Fork of Tennessee Creek on a footbridge. There are good, hard-packed campsites in the area. Cross another jeep trail, just past the stream. At **mile 3.7**, cross West Tennessee Creek on a bridge. There are campsites near the stream. At mile 4.1, the trail begins following an old jeep trail to the right. At **mile 4.8 E** , turn right at a poorly-marked intersection. And at **mile 5.4**, turn left at another unmarked intersection. The trail becomes less confusing past this point.

At **mile 6.3**, the trail begins following the bottom of Longs Gulch. This valley has a strong stream and many good camping possibilities. Cross the stream at **mile 6.6**, then enter the Holy Cross Wilderness Area at **mile 6.7 F** . There is a boundary sign and a trail register at this location. Cross the stream once more at **mile 6.9** and begin climbing out of the valley. Briefly enter the tundra near two small lakes at **mile 7.7** (11,490) **G** . There are high altitude campsites here. Re-enter the trees, then head downhill to a small stream with campsites at **mile 8.1** (11,260). Cross another stream at **mile 8.3**, then climb into the tundra again. Reach a high point at **mile 8.8** (11,640) **H** , then begin another descent. Ignore a side trail heading down the valley at **mile 9.4**, then cross another stream at **mile 9.6** (11,470) **J**. There are some small campsites here. Hit a well-marked intersection at **mile 10.0** and turn right. Cross a stream at **mile 10.2** on a footbridge. There are small campsites nearby. At **mile 10.5**, cross a small stream, then turn right at a well-marked intersection. Cross another small stream with good campsites just past this intersection. The trail goes by a small lake at **mile 10.7 K** , then another lake with good campsites at **mile 10.8** (11,110). At **mile 11.7**, the trail begins a steep descent via a series of switchbacks. Cross two small streams at **mile 11.8**, then leave the wilderness at **mile 13.0 L**. A trail register is located at **mile 13.5**, just before a bridge across the Lake Fork. Continue ahead to **mile 13.6 M** and a trailhead parking area (10,040), the end of Segment 9.

LEFT: *Sunrise at Porcupine Lakes.*

LEFT:
Skiing on the CT.

backpackers. Five of the huts were built with donations from family and friends to honor individuals who died serving the 10th Mountain Division during World War II.

The huts are situated between 9,700 and 11,700 feet and are designed for experienced backcountry travelers. Most of them operate in the winter between late November and late April, and then again for three months in the summer. Accommodations are best described as comfortably rustic, with bunks to sleep about 15 people in a communal setting. Huts are equipped with wood stoves for heating, propane for cooking, photovoltaic lighting, mattresses and utensils. You bring your own sleeping bag, food and clothing. Users melt snow in winter and collect water from streams in summer.

Over 300 miles of trails link the huts together and several sit close to the CT, including Janets Cabin, Vances Cabin, and Uncle Buds. Reservations are required. Contact The 10th at (970) 925-5775 or visit their website at www.huts.org. Please note that this site administers a system of huts, including those of the 10th as well as Alfred A. Braun Huts and Friends Huts.

10th Mountain Division Hut System

For backcountry skiing, snowshoeing, and snowboarding enthusiasts, there are a number of winter accesses for the CT, usually where the trail crosses a major pass at a regularly plowed highway. Undoubtedly the best of these is the Tennessee Pass access, at the start of Segment 9; not only for a reputation for excellent snow conditions, but also, this access sits smack in the middle of an extensive network of mountain huts run by the 10th Mountain Division Hut Association.

The 10th is a non-profit organization founded in 1980 by a group of backcountry recreationalists, including several veterans of the famed US Army's 10th Mountain Division which trained at nearby Camp Hale in the 1940s.

The hut system occupies a large triangle between Vail, Leadville, and Aspen. Styled after the European tradition of hut-to-hut travel, 29 huts within the system provide overnight shelter for backcountry skiers, snow boarders, snowshoers, mountain bikers, and

BELOW: *Janets Cabin near Searle Pass, Seg. 8.*

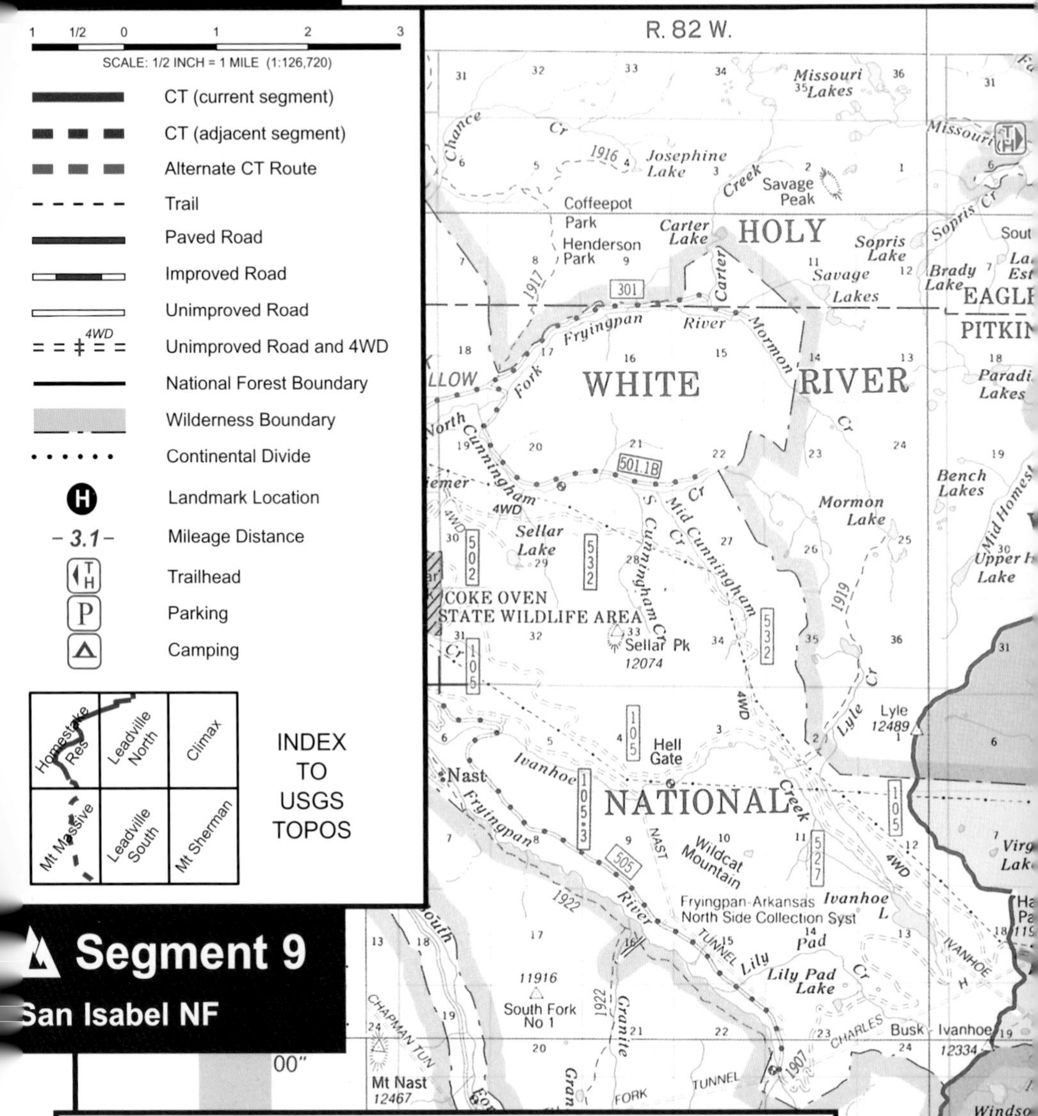

1 1/2 0 1 2 3
SCALE: 1/2 INCH = 1 MILE (1:126,720)
CT (current segment)
CT (adjacent segment)
Alternate CT Route
Trail
Paved Road
Improved Road
Unimproved Road
4WD
Unimproved Road and 4WD
National Forest Boundary
Wilderness Boundary
Continental Divide
Landmark Location
- 3.1 -
Mileage Distance
Trailhead
Parking
Camping
Homestake Res
Leadville North
Climax
Mt Massive
Leadville South
Mt Sherman
INDEX TO USGS TOPOS
R. 82 W.
Missouri Lakes
Josephine Lake
Savage Peak
Coffeepot Park
Henderson Park
Carter Lake
HOLY
Sopris Lake
Savage Lakes
Brady Lake
EAGLE
PITKIN
Paradise Lakes
Fryingpan River
WHITE
RIVER
NATIONAL
Mormon Lake
Bench Lakes
Upper Homestake Lake
Sellar Lake
COKE OVEN
STATE WILDLIFE AREA
Sellar Pk
12074
Lyle
12489
Hell Gate
Nast
Wildcat Mountain
Fryingpan-Arkansas North Side Collection Syst
Ivanhoe L
Lily Pad Lake
South Fork No 1
11916
Busk
Ivanhoe
12334
Mt Nast
12467
Windsor Lake
Notch
PAN

Segment 9

San Isabel NF

Landmark Comments	Mileage	Fr. Denver	Latitude	Longitude
A Begin Segment 9	0.0	143.1	39.363209	-106.311218
B Meet Treeline Ski Trail	1.1	144.2	39.354824	-106.325518
C Cross Wurtz Ditch	2.5	145.6	39.352121	-106.349086
D Cross Tennessee Cr.	3.5	146.6	39.347221	-106.359585
E Turn right at intersection	4.8	147.9	39.342158	-106.377728
F Enter Wilderness Area	6.7	149.8	39.329348	-106.404325
G Two small lakes	7.7	150.8	39.321847	-106.413816
H Reach high point	8.8	151.9	39.310144	-106.402422
J Cross stream	9.6	152.7	39.307737	-106.406260
K Go by small lake	10.7	153.8	39.298188	-106.419916
L Leave wilderness	13.0	156.1	39.288178	-106.438951
M End Segment 9	13.6	156.7	39.284955	-106.446187

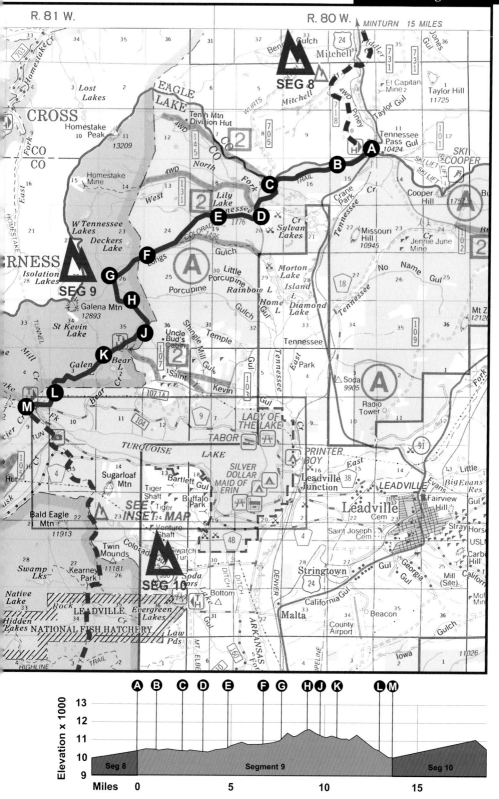

Segment 10
Timberline Lake & CT Trailhead
Halfmoon Creek

BELOW: *A through-hiker passes under a canopy of aspen.*

Distance: 13.0 miles
Elevation Gain: approx 1760 ft

USFS Maps: San Isabel National Forest, see pages 116-117.

USGS Quad Maps: Homestake Reservoir, Mount Massive.

Trails Illustrated map: # 127.

Jurisdiction: Leadville Ranger District, San Isabel NF.

Access from Denver:

Access from Durango:

Availability of Water:

Bicycling: see page 115.

Gudy's Tip

"*If your goal is to climb Mount Elbert or Mount Massive, get a very early start. Thunderstorms and lightening can roll in by noon during the summer. And by starting early, you'll avoid the crowd of peakbaggers.*" There is camping near the Halfmoon Creek Trailhead, a good "base camp" for climbing both of these fourteeners.

About This Segment

This trailhead and segment break is a change from previous editions of the CT guidebook. The previous trailhead at the Hagerman Pass Road access to the CT does not have any off road parking, while the Timberline Lake and Colorado Trail Trailhead has a nice off-road parking area for about 15 cars. So in this edition of the guidebook, the Timberline Lake and Colorado Trail Trailhead is now the breakpoint between Segments 9 and 10. There are a few adequate campsites around this trailhead and plenty of water. Previous editions of the CT guidebook have referred to this trailhead as the Lake Fork Trailhead, since it is on Lake Fork Creek. However, the Leadville Ranger District has upgraded the trailhead and refers to it as the Timberline Lake and Colorado Trail Trailhead.

In this segment, there are a couple of almost 1,000-foot climbs and descents; but at the end of the segment, the CT is at almost the same elevation as at the beginning. Along the way, you'll enter the beautiful Mount Massive Wilderness Area at about mile 3.0. At approximately mile 6.0, the CT crosses the Leadville National Fish Hatchery, one of the oldest hatcheries in the Federal system. It was established by Congress in 1889 and is still very active. The buildings are about 2 miles east of the CT's crossing of Rock Creek. At about the mile 10.0, a side-trail leads off to the top of Mount Massive (14,421), the second highest mountain in Colorado. For those interested in the side trip, it is 3.5 miles each way, with a little over 3,000 feet of vertical. This segment ends as you leave the wilderness area at the Halfmoon Creek Trailhead.

Trailhead/Access Points

Timberline Lake and Colorado Trail Trailhead 🚗 **:** This access road seems to have several names, depending or your source: Turquoise Lake Road, County Road-9, and FS-104. Turquoise Lake Road seems to be the most comprehensive, since it applies from the end of the 1000 block of W. 6th St. in downtown Leadville, all the way around Turquoise Lake and back to its starting point at W. 6th St. The trailhead is accessed from the westernmost point of the Turquoise Lake Road. So, to get to the trailhead from US-24, which runs through the center of Leadville, turn west on W. 6th St and follow it to the end of the 1000 block, curve right around the Lake City Recreation Center, then almost immediately turn left onto the Turquoise Lake Road. Follow it to its westernmost point and turn west onto the access road for the 100-yard drive to the parking area. It makes no difference whether you drive around the north side of the lake or the south, but the south is a little shorter.

Hagerman Pass Road Access 🚗 **:** Follow the instructions above to the Turquoise Lake Road. Follow it around the south side of the Lake. At 3.1 miles after crossing Sugarloaf Dam, Hagerman Pass Road exits at a shallow angle to the left. The CT crosses at 0.9 mile up this road. There is no parking space here.

Halfmoon Creek Trailhead 🚗 **:** See Segment 11.

Trail Description

ABOVE: *Boulder hopping at one of the many stream crossings in Segment 10.*

BELOW: *Hikers push on as snowflurries pelt them near Mount Massive.*

This segment begins at the trailhead parking area above Turquoise Lake, **mile 0.0 Ⓐ** . Just after leaving the parking area, an intersection with the trail to Timberline Lake presents itself. Turn left and cross a small stream after about 100 feet (10,050). Head up the hillside on the Colorado Trail. At **mile 0.4**, cross Glacier Creek on a good bridge. There are campsites in the vicinity. At **mile 1.2 Ⓑ** , cross Busk Creek (10,120) on another bridge. There is a fishing trail that leads to the left. Ignore this trail and continue ahead. Cross the Hagerman Pass Road at **mile 1.8** (10,340). The trail continues 100 feet to the left on the other side of the road. Just above the road at **mile 1.9** there is a scenic, dry campsite that overlooks Turquoise Lake

Pass by a trail register, then cross a small stream at **mile 2.5**. Another stream is crossed at **mile 2.8** (10,920), then a road at **mile 3.0**. Just beyond the road, pass under a power line. As the high point on the ridge is reached, a panoramic view of Mt. Elbert opens up ahead. Enter the Mount Massive Wilderness Area at **mile 3.3 Ⓒ** . The boundary is marked by a trail register. This wilderness was designated by Congress in 1980 and is 18,000 acres in size. Mt. Massive, at 14,421 feet in elevation, is the second highest peak in Colorado (Mt. Elbert is the highest at 14,440 feet).

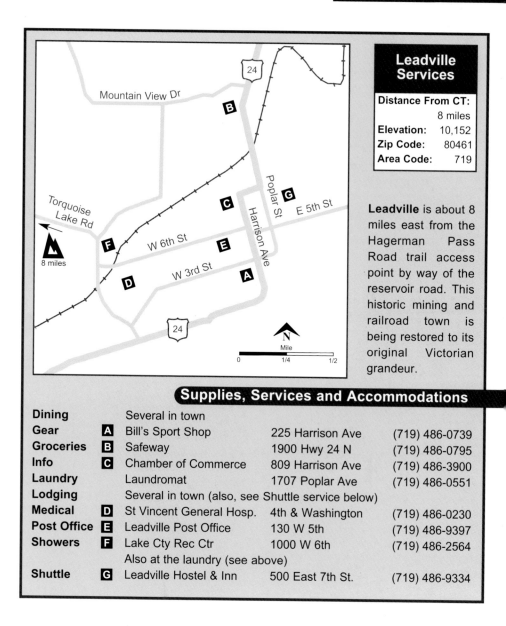

Leadville Services

Distance From CT:
8 miles
Elevation: 10,152
Zip Code: 80461
Area Code: 719

Leadville is about 8 miles east from the Hagerman Pass Road trail access point by way of the reservoir road. This historic mining and railroad town is being restored to its original Victorian grandeur.

Supplies, Services and Accommodations

Dining		Several in town	
Gear	**A**	Bill's Sport Shop	225 Harrison Ave	(719) 486-0739
Groceries	**B**	Safeway	1900 Hwy 24 N	(719) 486-0795
Info	**C**	Chamber of Commerce	809 Harrison Ave	(719) 486-3900
Laundry		Laundromat	1707 Poplar Ave	(719) 486-0551
Lodging		Several in town (also, see Shuttle service below)		
Medical	**D**	St Vincent General Hosp.	4th & Washington	(719) 486-0230
Post Office	**E**	Leadville Post Office	130 W 5th	(719) 486-9397
Showers	**F**	Lake Cty Rec Ctr	1000 W 6th	(719) 486-2564
		Also at the laundry (see above)		
Shuttle	**G**	Leadville Hostel & Inn	500 East 7th St.	(719) 486-9334

Just beyond the register is a small stream with a good campsite (11,060). Another stream, without a good campsite, is crossed at **mile 3.3**. Cross yet another stream at **mile 4.1**. There are good campsites here. Cross a old, abandoned jeep trail at **mile 4.2** ❶ Intersect another old road at **mile 5.1** ❷ and turn to the right. Follow to another "Y" intersection in about 300 feet (10,640). Again, bear to the right. A wooden sign, facing the road, shows the direction of the trail. A Forest Service sign, identifying the Colorado Trail and the Kearney Park Trail, is passed at **mile 5.2** (the overgrown trail to Kearney Park takes off across the meadow). Cross the old Fish Hatchery Road at **mile 6.0** ❸ and pass through a large, hard-packed camping area on the banks of Rock Creek (10,300). Cross the creek at **mile 6.2** on a good bridge. Then cross a small stream at **mile 6.5**. There are good campsites in the vicinity. Ignore a faint side trail at **mile 7.0**, then begin following a stream at **mile 7.4**. There are a few small campsites here. Cross the Highline Trail, leading to Native Lake, at **mile 7.7** ⓖ and cross another small stream at **mile 8.5**. There are no good campsites here, but some fairly good sites may be found about 0.1 mile further ahead. And there are even better sites to be found at **mile 8.8** ⓗ, where the trail crosses North Willow Creek on a bridge (11,040).

At **mile 9.8** ⓘ, intersect the trail to Mt. Massive (11,220). A good, dry camping area is found at **mile 10.0**, below the Mt. Massive Trail. A better campsite is at **mile 10.2** at Middle Willow Creek (11,030). These sites are often occupied by groups climbing Mt. Massive. Cross South Willow Creek at **mile 10.8** ⓚ and pass by an old mine building at **mile 11.3** (10,880), then begin a rapid descent at about **mile 11.7**. Reach the wilderness boundary at **mile 12.9**, then enter the trailhead parking area near Halfmoon Creek at **mile 13.0** ⓛ. Here, the segment ends at a crossing of Halfmoon Creek (10,060).

Climbing Mt. Elbert and Mt. Massive

The two highest peaks in the state are tempting side trips for many hikers on this stretch of the CT. No technical skills are required for either climb. Still, one must regard these as serious undertakings due to potentially exposed weather conditions and strenuous high altitude hiking. Be prepared — start early, bring warm clothing and rain gear, and turn back if you encounter bad weather or experience symptoms of altitude sickness.

The Hayden Survey named Mt Massive (14,421') in the 1870s, and despite several attempts since to substitute names of various individuals, the superior descriptive appellation has stuck. Mt. Elbert (14,433') was not so lucky. Like so many other mountains in Colorado, it was named for a politician, Samuel H. Elbert, who was initially appointed by President Lincoln in 1862 as secretary of the new Colorado Territory. After a succession of posts, Elbert became a Supreme Court justice when Colorado achieved statehood. Elbert the mountain is the second highest peak in the

contiguous United States — Mt Whitney in California tops it by only 60 feet.

Both summits can be reached by trail from the CT trailhead parking area on Halfmoon Creek Road (end of Seg. 10, start of Seg. 11). For Mount Massive, reverse Segment 10 of the CT for 3 miles and pick up the Mt. Massive Trail, which you follow west, then north to the summit. For Mount Elbert, go south on Segment 11 of the CT for 1.3 miles, then take the Mt. Elbert Trail another 2.5 miles west to the top. Either summit requires about 4,500 feet of elevation gain.

BELOW: *Sunrise from on top of Mount Elbert.*

Mountain Bicycle Detour

Holy Cross/Mount Massive Wilderness Detour —
Segments 9 and 10 (San Isabel NF): This detour avoids the Holy Cross and Mount Massive Wilderness Areas. The detour skips 24.1 miles of the hiking route.

Detour Description: Leave the trail at mile 2.5 of segment 9, where the CT crosses the Wurtz Ditch Road (10,420). Turn left on the road and follow it to an intersection with FS-100 at **mile 0.3** (10,390. Turn left here and follow the road to **mile 1.3**, where it intersects US-24 (10,150). Turn right on the highway and ride south. Reach an intersection with CO-91 at **mile 8.4** and bear right at the fork to Leadville (10,160). Leadville is a great place to stop and spend a night or two and re-supply.

Continue south of Leadville on US 24 to **mile 14.0** and turn right on CO-300 (9,560). At **mile 14.8**, turn left on FS-160 (9,560) and follow it to a sharp right turn at **mile 16.0** (9,480). This is Halfmoon Creek Road (FS-110). Proceeding up the road there are numerous campsites and FS campgrounds along the way. Follow the road southwest to **mile 21.5** and rejoin the Colorado Trail where it takes off to the left, just before a bridge on Halfmoon Creek. Segment 11 begins at this point (10,060).

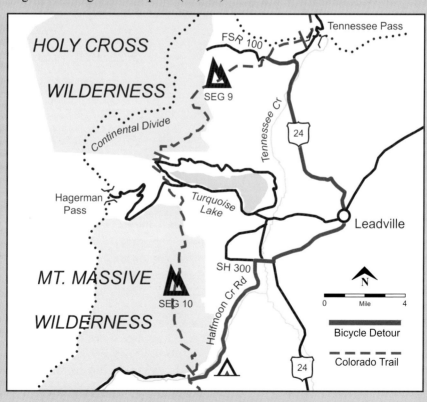

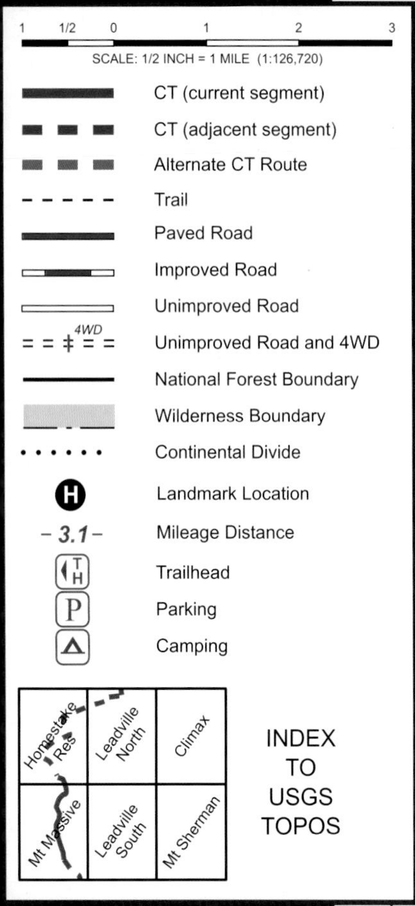

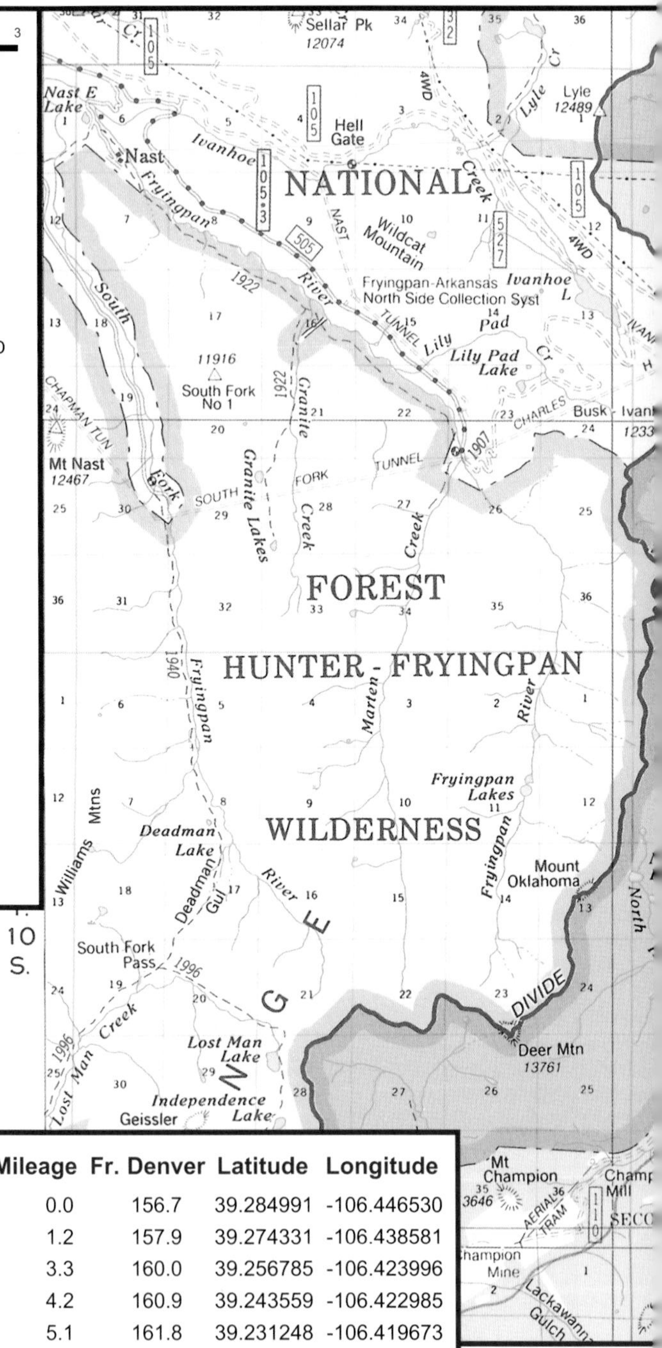

SCALE: 1/2 INCH = 1 MILE (1:126,720)

1 1/2 0 1 2 3	
▬▬▬▬▬	CT (current segment)
▬ ▬ ▬	CT (adjacent segment)
▬ ▬ ▬	Alternate CT Route
- - - - -	Trail
▬▬▬▬▬	Paved Road
▭▭▭	Improved Road
▭▭▭▭	Unimproved Road
= = ‡ = = (4WD)	Unimproved Road and 4WD
▬▬▬	National Forest Boundary
▬▬▬	Wilderness Boundary
• • • • • •	Continental Divide
H	Landmark Location
– *3.1* –	Mileage Distance
[TH]	Trailhead
[P]	Parking
[△]	Camping

INDEX TO USGS TOPOS

Homestake Res	Leadville North	Climax
Mt Massive	Leadville South	Mt Sherman

▲ Segment 10

San Isabel NF

Landmark Comments	Mileage	Fr. Denver	Latitude	Longitude
A Begin Segment 10	0.0	156.7	39.284991	-106.446530
B Cross Busk Creek	1.2	157.9	39.274331	-106.438581
C Enter wilderness	3.3	160.0	39.256785	-106.423996
D Cross jeep road	4.2	160.9	39.243559	-106.422985
E Intersect road and go right	5.1	161.8	39.231248	-106.419673
F Cross hatchery road	6.0	162.7	39.225858	-106.423964
G Cross Highline Trail	7.7	164.4	39.208323	-106.426796
H Cross North Willow Cr.	8.8	165.5	39.194863	-106.430149
J Intersect Mt. Massive Tr.	9.8	166.5	39.184327	-106.426737
K Cross S. Willow Creek	10.8	167.5	39.172337	-106.423442
L End of Segment 10	13.0	169.7	39.151623	-106.418690

Sellar Pk 12074

Nast E Lake

Nast

Ivanhoe

Hell Gate

NATIONAL

Wildcat Mountain

Fryingpan-Arkansas North Side Collection Syst

Ivanhoe

Lily Pad Lake

Mt Nast 12467

South Fork No 1

Granite Lakes

Busk

FOREST

HUNTER - FRYINGPAN

Marten

Fryingpan Lakes

Deadman Lake

WILDERNESS

Mount Oklahoma

South Fork Pass

Lost Man Lake

Independence Lake

Geissler

Deer Mtn 13761

Williams Mtns

Mt Champion 3646

Champion Mine

Lackawanna Gulch

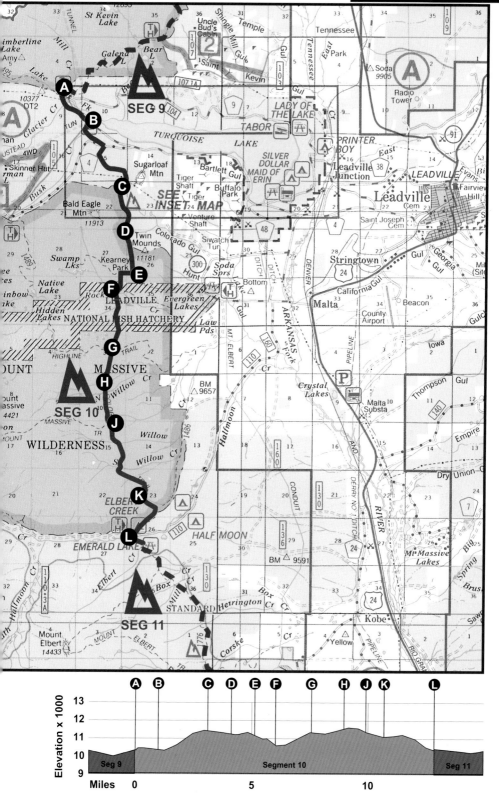

Segment 11
Halfmoon Creek to Clear Creek Road

BELOW: *Hikers descend into the Clear Creek valley, terminus of Segment 11.*

Distance: 21.5 miles
Elevation Gain: approx 1520 ft

USFS Maps: San Isabel National Forest, see pages 124-125.

USGS Quad Maps: Mount Massive, Mount Elbert, Granite, Winfield, Mount Harvard.

Trails Illustrated map: # 127.

Jurisdiction: Leadville Ranger District, San Isabel NF.

Access from Denver:

Access from Durango:

Availability of Water:

Bicycling:

Gudy's Tip

"The previous route over Hope Pass has been replaced by a more direct one. Those still choosing to climb Hope Pass know why it is so named: 'Hope I never have to go over that again with a full pack.'" In 2000, the access issues were finally resolved and the present, lower elevation route between the Lake Creek and Clear Creek drainages opened. The old Hope Pass route is now the Continental Divide Trail.

About This Segment

This segment begins by skirting the eastern base of Mount Elbert (14,433), the highest mountain in Colorado, at approximately the 10,000-foot level. Two of the most popular climbing routes up Mount Elbert depart from this section of the CT.

South of Mount Elbert, the CT goes around Twin Lakes Reservoir, part of the Pan-Ark Project which diverts water from the Western Slope to the Front Range via tunnels and the Arkansas River. The Mount Elbert Pump Station, located on the north shore of Twin Lakes Reservoir, generates electricity using a "pumped storage" technique. It involves using water from a higher reservoir to generate electricity when demand is high, then using electricity to pump the water back up to the higher reservoir when the demand for electricity is low. The Mount Elbert Pump Station previously provided a pleasant rest stop for hikers; but since 9/11, it has been closed to the public in the interest of national security. The access to the trail across the reservoir's dam was also closed; so now, the CT follows along the south side of CO-82 until it crosses Lake Creek on the highway bridge. Use caution, this is a narrow bridge with lots of high speed traffic. Then, the CT winds its way up the south shore of the reservoir to the Cache Creek Cutoff. The Cutoff was opened in 2000 after many years of negotiation to obtain an easement through this area. One big advantage of the Cache Creek Cutoff is that it eliminated 6 miles of dusty road walk. This segment terminates where the CT crosses Clear Creek Road, 1/8 mile west of the Colorado Division of Wildlife CG at the west end of Clear Creek Reservoir.

Trailhead/Access Points

Halfmoon Creek Trailhead 🚗 : Drive south from Leadville on US-24 for about 3.5 miles. Turn right (west) onto CO-300. Drive 0.8 mile, turn left (south) and continue 1.2 miles to an intersection. Take the right hand branch (FS-110). Continue 5.5 miles to the trailhead on the right hand side of the road, just after passing over a large culvert.

Lakeview Campground Trailhead 🚗 : Drive south from Leadville on US-24 for approximately 15 miles to CO-82. Turn right onto the highway for 4 miles. Turn right onto Lake Co Rd-24 for 1 mile to the Lake View Campground. Trailhead parking is provided in the campground.

Clear Creek Road Trailhead 🚗 : See Segment 12

Trail Description

This section begins at the Mount Massive Trailhead parking area on Halfmoon Creek, **mile 0.0** (10,065) ❹. From the parking area, walk to the Halfmoon Creek Road and cross the creek via the bridge on the road. The trail leaves to the south, immediately after crossing the creek. This is the re-entry point for mountain bikers who have just detoured around the Holy Cross and Mt. Massive Wilderness Areas. Follow the trail in a generally southerly direction. At **mile 0.4**, another trail from the Mount Elbert Trailhead merges from the left. Continue ahead, crossing a creek in a few hundred feet. Pass the ruins of a old log cabin at **mile 0.6**, then cross an old, unused irrigation canal at **mile 1.2**. At **mile 1.3** ❺, the Mount Elbert Trail leaves to

The Legacy of the Interlaken Resort

Seemingly isolated and forgotten today, it's hard to imagine that one of the most popular tourist destinations in Colorado before the 20th Century was Interlaken, nestled on the shores of the present-day Twin Lakes. The complex was started in 1879 and enlarged after James V. Dexter bought the lakeside resort and grounds in 1883 and transformed it into a popular summer retreat for those that rode the train to a nearby stop, then took the short carriage ride to the south shore location.

The Interlaken Hotel boasted some of the best amenities for the time with comfortable rooms and expansive views of mountains and lakes. There was a tavern, pool hall, barns and stables, and a unique six-sided

BELOW: *The old Interlaken Resort hotel sits on the shores of Twin Lakes with a backdrop of Mount Elbert.*

outdoor privy. An ice house, granaries, and laundry rounded out the facility. Guests came to fish, hunt, ride horses or just plain relax. Dexter build his own private cabin to reflect his nautical interests, including a cupola atop the second story with views in all directions.

Unfortunately, the resort rapidly fell into decline after the turn of the century when Twin Lakes were enlarged by irrigation interests. The entrance road was inundated and the large, but now shallow, lakes were less attractive to nature lovers. Eventually, the place was abandoned and the buildings began to deteriorate.

In 1979, as the reservoir was enlarged further, the Bureau of Reclamation stepped in and began to record and stabilize the historic district. Buildings that were to be inundated by the new dam were moved slightly uphill and extensively repaired. For CT hikers, the site is an interesting and short side trip that preserves a slice of Colorado history.

Twin Lakes, an old mining town and perhaps Colorado's oldest resort town, is approximately 1.0 mile west of the CT crossing on Hwy-82. The Twin Lakes Store is a delightful old general store, and now convenience/gas store, which provides the basics and has a very small post office within to serve the locals.

Twin Lakes Services

Distance From CT:	
	1 miles
Elevation:	9,210
Zip Code:	81251
Area Code:	719

Supplies, Services and Accommodations

Dining	Twin Lakes Nordic Inn	6435 Hwy 82	(719) 486-1830
Gear	Twin Lakes Store	6451 Hwy 82	(719) 486-2196
Groceries	See Twin Lakes Store above		
Laundry	Win Mar	Hwy 82 & Hwy 24	(719) 486-0785
Lodging	Twin Peaks Cabins	889 Hwy 82	(719) 486-2667
	Win Mar	Hwy 82 & Hwy 24	(719) 486-0785
	Twin Lakes Roadhouse/Lodge		(888) 486-4744
Medical	Nearest in Leadville		
Post Office	See Twin Lakes Store above		
Showers	Win Mar	Hwy 82 & Hwy 24	(719) 486-0785

the right (10,590). Stay on the left fork at this poorly-marked intersection. Cross another old trail at **mile 1.5**. Cross a small stream a few hundred feet further. A few small campsites are possible here. Cross Box Creek at **mile 1.8**. Pass an old jeep trail at **mile 1.9**, then cross Mill Creek on a bridge at **mile 2.0** (10,345) **C** . There are good, hard-packed campsites near Mill Creek. At **mile 2.3** and **mile 2.8**, cross old logging trails. Cross Herrington Creek at **mile 3.2** (10,320) **D** , then merge with another old logging trail, just beyond. There is a good hard-packed campsite near this intersection. Pass by a marshy area with several large beaver ponds at **mile 4.2**. At **mile 4.4**, turn right at an intersection marked by a 4X4 post and join the Mount Elbert Trail for 300 feet, until that trail leaves to the right. Continue ahead and slowly begin to descend through a forest of huge aspen trees. Pass by some more beaver ponds at **mile 4.7** (10,550) **E** . While camping might be possible here, the area is very buggy.

Just past the ponds, reach another intersection marked with a post and a Mount Elbert sign. Go right and cross a bridge then join a motorized jeep trail at **mile 4.8**. There are numerous campsites here, at a parking area for Mount Elbert hikers. The trail continues on the west side of the road, past the bridge, and stays to the west and south, parallel to the road for the next 2.4 miles, crossing two small streams. Watch for a junction at about two miles and keep to the right below the campground, on the trail, to where it passes under CO-82 at **mile 7.2** (9,320). This huge culvert has the distinction of being the only pedestrian underpass on the Colorado Trail. This also is the beginning of a long, and often, hot hike along the shores of Twin Lakes to a spot below the dam.

The trail starts out passing through a forest of large ponderosa pine, then passes to the left of the Mount Elbert Power Plant after crossing a road at **mile 7.8** (9,295) **F** . This hydroelectric facility pumps water from Twin Lakes to a reservoir up the mountainside during the nighttime hours when electricity is cheap, then produces electricity using the same water during the daytime when rates are higher. Leave the area of the power plant at **mile 8.1** by crossing a log fence, then cross a road at **mile 8.3**. Cross another road at **mile 8.8**. Continue ahead and cross a third road at **mile 9.7**. Other intersections with a road occur at **mile 10.6** and **mile 10.8**. Continue on ahead, eventually crossing the Twin Lakes Dam Road at **mile 10.9** **G** .

ABOVE: *Hiking through the sagebrush near the Twin Lakes Dam.*

The trail originally crossed the dam to the south, but the CT has been re-routed via a circuitous detour to the east, below the dam. (This was ordered by the Homeland Security Department in 2001 to protect the hydroelectric facility.) Follow the trail across the dam road and eventually join the paved highway, then carefully cross Lake Creek on the highway bridge (9,170). Turn right just past the bridge at **mile 11.4** and pass through a gate. From here, the trail meanders along the creek and through a marshy area until it joins a gravel road at **mile 11.7**. Turn right and pass by the dam on the road at **mile 12.0**. The road forks at **mile 12.2** (9,230) **H** . Take the right fork here. At **mile 12.4**, the trail leaves the road and follows the south shore of the reservoir for about 1.3 miles. Then at **mile 13.7** **J** , turn left at a intersection marked with a post (9,210). The CT turns sharply off to the south and heads up the hill away from the lake. The Continental Divide Trail (and the old CT route) splits off here and follows the trail along the lake, eventually passing over Hope Pass. The old Interlaken Resort is a interesting side trip of about 1 mile along the lake shore.

Follow the trail to the ridge, then descend to a jeep trail at **mile 14.5** (9,710). Turn right here. Signs at this intersection are stolen occasionally and hikers can get lost by heading left and downhill. Be sure to turn uphill, to the right and northwest. Ignore a logging trail to the left at **mile 14.7**. Reach a poorly-marked intersection at **mile 14.9** and turn to the left. Cross a seasonal stream at **mile 15.9** (9,840) **Ⓚ**. There are possible campsites in the area. Cross a road at **mile 16.2**, then cross a stream at **mile 16.3**, followed by an old trail at 400 feet beyond. A large hard-packed campsite is located 300 feet below the trail along the stream. This stream may not be running in dry weather. Intersect a road at **mile 16.5**, then enter a spectacular aspen forest. Cross a stream at **mile 16.7** (9,930). A confusing set of intersections begins by turning left on a road at **mile 17.3**, then turning right on another jeep trail at **mile 17.4** (9,810). This road hits another jeep trail in 100 feet. The trail angles off from this road to the left. At **mile 17.6**, another small trail comes in from the left. This intersection is not confusing, but might be helpful for those navigating through the previous maze of roads. Cross an irrigation ditch at **mile 18.1** **Ⓛ** on a rickety wood bridge. There are campsites here, assuming that there is water in the canal.

Intersect another old logging trail at **mile 18.3** (9,425) and follow it to the right, then pass by another logging trail on the left at **mile 18.5**. Cross a seasonal stream at **mile 18.6**, then follow the right fork at a intersection ahead. Pass under a power line and turn right on the power line road at **mile 18.9** (9,370). Cross Cache Creek in about 300 feet. Continue along the road to **mile 19.4**, to a point where the power line makes a sharp bend to the left (9,500). Go straight ahead, leaving the road. At **mile 20.1** **Ⓜ** , turn left at an intersection marked with a post. Bear to the right and leave the old road on a single-track trail at **mile 20.2**, then gain the top of the ridge in 200 more feet (9,850). Begin descending into the Clear Creek drainage. Cross an old canal at **mile 20.6**, turning right at the jeep road and staying below the road for the next several hundred feet. The trail then crosses the road and descends the hillside to the trailhead at the Clear Creek Road at **mile 21.5** (9,000) **Ⓝ** .

LEFT: *There are several beautiful aspen-lined walks in Segment 11.*

SCALE: 1/2 INCH = 1 MILE (1:126,720)

———	CT (current segment)
▬ ▬ ▬	CT (adjacent segment)
▬ ▬ ▬	Alternate CT Route
- - - - -	Trail
———	Paved Road
⊏——⊐	Improved Road
⊏——⊐	Unimproved Road
= = ‡ = = 4WD	Unimproved Road and 4WD
———	National Forest Boundary
▬ - ▬	Wilderness Boundary
• • • • •	Continental Divide
H	Landmark Location
– 3.1 –	Mileage Distance
(T/H)	Trailhead
P	Parking
▲	Camping

INDEX TO USGS TOPOS

Mt Massive, Leadville South, Mt Sherman, Mt Elbert, Granite, South Peak

▲ Segment 11
San Isabel NF

	Landmark Comments	Mileage	Fr. Denver	Latitude	Longitude
A	Begin Segment 11	0.0	169.7	39.151623	-106.418690
B	Intersect Mt. Elbert Tr.	1.3	171.0	39.144016	-106.407542
C	Cross Mill Creek	2.0	171.7	39.136865	-106.401135
D	Cross Herrington Cr.	3.2	172.9	39.124316	-106.390187
E	Pass beaver ponds	4.7	174.4	39.106019	-106.394501
F	Cross road	7.8	177.5	39.094819	-106.354161
G	Cross dam road	10.9	180.6	39.082364	-106.302990
H	Take right fork	12.2	181.9	39.073660	-106.304542
J	Turn left at intersection	13.7	183.4	39.075180	-106.331788
K	Cross stream	15.9	185.6	39.060306	-106.325006
L	Cross irrigation ditch	18.1	187.8	39.039574	-106.308826
M	Turn left at intersection	20.1	189.8	39.022743	-106.304576
N	End Segment 11	21.5	191.2	39.017860	-106.298147

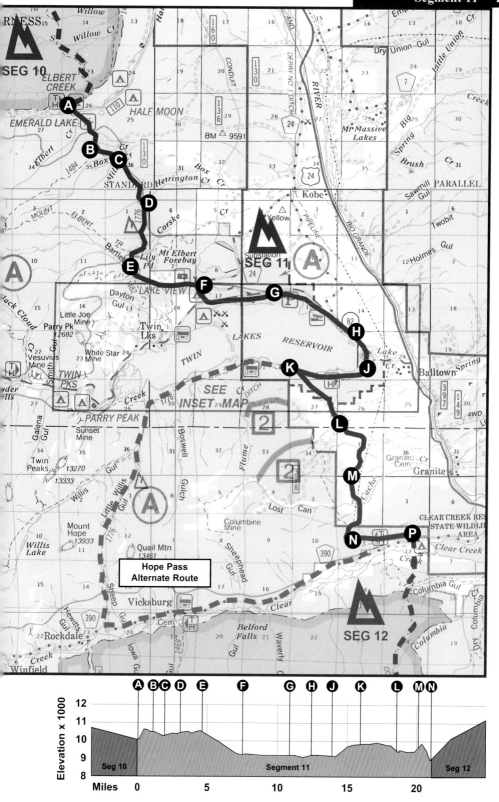

Segment 12
Clear Creek Road to North Cottonwood Creek

BELOW: *Hiking through a clear cut in the Collegiate Peaks area.*

Distance: 18.5 miles
Elevation Gain: approx 4520 ft

USFS Maps: San Isabel National Forest, see pages 132-133.

USGS Quad Maps: Granite, Mount Harvard, Harvard Lakes, Buena Vista West.

Trails Illustrated map: # 129.

Jurisdiction: Leadville Ranger District, San Isabel NF.

Access from Denver:

Access from Durango:

Availability of Water:

Bicycling: see page 131.

Gudy's Tip

"*If you have the time, a hike up Pine Creek into Missouri Basin is a rewarding side-trip. In this emerald-clad basin, you are seemingly in the very heart of the sky-touching Collegiates, surrounded by four 14ers — Harvard, Missouri, Belford and Oxford.*" This long day trip is about 5.5 miles each way into Missouri Basin, one of the largest alpine basins in the Sawatch Range.

In this segment, the CT continues its path along the eastern flank of the Sawatch Range with more spectacular ups and downs than the previous segment. In fact, you will spend a considerable amount of time above the 11,000-foot level. Three fourteeners (Mounts Oxford, Harvard and Columbia) are within 3 miles of the CT along this segment. Approximately 16 miles of this segment are within the Collegiate Peaks Wilderness Area, so bicyclists need to divert to the bicycle detour. It is a beautiful area with plenty of water and campsites, so there is no need to hurry up or down its several steep climbs.

This portion of the CT was re-routed in 2007 to avoid the private property of the Clear Creek Ranch. This required almost 3 miles of new trail construction and an 80-foot-long bridge across Clear Creek, built by eight crews of Colorado Trail Foundation volunteers.

Trailhead/Access Points

Clear Creek Road Trailhead Access 🚗 : Drive north from Buena Vista for approximately 17 miles. Turn left on Chaffee Co Rd-390. Drive 2.5 miles to a small, rough parking area, just west of the Colorado Division of Wildlife CG. Three large boulders on the south side of the road mark this trailhead and small parking area. There are Colorado Trail markers on both sides of the road.

North Cottonwood Creek Road Trail Access 🚗 : See Segment 13.

Supplies, Services and Accommodations

Available in Buena Vista (see Segment 13).

Trail Description

This segment begins at the Clear Creek Trailhead **A** , consisting of a small parking area on the south side of the Clear Creek Road, marked by three large boulders, **mile 0.0** (9,000). This trailhead is just east of the pole fence marking the boundary of the Clear Creek Ranch.

Begin the segment by going between the boulders and following the well-marked trail south and then east, following the creek to a steel brdige crossing the creek. Colorado Trail Foundation crews placed this bridge during the summer of 2007. The trail continues on the south side of the creek, climbing out of the Clear Creek Valley. In about a mile, you will pass udner the powerline at **mile 1.5** and cross an old jeep trail at **mile 1.9** (9,650) **B** in a sagebrush meadow at a well-marked intersection. Cross a seasonal stream at **mile 2.7**, then a spring-fed stream at **mile 4.0** (10,910) **C** . A small camp might be possible here. Cross two more small streams at **mile 4.4** and **mile 4.5**. None of these water sources should be deemed reliable in a very dry year.

Collegiate Peaks

The impressive collection of skyscraping fourteeners with names like Harvard, Columbia, Yale and Princeton are collectively known as the Collegiate Peaks, a subset of the greater Sawatch Range. First surveyed by a team led by Professor Josiah Dwight Whitney (for whom California's Mount Whitney is named) from Harvard. They started the tradition of naming these fourteeners for Ivy League universities after climbing Mount Harvard (14,420) in 1869. Mount Yale (14,196) was named after Whitney's alma mater. Later climbers continued the practice, adding Princeton, Oxford and Columbia.

Despite their proximity, most of the Collegiate fourteeners don't lend themselves to a day climb from the Colorado Trail. The best opportunity is on Mount Yale in Segment 13. At about mile 3.4 of that segment, the CT gains the long east ridge of Yale, offering a moderate route to the summit with a bit of rock hopping and a few false summits along the way. However, for non-climbers there are outstanding views of these giants at several vantage points on the CT.

Top out on the ridge **❶** at **mile 4.9** in a robust stand of bristlecone pines, mixed with fir (11,655). The trail now descends into the valley via a series of switchbacks. At **mile 6.5 ❷**, a trail joins the Colorado Trail from the northwest. Continue ahead and to the south. As you pass through the valley there are numerous good, hard-packed campsites along Pine Creek for the next 0.25 mile.

The trail intersects another trail coming up Pine Creek at **mile 6.6** (10,430). Here, the Colorado Trail crosses the creek on a good wooden bridge. Cross a smaller stream at **mile 6.8**, as you climb up out of the valley

BELOW: *Collegiate Wilderness Area boundary near Pine Creek.*

(10,525). There are good campsites in the vicinity. Cross a side trail at **mile 8.1** (10,560) **F** and continue ahead on the main trail. The side trail goes to Rainbow Lake, about 0.3 miles to the southwest. At **mile 9.1**, reach the edge of the tundra, then reach a high point (11,870) with nice views of the summit of Mt. Oxford. Head downhill, passing a small spring at **mile 9.4**. Cross Morrison Creek at **mile 9.8** (11,570) **G** , a good water source with some small campsites nearby. At **mile 10.5**, the Wapaca Trail comes in from the east (11,530). Continue ahead. At **mile 11.8**, cross Frenchmen Creek **H** , where there are many good, hard-packed campsites in the area (11,030). Intersect the Frenchmen Creek Trail at **mile 11.9**. Continue straight ahead, ignoring two well-traveled trails leading to the left and downhill. This intersection has been confusing to a number of trail users.

Cross another small stream at **mile 12.0**. Cross a side trail that is actually an old mining road at **mile 14.2** (10660) **I** . Continue straight ahead. Cross Three Elk Creek at **mile 15.2** (10,280'), then cross the Elk Creek Trail at **mile 15.4** **K** . Just past this intersection, go by Harvard Lake which is on the left (10,240). There are good campsites here. Ignore a trail leading around the lake and take a fork to the right. Cross a small stream at **mile 15.7** (10,160), then cross Powell Creek at **mile**

Gunnison Spur

The Colorado Trail Foundation has been working for a number of years on the completion of the Gunnison Spur to the Colorado Trail. It is planned that it will begin on the south side of Twin Lakes and proceed over Hope Pass, then up the South Fork of Clear Creek and over the Continental Divide near Lake Ann, down the high ground between Illinois Creek and Texas Creek, and up the Taylor River to a foot bridge across the Taylor just south of Dinner Station Campground. From there it will generally follow the high ground between the Taylor River and Brook Trail Creek/Clear Creek to where they join near One Mile Campground. From there it will proceed south via various jeep tracks and trails in the Beaver Creek drainage before turning southwest to Signal Peak and on to the trailhead at Western State College in Gunnison. The estimated distance for the Spur when completed is about 50 miles.

The Gunnison Spur has been signed but vandalism has taken a toll. Motorized traffic has also presented some problems, so that the CTF has not yet produced an official map or guide for the Spur, nor begun maintenance of it. It is still a work in progress with an uncertain completion date.

BELOW: *The Three Apostles, landmarks along the Gunnison Spur, in the South Fork of Clear Creek.*

15.9. Pass by a side trail to the A/U Ranch at **mile 16.5** (9,960) **Ⓛ** . Stay to the right for the Colorado Trail. The trail to the ranch is heavily used by horseback riders.

At a switchback at **mile 17.8**, horse traffic leaves the Colorado Trail on another side trail to the A/U Ranch (9,865). Stay to the right and descend into the valley. Pass a trail register at **mile 18.2** (9,430), then turn right on a county road. Follow the road uphill to the trailhead at **mile 18.5** (9,400) **Ⓜ** . Here, you'll find toilets, a large parking area and several interpretive signs.

BELOW: *CT hikers check their location in the CT Databook.*

Collegiate Peaks Wilderness Detour — *Segment 12 and 13 (San Isabel NF):* This is a mandatory detour to avoid the Collegiate Peaks Wilderness Area. Part of it is on busy US-24 and you'll have a hard time watching for traffic when your attention is drawn to the wonderful views of the giant Collegiate Peaks that line the west side of the road. While you may stay on US-24, it is more pleasant to turn onto Chaffee County Rd-371 for the 10 mile pedal into Buena Vista.

Detour Description: Start this detour at the end of Segment 11 (start of Segment 12) on Chaffee CO Rd-390. Ride east to **mile 3.0** and turn right (south) onto US-24. Continue on the highway to **mile 8.9**, then exit left onto Chaffee Co Rd-371. At this point, cross over the Arkansas River on Rd-371 and follow the abandoned railbed of the Colorado Midland to Buena Vista at **mile 18.8**.

Cross the river into town and go right on Main Street (west), past the intersection with US-24, onto Chaffee Co Rd-306 (the Cottonwood Pass Road). Continue to the Avalanche Trailhead parking area at **mile 28.4**, re-joining the Colorado Trail at mile 6.6 of Segment 13.

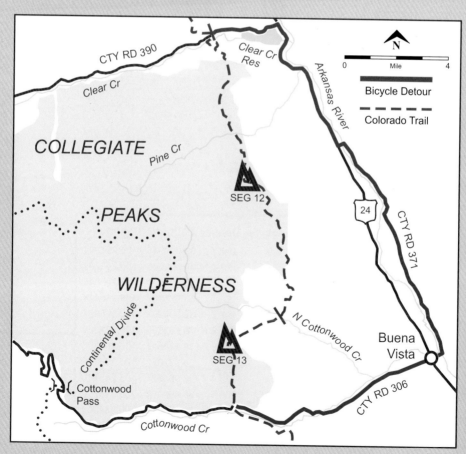

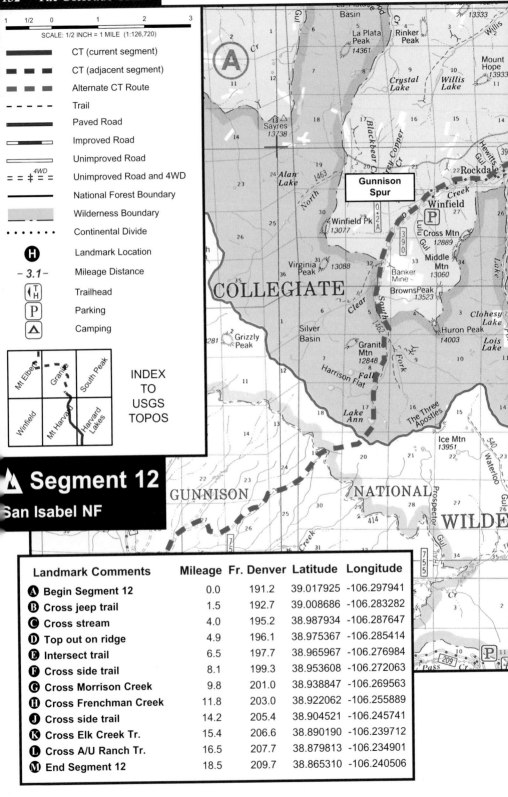

SCALE: 1/2 INCH = 1 MILE (1:126,720)

	CT (current segment)
	CT (adjacent segment)
	Alternate CT Route
	Trail
	Paved Road
	Improved Road
	Unimproved Road
	Unimproved Road and 4WD
	National Forest Boundary
	Wilderness Boundary
	Continental Divide
H	Landmark Location
– 3.1 –	Mileage Distance
Trailhead
P	Parking
▲	Camping

INDEX TO USGS TOPOS

Mt Elbert · Granite · South Peak
Winfield · Mt Harvard · Harvard Lakes

▲ **Segment 12**

San Isabel NF

Landmark Comments	Mileage	Fr. Denver	Latitude	Longitude
Ⓐ Begin Segment 12	0.0	191.2	39.017925	-106.297941
Ⓑ Cross jeep trail	1.5	192.7	39.008686	-106.283282
Ⓒ Cross stream	4.0	195.2	38.987934	-106.287647
Ⓓ Top out on ridge	4.9	196.1	38.975367	-106.285414
Ⓔ Intersect trail	6.5	197.7	38.965967	-106.276984
Ⓕ Cross side trail	8.1	199.3	38.953608	-106.272063
Ⓖ Cross Morrison Creek	9.8	201.0	38.938847	-106.269563
Ⓗ Cross Frenchman Creek	11.8	203.0	38.922062	-106.255889
Ⓙ Cross side trail	14.2	205.4	38.904521	-106.245741
Ⓚ Cross Elk Creek Tr.	15.4	206.6	38.890190	-106.239712
Ⓛ Cross A/U Ranch Tr.	16.5	207.7	38.879813	-106.234901
Ⓜ End Segment 12	18.5	209.7	38.865310	-106.240506

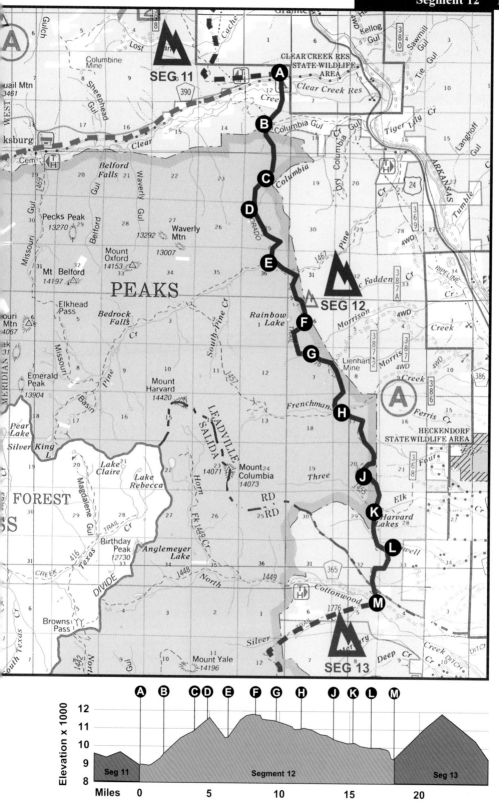

Segment 13
North Cottonwood Creek Road to Chalk Creek Trailhead

BELOW: *A view of Mount Princeton from near treeline on Mount Yale.*

Distance: 22.8 miles
Elevation Gain: approx 3720 ft

USFS Maps: San Isabel National Forest, see pages 140-141.

USGS Quad Maps: Buena Vista West, Mount Yale, Mount Antero.

Trails Illustrated map: # 129.

Jurisdiction: Salida Ranger District, San Isabel NF.

Access from Denver:

Access from Durango:

Availability of Water:

Bicycling: ✖   see page 131.

Gudy's Tip

"*Watch out for the missed signs at the Chalk Cliffs. The route along the road is a solution to skirt private property.*"

Be respectful of a long stretch of private property, as the trail descents into the Chalk Creek valley. Although CT travel here is primarily on public roads, there is no camping available on the surrounding private land. Ideally, the CTF will find a future solution to avoid this section.

About This Segment

After a rather idyllic and benign beginning, this segment suddenly gets serious and climbs nearly 3,000 feet in the next 3 miles. Once you reach the top of the east ridge of Mount Yale, there are some pretty decent views in all directions, particularly if you take a short walk to the top of the knoll to the east of the saddle. If the summit of Mount Yale (14,196) interests you, it can be reached via the ridge to the west. There is no trail; but it's a pretty decent scramble. Allow about 4 hours for the round trip — there are a couple of discouraging false summits along the route.

Just after leaving the saddle, heading south on the CT, pass an interesting *bristlecone pine* forest. The trip down from this ridge is as steep as the trip up. After arriving at the Avalanche Trailhead, where bicyclists can rejoin the CT after their detour around the Collegiate Peaks Wilderness Area, it is a relatively flat walk for the next three miles. Then, after a short climb, the CT contours its way around the base of Mount Princeton. At mile 17, rejoin civilization as you walk through the corner of a youth camp. Here, you start a 6-mile road walk, in order to get through private property and down the steep valley side of Chalk Creek. The Colorado Trail Foundation has been searching for years for a way to improve this section; but so far, no success. The saving grace of this section is the possibility of a soak at the Mount Princeton Hot Springs Resort. This segment terminates at a trailhead parking area on the south side of Chaffee County Rd-162.

Caution, there is NO camping sites for the next 6.5 miles after encountering private property at the youth camp at mile 17 of this segment!

Trailhead/Access Points

North Cottonwood Creek Trailhead : From US-24 at the north end of Buena Vista, turn west on Crossman Street (7 blocks north of the stoplight and across the highway from the *Trailhead Outdoor Gear* store. Crossman Street is also known as Chaffee County Rd-350). Follow it for 2 miles to its end, where it "T"s into Chaffee County Rd-361. Turn right (north), proceed 0.9 mile and make a sharp left turn (south) on to a gravel road, Co Rd-365. The road soon turns west and continues for 3.5 miles (some of them very rough and rutted) to the *northbound* CT trailhead. A trail register and sign identify it and there is a small informal parking area on the south side of the road. Continue 0.1 mile to the *southbound* trailhead on the south side of the road. It can be identified by the presence of a large gravel parking lot, interpretive signs and a FS toilet. There is also an even larger parking lot on the north side of the road, suitable for horse trailers. This area is the official end of Segment 12 and the beginning of Segment 13.

Avalanche Trailhead : From US-24 in Buena Vista, turn west at the stoplight onto the Cottonwood Pass Road (Main Street, which becomes Chaffee Co Rd-306 at the edge of town). Drive 9.5 miles to the Avalanche Trailhead on the north side of the highway. You may spot "Colorado Trail" signs on both sides of the highway at about 0.2 mile before the trailhead entrance sign on the right hand side. The CT crosses the parking area near the middle.

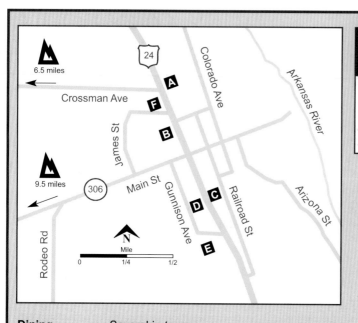

Buena Vista Services

Distance From CT:	
	9.5 miles
Elevation:	7,954
Zip Code:	81211
Area Code:	719

Dining		Several in town.		
Gear	A	Trailhead Ventures	707 Hwy 24 North	(719) 395-8001
Groceries	B	City Market	438 Hwy 24 Nouth	(719) 395-2431
Info	C	Chamber of Commerce	343 Hwy 24 South	(719) 395-6612
Laundry	D	Morrison's Laundromat	410 Hwy 24	no phone
Lodging		Several in town.		
Medical	E	Mountain Medical Centre	36 Oak	(719) 395-8632
Post Office	F	Buena Vista Post Office	110 Brookdale Ave	(719) 395-2445

Supplies, Services and Accommodations

Buena Vista, as might be gathered by its Spanish name, is a beautiful place to visit because of its mild year-round climate and striking location in the Arkansas Valley, between the mineralized Mosquito Range and the towering Sawatch. The town is an ideal resupply point for long-distance trekkers because the CT through here is approximately halfway between Denver and Durango. The most direct way to reach Buena Vista from the CT is to follow Chaffee Co Rd-306 approximately 9.5 miles east from Avalanche Trailhead.

Cottonwood Lake Road Access 🚗 : From the stoplight in Buena Vista described above, proceed west on the Cottonwood Pass Road for approximately 8 miles. Turn left onto the Cottonwood Lake Road (Chaffee Co Rd-344). After about 0.2 mile, the CT crosses this road. There is a small primitive parking area on the left hand side.

Chalk Creek Trailhead 🚗 : See Segment 14.

Trail Description

Begin this segment at the North Cottonwood Creek Trailhead on FS-365, **mile 0.0 Ⓐ**. This is a large trailhead area with ample parking and toilets. The trail begins by a sign just to the east of the toilet. Cross North Cottonwood Creek on a substantial wood bridge (9,360). At **mile 0.1**, pass by a trail register. Beyond is a good campsite close to the stream. The steep trail follows the drainage up through a mixed spruce and fir forest. At **mile 2.0 Ⓑ**, the trail begins following Silver Creek (10,970). There are good, flat campsites along the trail for the next half mile. Campers are reminded to camp at least 100 feet from the stream and trail. Pass by a faint climbers trail at **mile 2.2**. Cross the creek at **mile 2.5** and begin a short climb. This creek crossing is the last water for about 3.8 miles.

Enter the Collegiate Peaks Wilderness Area at **mile 2.7 Ⓒ** and gain the top of Mount Yale's long east ridge at **mile 3.4** (11,905) Ⓓ. There is a dry, hard-packed campsite to the right. At **mile 3.6**, enter a mixed bristlecone pine and fir forest. The trail descends steeply in places. At **mile 5.6**, a horse trail joins from the east at a switchback. Leave the wilderness at **mile 6.3 Ⓔ** near a small stream, the last water source for northbound hikers for 3.8 miles. Pass a trail register at **mile 6.4**, then cross a stream and arrive at the Avalanche Trailhead at **mile 6.5**. (This is easily the largest trailhead parking area along the entire Colorado Trail, rivaling some major shopping centers.) There are toilets here.

After passing across the parking area, pick up the trail again at a sign. Follow the trail to the Cottonwood Pass Road (FS-306) at **mile 6.6**. This is a convenient spot for mountain bikers to re-join the trail after detouring around the Collegiate Peaks Wilderness Area. Follow a small road directly across and take the trail to the left. Cross to the north side of Cottonwood Creek on a sturdy bridge at **mile**

RIGHT: *A CT hiker enjoys a peaceful aspen forest.*

ABOVE: *Hiking up in the clouds on Mt. Yale's east ridge.*

6.7. The trail heads to the east here, just north of private land along the shores of Rainbow Lake. Trail users are asked to stay on the trail and respect the private property. Cross a small stream at **mile 7.5 ❻**. There are no campsites here. Pass an intersection with a horse trail at **mile 8.2**. The horse trail goes down by the creek. Stay high on the Colorado Trail. Cross the Cottonwood Lake Road (FS-344) at **mile 8.9 ❼**, then cross South Cottonwood Creek at **mile 9.0**. This is the last reliable water source for 4.5 miles.

The trail follows the creek for about 0.5 mile. There are many good, hard-packed campsites in this area. Begin to leave the creek at **mile 9.4**, then cross a road (FS-343) at **mile 9.5**. Go by a trail register after crossing the road. The trail forks at **mile 10.1 ❽**. Take the right fork. Merge with a jeep trail at **mile 11.0**, then leave the road to the left at **mile 11.1**. Take yet another left at an intersection at **mile 11.2** and reach a saddle at **mile 11.7** (9,880) **❾**. Continue ahead past the saddle to **mile 11.8**, then turn left and follow the trail as it contours along the ridge. Cross a stream at **mile 13.5** (9,930) **❿**, then cross another stream with some possible, small campsites at **mile 14.0** (10,000). Intersect some jeep trails at **mile 15.3** and **mile 15.5**. Cross a small stream at **mile 15.7** (9,530) **⓫**. Pass under a power line at **mile 16.7**, then hit a road (C0 Rd-322) at **mile 16.9** (9,500). This is the start of a lengthy section on private land, where the trail follows roads.

Mount Princeton Hot Springs

The spot was long frequented by Native Americans before taken over and first developed by whites in 1860. The Mount Princeton Hot Springs Resort boomed and busted in response to the fortunes of area mines, the coming of the railroad and its subsequent final departure in 1926. The elaborate hotel on the site was taken down for scrap lumber in 1950. But you can't keep a good place down, or as they say at the resort, "The 135 degrees at the surface will melt your cares away." The three pools are open every day of the year ($10/per adult as of 2005).

Follow the road down and pass under a sign and through a private camp at **mile 18.2 ⓜ**. The pavement begins here. Follow the road to **mile 19.0 ⓝ** and turn to the right onto Co. Rd-321 (8,620). Follow this to **mile 20.3** and intersect Co. Rd-162 near Princeton Hot Springs. Hikers may wish to stop here for a dip in the legendary springs. Turn off of the road onto Bunny Lane (Co. Rd-291) at **mile 21.7**. Follow this dirt road through a neighborhood to the end of the segment **ⓟ** at **mile 22.8** (8,390). This is the Chalk Creek Trailhead and the end of private land.

Mountain Bicycle Detour

Raspberry Gulch Detour — *Segments 13 and 14 (San Isabel NF):* There is a mandatory detour for cyclists that begins in Segment 12 and ends at mile 6.6 of Segment 13 (see page 131). The rest of Segment 13 is ridable; but we offer this *optional* detour in Segment 13 and 14 for those who may prefer smooth, graded county roads to the trail, and because the steep switchbacks at the beginning of Segment 14 can be a challenge for some riders. (This detour was once advised to avoid a poorly-maintained section of the trail in the northern part of Segment 14; but the trail was rerouted in 1989 and the detour is not as critical now.)

Detour Description: Follow the CT to mile 20.3 in Segment 13 and turn left (east) onto Chaffee Co. Rd-162. Ride to **mile 0.7** and turn southeast, then east, on Rd-270, which soon takes on a southerly heading. Continue to **mile 4.6** and go right (west) on Rd-272. Turn left (south) at an intersection at **mile 6.6** and pedal on Rd-272 to **mile 8.2** and the Browns Creek Trailhead. Continue up the Browns Creek Trail to **mile 9.6** and rejoin the CT at mile 6.4 on Segment 14.

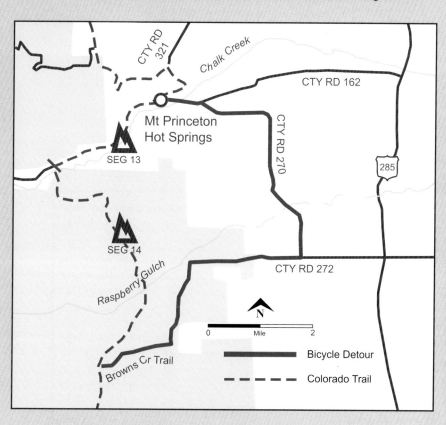

Legend

SCALE: 1/2 INCH = 1 MILE (1:126,720)

- CT (current segment)
- CT (adjacent segment)
- Alternate CT Route
- Trail
- Paved Road
- Improved Road
- Unimproved Road
- Unimproved Road and 4WD
- National Forest Boundary
- Wilderness Boundary
- Continental Divide
- **H** Landmark Location
- – 3.1 – Mileage Distance
- Trailhead
- P Parking
- Camping

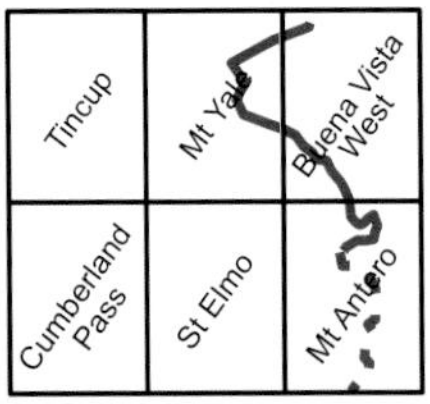

INDEX TO USGS TOPOS

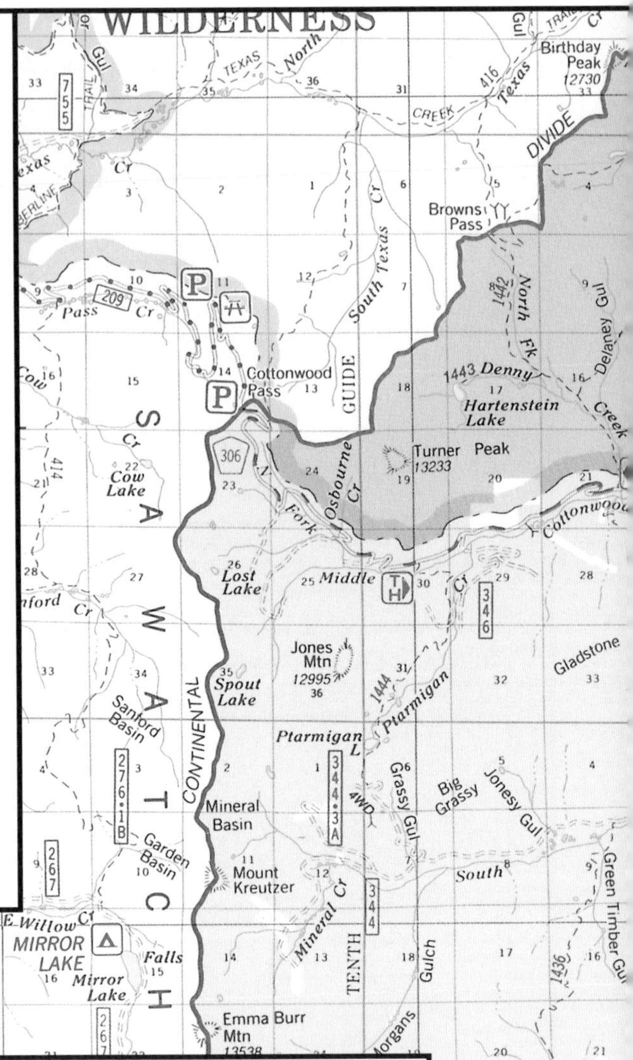

Tincup | Mt Ya... | Buena Vista West
Cumberland Pass | St Elmo | Mt Antero

▲ Segment 13
San Isabel NF

T. 15 S.

Landmark Comments	Mileage	Fr. Denver	Latitude	Longitude
Ⓐ Begin Segment 13	0.0	209.7	38.865310	-106.240506
Ⓑ Trail follows Silver Cr.	2.0	211.7	38.856105	-106.266732
Ⓒ Enter wilderness area	2.7	212.4	38.852230	-106.277184
Ⓓ Top out on ridge	3.4	213.1	38.847546	-106.281314
Ⓔ Leave wilderness area	6.3	216.0	38.816113	-106.277737
Ⓕ Cross stream	7.5	217.2	38.808184	-106.265080
Ⓖ Cross road	8.9	218.6	38.802061	-106.246868
Ⓗ Take right fork	10.1	219.8	38.802770	-106.234450
Ⓙ Reach saddle	11.7	221.4	38.794230	-106.227016
Ⓚ Cross stream	13.5	223.2	38.776974	-106.219858
Ⓛ Cross stream	15.7	225.4	38.758183	-106.198633
Ⓜ Pass private camp	18.2	227.9	38.740012	-106.175370
Ⓝ Reach Co. road	19.0	228.7	38.742571	-106.161679
Ⓟ End Segment 13	22.8	232.5	38.716778	-106.199532

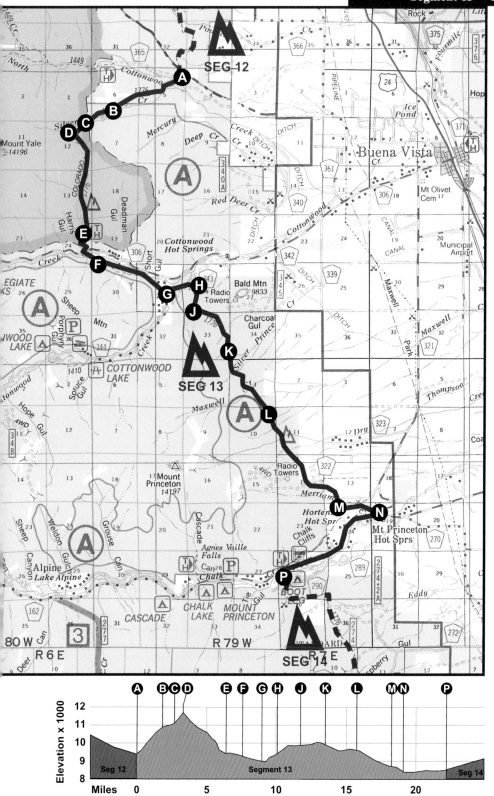

Segment 14
Chalk Creek to US-50

BELOW: *A mountain biker makes for the bridge at Chalk Creek.*

Distance: 20.9 miles
Elevation Gain: approx 3320 ft

USFS Maps: San Isabel National Forest, see pages 146-147.

USGS Quad Maps: Mount Antero, Maysville.

Trails Illustrated map: # 130.

Jurisdiction: Salida Ranger District, San Isabel NF.

Access from Denver: 🚗

Access from Durango: 🚗

Availability of Water: ☕

Bicycling: 🚲   see page 139.

Gudy's Tip

"*The short, but often overlooked, five-mile stretch between Shavano Campground and US-50 wanders through lovely aspen and lodgepole pine forests.*" Through-hikers should note that Cree Creek, crossed at mile 19.4, is the last decent camping spot north of the highway.

About This Segment

This segment travels through the southern end of the Sawatch Range. Although there are still several fourteeners nearby (Antero, Shavano & Tabeguache), the CT takes a much less rigorous route through the area. After the initial climb of 900 feet in the first 1.5 mile to get out of the Chalk Creek Valley, the CT ambles along between the 9,000 and 10,000-foot levels for the next 16 miles, before starting a descent to US-50. Water sources are not quite as frequent as in previous sections, but there is still plenty of it. Good campsites are not a problem either. So, amble along and enjoy the great views of the lower Arkansas valley and the northern Sangre de Cristo Range.

Trailhead/Access Points

Chalk Creek Trailhead : Drive south from Buena Vista on US-285 to Nathrop. Turn right (west) onto Chaffee Co. Rd-162 for approximately 7 miles. The trailhead is on the left side of the road, slightly below road level.

Browns Creek Trailhead : Drive south from Nathrop on US-285 for about 3.2 miles. Turn right (west) on Chaffee Co. Rd-270 for 2 miles to a point where it turns north. Continue straight ahead onto Rd-272 for 2 miles to where it turns south (left) at an intersection. Continue south on Rd-272 for 1.6 more miles to the Browns Creek Trailhead. From there, walk west on a trail for 1.4 miles to intersect the CT.

Angel of Shavano Trailhead : From the intersection of US-285 and US-50 at Poncha Springs, drive west on US-50 for about 6 miles. Turn right (north) onto Chaffee Co. Rd-240 (North Fork South Arkansas River Road). Proceed on Rd-240 for 3.8 miles to the trailhead parking area opposite the Angel of Shavano Campground.

US-50 Trail Access : See Segment 15.

Trail Description

This segment begins at the Chalk Creek Trailhead, **mile 0.0** (8,390) **Ⓐ**. There are signs identifying the trail and two small parking areas. After leaving the trailhead, go south across a bridge and begin hiking uphill. The water here is the last reliable source until Browns Creek, some 6.6 miles ahead. Pass the Bootleg Trail at **mile 0.1** and continue ahead. Ignore an intersection with a horse trail at **mile 0.3**, which leaves to the east, and continue up the well-defined trail. Cross FS-290 at **mile 0.4**. This intersection is marked with a Forest Service sign for "Raspberry Gulch". At **mile 0.7**, pass near a jeep road that is 100 feet to the right. Reach a small saddle at **mile 1.2**. The trail turns left (east) and follows the ridge to **mile 1.4** (9,310) **Ⓑ**. Begin slowly descending, towards the east, to **mile 2.1** (9,020), then turn to the right (south) and down a steep, rocky and eroded gully. The trail is poorly marked here. Pass by a fenced area at **mile 2.3**. Cross FS- 274 at **mile 2.5 Ⓒ**. Follow the trail as it contours along the gentle hillside. Cross FS-273 at **mile 4.0 Ⓓ**. Ignore a side trail that merges from the east at **mile 4.8**. Cross another trail at **mile 5.6**.

At **mile 6.1 Ⓔ**, hit the Little Browns Creek Trail (FS-1430) and turn sharply to the left at a well-marked intersection. Follow to **mile 6.4** (9,670) and intersect the

Salida Services

Distance From CT:	
	13 miles
Elevation:	7,036
Zip Code:	81201
Area Code:	719

Salida, the old railroad town, and now, main commercial center for the lower Arkansas valley, is about 13 miles east of the CT crossing on US-50. **Poncha Springs**, 8 miles east of the crossing, has a restaurant and a small convenience store. Monarch Spur RV Park, about 1 mile east of the CT on Hwy 50, has camping and showers. The Monarch Mountain Lodge, about 4.5 miles west of the CT on Hwy-50, has lodging and a mail drop.

Supplies, Services and Accommodations

Bus	A	TNM & O (Greyhound)	735 Blake St	(719) 539-7474
Dining		Several in town		
Gear	B	Headwaters Outdoor	228 North F St	(719) 539-4506
Groceries	C	Safeway	232 G St	(719) 539-3513
	D	Salida Food Town	248 W Hwy 50	(719) 539-7500
Info	E	Chamber of Commerce	406 W Rainbow Blvd	(719) 539-2068
Laundry	F	Lazrine's Coin-op	E St and 14th St	(719) 539-3659
Lodging		Several in town		
Medical	G	Heart of Rockies Med. Ctr.	448 East 1st St	(719) 539-6661
Post Office	H	Salida Post Office	310 D St	(719) 539-2117
Showers	J	Salida Hot Springs	410 W Hwy 50	(719) 539-6738

Browns Creek Trail, then turn right on the trail. At **mile 6.6**, cross Little Browns Creek on a bridge, then turn left at a well-marked intersection (9,620). There is a good, hard-packed campsite here. (Northbound hikes should obtain water here, as this is the last reliable source until Chalk Creek, some 6.6 miles away.) Cross another small stream at **mile 6.7**. A small campsite is just to the east (downhill), along the stream. Cross Browns Creek on a new log bridge that was built in the summer of 2005 at **mile 6.8** (9,615) **F**.

Cross the Wagon Loop Trail at **mile 6.9** and continue ahead to the south. Cross Fourmile Creek at **mile 8.7** (9,780) **G**. While there are no campsites close to the creek, there is one a few hundred feet further along the trail. At **mile 9.4**, the trail briefly touches the side of FS-275. Cross Sand Creek on a bridge at **mile 9.9** (9,615). There is a good campsite in the vicinity. Some good views of Mt. Shavano open up around **mile 11.8**. Cross a stream at **mile 12.2** (9860) **❶** , with campsites in the vicinity. Cross another stream at **mile 12.4**, also with camp possibilities. There is a trail register here. Past this stream, the trail turns into a old jeep trail. Intersect the well-marked Mt. Shavano Trail at **mile 12.7** (9,885) **❶** . At **mile 13.0**, pass through a Forest Service gate into an open meadow with a new log fence, preventing motorized access to the trail. A new side trail takes off to the left at **mile 13.3** and leads to a large car-camping and trailhead area on FS- 252. Continue ahead at this intersection.

Cross FS-254 at **mile 13.3** (9,810), then cross a stream at **mile 13.4**. Cross a seasonal stream at **mile 13.9** and another at **mile 14.5**, then arrive at a large trailhead parking area on CR-240 above Maysville (9,210). Head west along the edge of the parking area on a faint trail to the west. The trail briefly re-enters some trees, then crosses the road at **mile 15.0** at a well-identified intersection. Pass just west of Angel of Shavano Campground, then cross a bridge over the North Fork of the Arkansas at **mile 15.3** (9,135) **❶**. The trail begins a section of steep switchbacks out of the valley. Reach the top of the ridge at **mile 16.6** (9,715) **❶** . The trail skirts the edge of a re-planted, logged-over area at **mile 17.6**. A series of carsonite posts mark the trail as it crosses several old logging tracks entering the cut area. The CT then leaves the cut area and heads downhill to Lost Creek at **mile 17.8** (9445). There are good campsites here. Just beyond the creek, cross the Lost Creek Road, no longer a passable road. At **mile 18.9**, cross a road next to a huge, circular meadow (9,350). This is "Goat Waddi", where goat herders once held annual reunions. The trail goes directly across the FS road , then circles around the north and west side of the meadow. Just beyond the meadow, cross FS- 248 at **mile 19.1**. At **mile 19.4**, drop into a valley and cross a small stream via a log bridge near some ponds (9,205). There are a few small campsites in the vicinity.

At **mile 19.7** **❶** , cross a double powerline (9,325) and begin to descend the steep hillside to US-50 below. The trail follows the old power line road to **mile 20.0**, then leaves to the left on a single-track trail. Continue along the trail, dropping rapidly into the valley. Cross a old railroad grade at **mile 20.3**, then reach US-50 at **mile 20.4** (8,870). Turn briefly to the east here and walk 200 feet along the highway to the intersection with the Fooses Creek Road (FS-225). The segment ends here at **mile 20.9 ❶** (8,865).

Mount Shavano

Want to climb a fourteener (or two) as part of your Colorado Trail trek? The Mount Shavano Trail, which intersects the CT at **mile 12.7** (9,885), is the recommended route by the Colorado Fourteeners Initiative. Follow the Mt. Shavano Trail west about 3.5 miles to the saddle just south of Mount Shavano. From this spot, the trail is not clearly marked, but follow the ridge to the top of Mount Shavano (14,229) — about 0.3 miles. From the top of Shavano, travel northwest along the connecting ridge to Tabeguache Mountain's summit (14,155), less than 1.0 mile away. Return via the same route. Although technically easy and on a trail most of the way, don't underestimate the difficulties. Get an early start and be in shape for 5,000 feet of elevation gain and an arduous, 10-mile round trip.

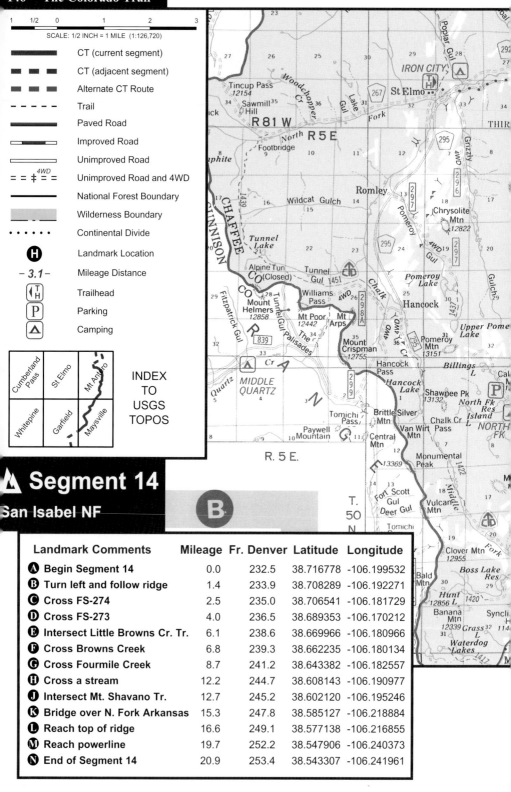

1 1/2 0 1 2 3

SCALE: 1/2 INCH = 1 MILE (1:126,720)

CT (current segment)

CT (adjacent segment)

Alternate CT Route

Trail

Paved Road

Improved Road

Unimproved Road

Unimproved Road and 4WD

National Forest Boundary

Wilderness Boundary

Continental Divide

H Landmark Location

– 3.1 – Mileage Distance

Trailhead

Parking

Camping

INDEX
TO
USGS
TOPOS

| Cumberland Pass | St Elmo | Mt Antero |
| Whitepine | Garfield | Maysville |

▲ Segment 14

San Isabel NF

B

Landmark Comments	Mileage	Fr. Denver	Latitude	Longitude
A Begin Segment 14	0.0	232.5	38.716778	-106.199532
B Turn left and follow ridge	1.4	233.9	38.708289	-106.192271
C Cross FS-274	2.5	235.0	38.706541	-106.181729
D Cross FS-273	4.0	236.5	38.689353	-106.170212
E Intersect Little Browns Cr. Tr.	6.1	238.6	38.669966	-106.180966
F Cross Browns Creek	6.8	239.3	38.662235	-106.180134
G Cross Fourmile Creek	8.7	241.2	38.643382	-106.182557
H Cross a stream	12.2	244.7	38.608143	-106.190977
J Intersect Mt. Shavano Tr.	12.7	245.2	38.602120	-106.195246
K Bridge over N. Fork Arkansas	15.3	247.8	38.585127	-106.218884
L Reach top of ridge	16.6	249.1	38.577138	-106.216855
M Reach powerline	19.7	252.2	38.547906	-106.240373
N End of Segment 14	20.9	253.4	38.543307	-106.241961

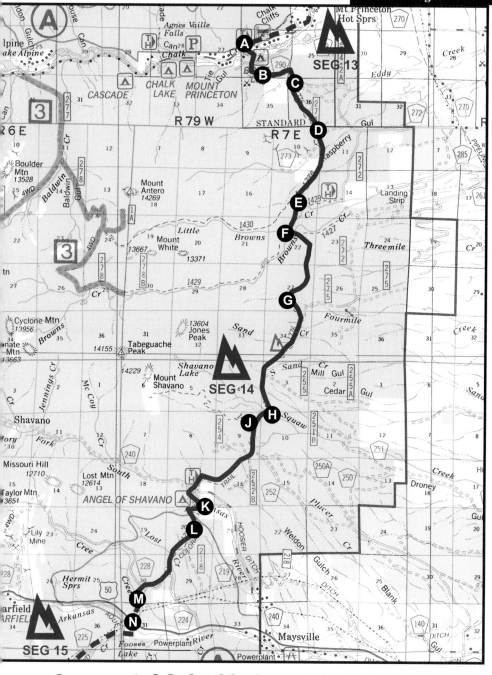

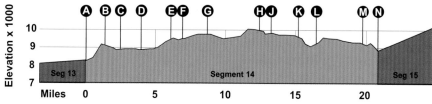

Segment 15
US-50 to Marshall Pass

BELOW: *A hiker tops out above Fooses Creek and enjoys the endless views.*

Distance: 14.2 miles
Elevation Gain: approx 3440 ft

USFS Maps: San Isabel NF, Gunnison NF, see pgs. 152-153.

USGS Quad Maps: Maysville, Garfield, Pahlone Peak, Mount Ouray.

Trails Illustrated map: #130, 139.

Jurisdiction: Salida Ranger District, Gunnison Ranger District.

Access from Denver:

Access from Durango:

Availability of Water:

Bicycling:

Gudy's Tip

"*Once up on the Divide, you'll have unobstructed views in every direction. Three of our mightiest mountain ranges— the Sawatch, the San Juan, and the Sangre de Cristo — reach for the sky.*" The Divide is lofty — and remote. There are no towns closeby for convenient re-supply and cell phones are unlikely to work in an emergency. The next 100 miles is the least traveled portion of the CT.

About This Segment

This segment begins a 100-mile section of the CT without any convenient re-supply points. Be sure you are prepared; it's fairly lonely country. The first 8 miles are a pleasant walk in the forest, although definitely climbing. Then the CT takes a short, steep ascent that puts you above timberline and onto the crest of the Continental Divide. The views are great. Through hikers will stay very close to the Divide for the next 150 miles. This has some good points — scenic views — and some cautions — low availability of water. There is very little of it to be found on the crest of the Divide, but some can usually be found within 0.25 mile on either side of the crest. If you follow the suggestions in the guidebook, you will hardly ever have to deviate very far from the CT to re-supply with water.

This segment of the CT has the only wooden shelter for the benefit of hikers and it predates the CT. At one time, the Colorado Trail Foundation considered a system of shelters along the trail but finally decided, given the high-quality of modern backpacking gear, that these were not needed or even desired. This segment ends at the Marshall Pass Road (FS-200) about 0.2 mile east of the Divide. This is a popular recreation area and you are not likely to be alone if you decide to camp there.

Trailhead/Access Points

US-50 South Fooses Creek Trailhead : From the intersection of US-285 and US-50 at Poncha Springs, drive west on US-50 for approximately 9 miles to the Fooses Creek Road (Chaffee County Rd-225). There is a wide shoulder on the south side of US-50 that can provide for limited parking. The official beginning of Segment 15 is here. The CT follows Fooses Creek Rd for 2.8 miles to a limited trailhead parking area. If you decide to drive to the trailhead, the road is rather primitive, but most cars can usually make it. Take the left fork at all junctions in route.

Marshall Pass Trailhead : See Segment 16.

Supplies, Services and Accommodations

Available in **Salida** (see Segment 14 on page 144.)

Trail Description

This segment begins at the intersection of US-50 and Fooses Creek Road (FS-225), **mile 0.0** (8,865) **A**. Follow the dirt road to the southwest. At **mile 0.2**, take a fork to the left and cross the South Fork of the Arkansas River on a bridge, crossing a cattle guard just past the bridge. This is private property on both sides of the road and hikers should stay on the main road. Cross Fooses Creek on a bridge at **mile 0.4** (8,795) and pass by a small reservoir at **mile 0.8** (8,930) **B**. This is part of a hydroelectric project that furnishes power to the Salida area. Public lands begin at the reservoir; but there are no good campsites for about a mile further

Pass by a public toilet at **mile 0.9** and cross Fooses Creek on a large culvert at **mile 1.1**. Enter an area where camping is allowed at **mile 2.0** **C**. Stay along this

main road to **mile 2.7** (9,580) where you will turn left on another small road (FS-225C). Take another left fork in about 500 feet to the Fooses Creek trailhead area. Cross the creek at **mile 2.9** (9,560) **D** . This area has numerous, hard-packed campsites near the creek. Cross the creek again at **mile 3.5**, and a smaller creek at **mile 3.7**. There are small campsites in the vicinity. Cross Fooses Creek once again at **mile 4.3** **E** . Again, there are small campsites. There is another good campsite near the trail at **mile 4.9** (10,165), where the stream is just below. Cross the stream again at **mile 5.0** and cross side streams at **mile 5.5** and **mile 6.2**. There are small campsites at both streams. More streams with campsites are encountered at **mile 6.7** (10,750) **F** , **mile 7.4**, and **mile 7.7**.

Cross Fooses Creek one final time, then begin climbing one of the steepest grades on the Colorado Trail at **mile 8.2** (11,440). Gain the crest of the Continental Divide at **mile 8.6** (11,910) **G** where the Colorado Trail merges with the Monarch Crest Trail. This is the re-entry point for the Continental Divide Trail as well. Turn left here at a well-marked intersection. There are fantastic views from this vantage point high on the divide, including the first glimpse of the San Juan Mountains far to the southwest.

The trail leads generally southeast along the Divide to **mile 10.3** (11,500) **H** .

ABOVE: *Crossing Fooses Creek.*   **BELOW:** *Fall colors along the CT.*

Here a signpost points to the Greens Creek Trail, and a small shelter cabin sits just east of the trail. If you should decide to camp at the cabin, water is available a short distance east along the Greens Creek Trail. From the cabin, the trail makes a more southerly turn and leaves the ridge of the Divide. A crosstrail to Agate Creek to the west and Cochetopa Creek to the east is encountered at **mile 11.4** (11810 **❿** . The summit of 13,971-foot Mt. Ouray is most often climbed via the Cochetopa Creek Trail — by following the trail to the Divide and traversing the ridge to the peak.

Cross a small stream with campsites nearby at **mile 12.7 ❻** . Join an old jeep trail at **mile 12.9** (11,410) and follow it downhill. Pass by the ruins of a mining shack at **mile 13.1**. This old structure was standing in 1990, but has collapsed since then. Cross a cattle guard at **mile 13.8** (10,980), followed by a irrigation canal at **mile 14.0**. Continue downhill on the jeep road to **mile 14.2** (10,825) **❿** , where the segment ends at a parking area on the Marshall Pass Road (FS-200). The parking area has a toilet and space for 10-12 cars.

Continental Divide National Scenic Trail

The Continental Divide National Scenic Trail (CDNST) passes through five western states from Canada to Mexico, as it winds a path through the majestic Rocky Mountains and encounters some of America's most dramatic scenery.

The CT and the CDNST are contiguous for about 200 miles in Colorado, including a long section that begins in Seg. 15 near Marshall Pass and diverges, over 100 miles later, near Stony Pass in Segment 23.

First envisioned by several far-sighted groups and individuals, including Benton Mackaye, founder of the Appalachian Trail, the 3,100-mile CDNST is still only about 70% complete today. The Colorado portion has one of the highest completion rates at 90%. The trail achieves its highest point in Colorado, passing over 14,270-foot Grays Peak, and includes a network of trails 759 miles long, beginning in Mount Zirkel Wilderness at the Wyoming border and entering New Mexico through the spectacular San Juans.

The Continental Divide Trail Alliance (CDTA) estimates that only about a dozen people undertake the entire six-month journey from Canada to Mexico each year. As is the same for the CT, few individuals finish the entire Colorado portion of the CDNST but thousands enjoy day hikes or week-long backpacks on segments of it.

ABOVE: *CDT sign near Fooses Creek.*

The first complete hike of the length of Colorado's Continental Divide was done by Carl Melzer, his son, Bob, and Julius Johnson in 1936. This was truly a pioneering trip, considering the incomplete maps and sketchy information available to them at that time. (The Melzers had a string of accomplishments. They were also the first to climb all of Colorado's 14ers in one summer (1937) and the first to climb all of the 14ers in the 48 states (1939) — all before Bob was 11 years old!)

For more information about the trail, contact CDTA at 303-838-3760 or visit their website at www.cdtrail.org.

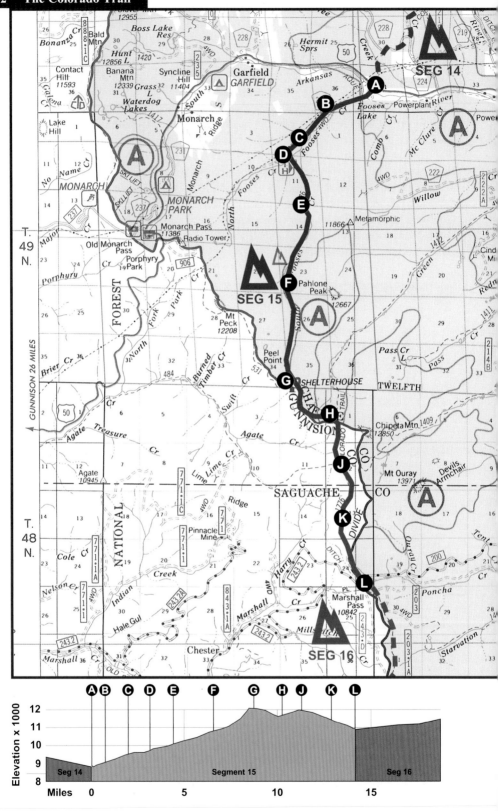

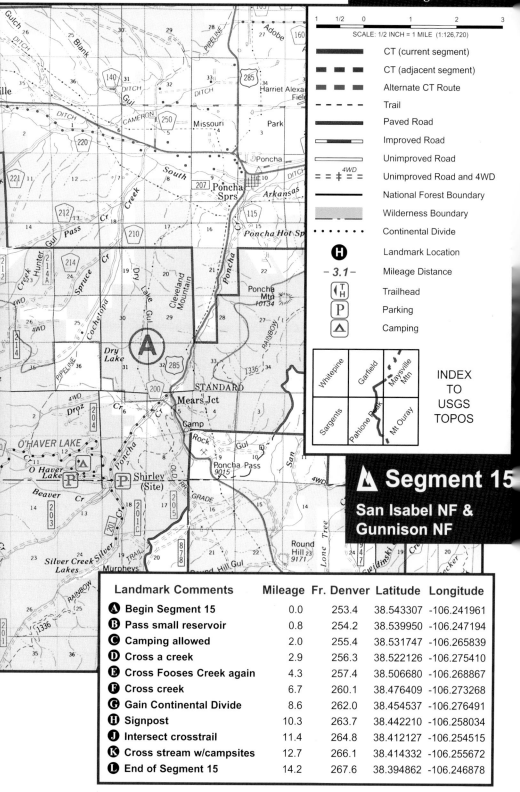

1	1/2	0	1	2	3

SCALE: 1/2 INCH = 1 MILE (1:126,720)

CT (current segment)
CT (adjacent segment)
Alternate CT Route
Trail
Paved Road
Improved Road
Unimproved Road
Unimproved Road and 4WD
National Forest Boundary
Wilderness Boundary
Continental Divide
H Landmark Location
- *3.1* - Mileage Distance
Trailhead
Parking
Camping

INDEX TO USGS TOPOS

Whitepine | Garfield | Maysville Mtn
Sargents | Pahlone Peak | Mt Ouray

▲ Segment 15

San Isabel NF & Gunnison NF

Landmark Comments	Mileage	Fr. Denver	Latitude	Longitude
A Begin Segment 15	0.0	253.4	38.543307	-106.241961
B Pass small reservoir	0.8	254.2	38.539950	-106.247194
C Camping allowed	2.0	255.4	38.531747	-106.265839
D Cross a creek	2.9	256.3	38.522126	-106.275410
E Cross Fooses Creek again	4.3	257.4	38.506680	-106.268867
F Cross creek	6.7	260.1	38.476409	-106.273268
G Gain Continental Divide	8.6	262.0	38.454537	-106.276491
H Signpost	10.3	263.7	38.442210	-106.258034
J Intersect crosstrail	11.4	264.8	38.412127	-106.254515
K Cross stream w/campsites	12.7	266.1	38.414332	-106.255672
L End of Segment 15	14.2	267.6	38.394862	-106.246878

Segment 16
Marshall Pass to Sargents Mesa

BELOW: *Early morning at Marshall Pass.*

Distance: 15.2 miles
Elevation Gain: approx 3080 ft

USFS Maps: San Isabel NF, Gunnison NF, Rio Grande NF, see pages 158-159.

USGS Quad Maps: Mount Ouray, Bonanza, Chester, Sargents Mesa.

Trails Illustrated map: # 139.

Jurisdiction: Salida, Gunnison and Saguache Ranger Districts.

Access from Denver:

Access from Durango:

Availability of Water: ☕

Bicycling: 🚲

Gudy's Tip

"Sargents Mesa teems with its hundreds of grazing elk and numerous trout-filled beaver ponds." The high mesas and rolling uplands along the Divide, extending from Marshall Pass to the La Garita Wilderness and known as the Cochetopa Hills, are excellent elk and mule deer habitat. Bighorn sheep are found around the pass and points north. Early morning or dusk are prime viewing times.

About This Segment

This segment of the CT and the next two segments are mostly open to motorized traffic. This is because, in the hurry to get the Colorado Trail opened, it was decided to follow an existing motorized route until a separate route could be located. So far, that goal has proven elusive. Be alert for motorcycles approaching at high speed in mid-summer. Water sources are a little scarce in this segment. Silver Creek, about 3.6 miles in, has water at about 0.25 mile east of the CT. As you climb the flank of Windy Peak on the CT, you can spot a very green area about 0.25 mile south of you, at the foot of the slope. That has been a reliable spring. About 11 miles in, cross Tank Seven Creek, which also is a good source of water. Walking up the meadow and approaching Sargents Mesa, there have always been a couple of stock tanks with water (if you are not fussy and have a good filter.) From Sargents Mesa, it is about 7 miles to water at Baldy Lake in the next segment.

There are many logging roads and other trails winding through this segment. The CT stays very close to the Divide. If you find yourself on a trail leaving the Divide and heading down, you have possibly made a mistake. Time to get out the map and compass, or the GPS if you are so equipped. Don't feel bad, many hikers have reported taking unwanted side trips in this area.

Trailhead/Access Points

Marshall Pass Trailhead 🚗 *:* Drive about 5 miles south of Poncha Springs on US-285 and turn west (right) at the Marshall Pass and O'Haver Lake Campground turnoff. The road starts out as Chaffee County Rd-200 and, somewhere towards the top of the pass, morphs into FS-200. It is about 13 miles from the highway to the summit of Marshall Pass. About 0.2 mile short of the pass is a parking area for about a dozen cars with a FS toilet nearby. This is the trailhead for the end of Segment 15 and the beginning of Segment 16.

Sargents Mesa Trail Access 🚙 *:* See Segment 17.

Supplies, Services and Accommodations

There is no convenient re-supply point in this segment.

Trail Description

This segment begins at the parking area on Marshall Pass **A**, mile **0.0** (10,825). The beginning of this segment is slightly confusing. Follow the Marshall Pass Road west for 0.2 miles to an intersecting jeep trail and turn off to the left (south). Immediately after leaving the road, there is another intersection. Take the left fork. This leads to another confusing intersection at **mile 0.3**. Go straight ahead across the intersection and up the hill. A wood sign marks the trail here. In a few hundred feet, reach a large post with a Forest Service sign board marking the trail. At **mile 0.4**, the trail becomes a single track and the jeep roads are left behind for a while. Follow the trail south to **mile 2.4 B** where it merges with a jeep trail. Go to the left and

The CT in Segment 16 and the Silver Creek Trail #1407 are portions of a mountain bike ride considered by *Bicycle* magazine to be one of the top five rides in the entire country. The Monarch Crest Trail descends an epic 3,500 feet from tundra to sagebrush desert, covering roughly 40 miles of mostly single-track.

Riders begin atop Monarch Pass (facilitated by a shuttle service out of Poncha Springs) and follow the Continental Divide Trail south to intersect the Colorado Trail atop Fooses Creek. Segment 15 is pedaled to Marshall Pass, then it's on to Segment 16. Riders drop off the Divide on the Silver Creek Trail/Rainbow Trail system to reach US-285, far in the valley below. A swift ride down the highway returns riders to Poncha Springs. *Whew!*

BELOW: *Cabin above Tank Seven Creek.*

then, straight ahead. This begins a motorized section of the trail where you are likely to encounter motorcycles and ATV traffic.

At **mile 2.8**, cross an abandoned logging trail at a well-marked intersection. Pass the Silver Creek Trail #1407 ❸ at **mile 4.1** (11,235). There is a campsite with water at about 0.25 mile down Silver Creek. At **mile 4.2**, the road becomes a single-track trail and the jeep road is closed. Cross a seasonal stream at **mile 4.5** (11,540). There is no campsite here. At **mile 4.7** ❹, pass through a Forest Service gate. An old trail sign here marks the Summit Trail, the same as the Colorado Trail at this point. The gate sits squarely at the top of the Divide, as the trail briefly moves to the eastern watershed.

Reach a high point at **mile 5.3** (11,570), then begin a steep descent at **mile 5.7**, as the trail zig-zags back and forth along the spine of the Continental Divide. Cross a jeep trail at **mile 7.1** (10,905) ❺. A Forest Service sign here identifies the Continental Divide Trail, but not the CT. At **mile 8.9** (10,625) ❻, the trail follows a pipeline cut for 200 feet, then abruptly exits to the right at a confusing

intersection. At **mile 11.0**  , pass by the Tank Seven Cutoff Trail #760 (10,582). Continue straight ahead. Begin a short downhill section. At **mile 11.6**, cross Tank Seven Creek (10,350) ❶. This is the last reliable water source until Baldy Lake, some 11.5 miles ahead in Segment 17.

There are several places to camp in the vicinity. Turn left immediately after crossing the creek

ABOVE: *Hiking along the Divide.*

on an old closed road. Pass by the ruins of an old ranching operation at **mile 12.2** (10,795). Cross FS-578 at **mile 12.8** ❶ and continue straight ahead. Cross another Forest Service road at **mile 13.8** (11,105). At **mile 14.7**, the Big Ben Trail #488 takes off to the right at a well-marked intersection (11,390). Continue ahead to **mile 15.2**, where the segment ends at the intersection of FS-855 (11,620) ❸ . This is probably the loneliest and poorest-marked trailhead on the entire Colorado Trail. Most through-hikers will choose to continue on and camp near Baldy Lake, 7.4 miles to the west.

The Legacy of Marshall Pass

In 1873, troubled be a toothache and in a big hurry to get to a dentist in Denver, Army Lieutenant William Marshal "discovered" this shortcut. Of course, for centuries bands of Ute Indians had been using the several gaps in this relatively low section of the Continental Divide between the soaring Sawatch and San Juan Ranges to travel between the intermountain parks and their lands to the west. Famed road and rail builder Otto Mears constructed the first wagon road over the pass, following existing paths, then sold it to the Denver and Rio Grande,

which laid rails over it in1881.

General William Palmer's D&RG was in a battle with John Evans' Denver South Park and Pacific to be the first to reach Gunnison, then tap the mineral-rich San Juans. While the DSP&P took the shorter route on paper, by tunneling under the Sawatch Range, Palmer choose the relatively low pass with modest grades for his route. The D&RG won the race, pulling into Gunnison to an exuberant crowd on August 8, 1881, as the DSP&P labored for another year on their ill-fated Alpine Tunnel.

The rails are long gone today, but Chaffee Co Rd.-200 follows the old trackbed.

Segment 16

Gunnison NF

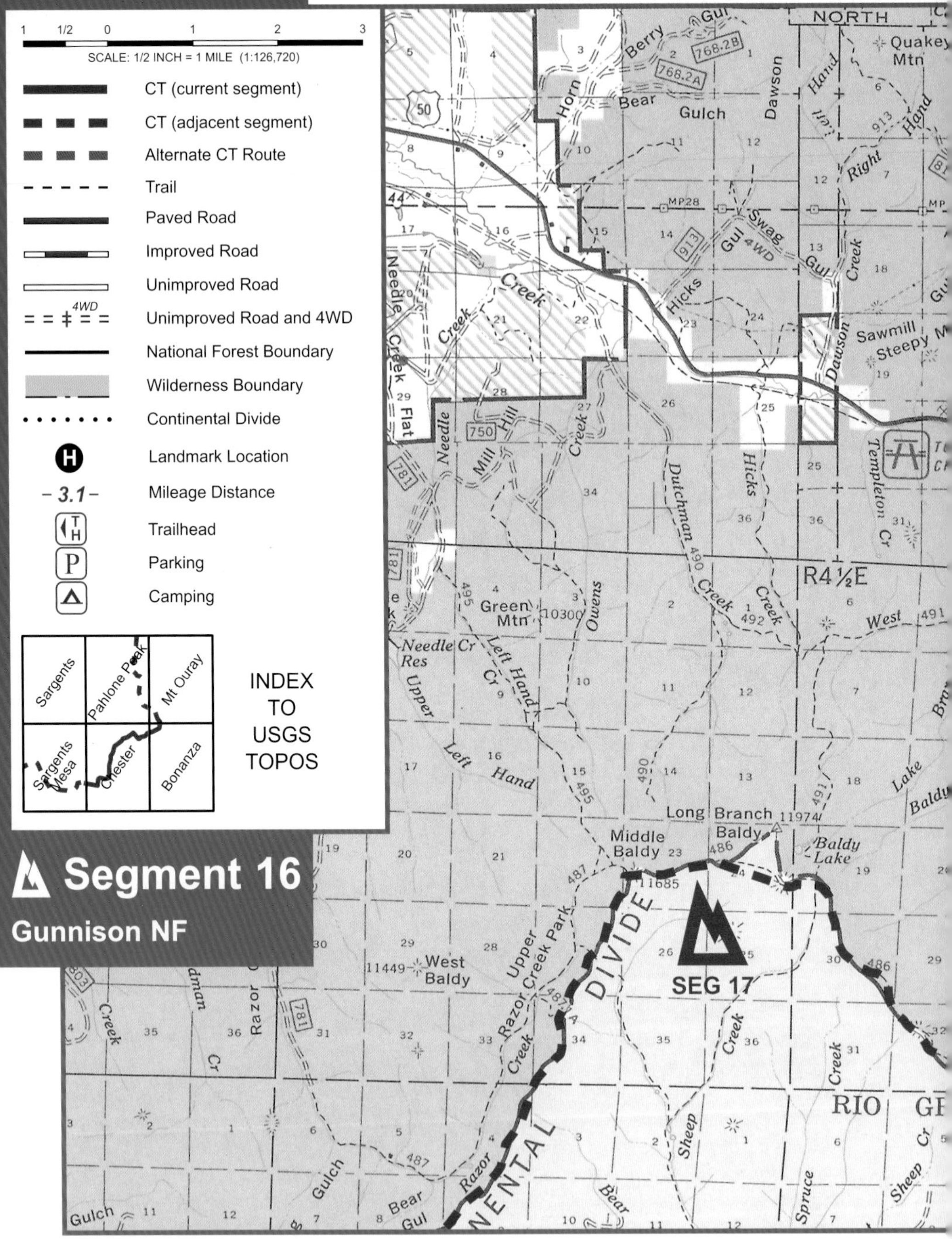
1 1/2 0 1 2 3
SCALE: 1/2 INCH = 1 MILE (1:126,720)
CT (current segment)
CT (adjacent segment)
Alternate CT Route
Trail
Paved Road
Improved Road
Unimproved Road
4WD
Unimproved Road and 4WD
National Forest Boundary
Wilderness Boundary
Continental Divide
Landmark Location
– 3.1 –
Mileage Distance
Trailhead
Parking
Camping
Sargents
Pahlone Peak
Mt Ouray
Sargents Mesa
Chester
Bonanza
INDEX TO USGS TOPOS
NORTH
Quakey Mtn
Berry Gul
Bear Gulch
Horn
Dawson
Left Hand
Right Hand
Swag Gul
Hicks
Creek
Needle Creek
Sawmill
Steepy Mtn
Flat
Mill Hill
Dutchman Creek
Templeton Cr
R4½E
Green Mtn
10300
Owens
Needle Cr Res
Upper Left Hand
Left Hand Cr
West
Lake
Baldy
Long Branch Baldy 11974
Middle Baldy
Baldy Lake
11685
DIVIDE
SEG 17
11449 West Baldy
Upper Creek Park
Razor Creek
Razor Cr
Sheep Creek
Spruce
RIO GR
CONTINENTAL
Bear Gul
Gulch
50
768.2B
768.2A
913
750
781
803
490
492
495
486
487
491
MP28
4WD

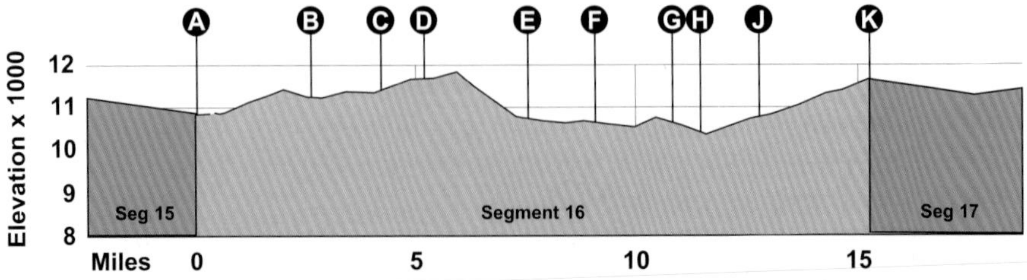
A
B
C
D
E
F
G
H
J
K
Elevation x 1000
12
11
10
9
8
Seg 15
Segment 16
Seg 17
Miles
0
5
10
15

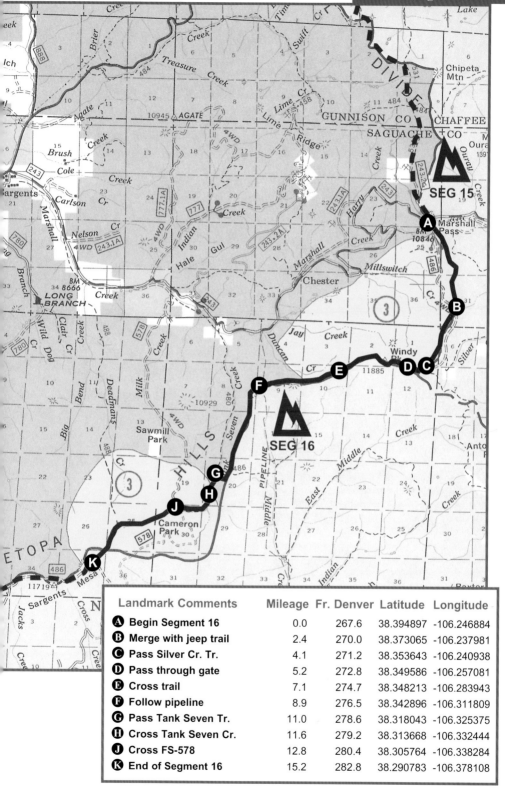

Landmark Comments	Mileage	Fr. Denver	Latitude	Longitude
Ⓐ Begin Segment 16	0.0	267.6	38.394897	-106.246884
Ⓑ Merge with jeep trail	2.4	270.0	38.373065	-106.237981
Ⓒ Pass Silver Cr. Tr.	4.1	271.2	38.353643	-106.240938
Ⓓ Pass through gate	5.2	272.8	38.349586	-106.257081
Ⓔ Cross trail	7.1	274.7	38.348213	-106.283943
Ⓕ Follow pipeline	8.9	276.5	38.342896	-106.311809
Ⓖ Pass Tank Seven Tr.	11.0	278.6	38.318043	-106.325375
Ⓗ Cross Tank Seven Cr.	11.6	279.2	38.313668	-106.332444
Ⓙ Cross FS-578	12.8	280.4	38.305764	-106.338284
Ⓚ End of Segment 16	15.2	282.8	38.290783	-106.378108

Segment 17
Sargents Mesa to Colorado Hwy-114

BELOW: *Grazing cows are common along the CT on Sargents Mesa.*

Distance: 20.4 miles
Elevation Gain: approx 2440 ft

USFS Maps: Rio Grande NF, Gunnison NF, see pgs. 164-165.

USGS Quad Maps: Sargents Mesa, West Baldy, North Pass.

Trails Illustrated map: # 139.

Jurisdiction: Saguache Ranger Dst. and Gunnison Ranger Dst.

Access from Denver:

Access from Durango:

Availability of Water:

Bicycling:

Gudy's Tip

"*B aldy Lake after Sargents Mesa is worth the half-mile detour; it's a watery haven along a dry segment of the trail.*" You'll need to plan your camps and water needs carefully on this segment. The only reliable water sources are at Baldy Lake at mile 7.0 and Lujan Creek at mile 18. All water sources should be treated as suspect because of livestock use.

About This Segment

This segment continues to travel along the crest of the Continental Divide. That means that water sources are scarce. There are no reliable water sources before Baldy Lake, which is 7 miles along the trail. The next one beyond is Lujan Creek, beginning at mile 18. This segment reaches its high point at the crest of Middle Baldy Peak, where there are great views of the Gunnison Basin. To get around the steep southwest face of Middle Baldy, the CT starts the decent in a northwesterly direction, but soon curves around to the south, entering the drainage of Razor Creek for a mile or so. As soon as it clears the steep face of Middle Baldy, the CT rejoins the crest of the Divide and stays there until its decent into the Lujan Creek drainage. This segment ends on the south shoulder of CO-114, 0.4 mile southwest of where the Lujan Creek Road meets the highway.

Trailhead/Access Points

Sargents Mesa Trailhead Access (FS-855) 🚙 : From the small town of Saguache on US-285 in the San Luis Valley, proceed northwest on CO-114 for 10.5 miles. Take the right-hand branch of the "Y" onto Saguache Co Rd-EE38. Proceed 0.8 mile to the next "Y" and take the left branch, continuing on Rd-EE38. Continue up the Jacks Creek valley for 5 miles where Rd-EE38 makes a sharp right, climbing out of the valley and becoming FS-855. Follow FS-855 for about 10, winding miles to a large, open meadow where it degenerates; but was reported much improved in 2006. Turn left and continue 0.7 mile along the edge of the forest to the official beginning of this segment. The Rio Grande National Forest map is very helpful in clarifying this route.

Lujan Creek Road Trail Access 🚗 : From Saguache on US-285 in the San Luis Valley, drive west on CO-114 for approximately 30 miles to North Pass. Continue 1.1 miles down from the pass to the Lujan Creek Road (Saguache Co Rd-31CC/FS-785), on your right. Follow this narrow, slick-when-wet shelf road for 2 miles up the Lujan Creek Valley, where it makes an abrupt right turn up a switchback. Avoid the jeep road that departs to your left. Continue 0.1 mile to cross a cattle guard. Branch left here for 0.1 mile to where the CT comes down from the mountain.

Colorado Hwy-114 Trail Access 🚗 : See Segment 18.

Supplies, Services and Accommodations

There is no convenient supply point for this segment.

Trail Description

This segment begins at the obscure, Sargents Mesa trailhead on FS-855 at the intersection with FS-486, **mile 0.0** (11,620) **Ⓐ** . Follow FS-486 to the south. There is a Continental Divide Trail post, CDT 813, marking the way. The trail follows the old jeep trail to **mile 2.3 Ⓑ** , where the CT abruptly leaves the jeep road to the right.

ABOVE: *Alpine sunflowers*

Many hikers have missed this intersection in the past, but a new sign and post should help.

The trail crosses a grassy area, and may be difficult to spot at first. At **mile 2.4**, cross the Long Branch Trail #489 and continue straight ahead. The trail soon becomes easier to follow, as it continues along the forested ridge of the divide. At **mile 6.9 ©**, reach the Baldy Lake Trail intersection (11,515). The lake (11,260) is 0.5 mile to the west along a good trail. This is a popular camp spot and is the only reliable water source until Lujan Creek, some 11 miles ahead.

Continue along the crest of the Divide in a series of ups and downs. Cross near the summit of Middle Baldy Peak at **mile 9.1** (11,685), then drop down to an intersection with the Dutchman Creek Trail at **mile 9.8** (1,1380) **Ⓓ**. Bear to the left at this intersection. Cross Razor Creek at **mile 10.5 Ⓔ**. This creek is seasonal and may be dry. Follow the creek bed to **mile 10.8**, where the trail intersects the Razor Creek Trail #487 (10,850). Go to the left here, leaving the valley and heading back up to the ridge. After reaching the ridge, cross a trail at **mile 11.5 Ⓕ** which goes

BELOW: *Cairn along the Continental Divide.*

to the Razor Creek Trailhead.

Continue ahead, and at **mile 12.5**  , bear left at the intersection of Razor Creek Spur Trail #87.1A (11,070). This spur drops back into the Razor Creek drainage. Continue along the mostly forested ridge. Head up a series of steep switchbacks at **mile 15.1** (10,560), then join an old jeep road at **mile 16.5** (11,070). Reach the Lujan Creek Trailhead at **mile 17.8** (10,340). This trailhead

ABOVE: *Open parks are typical for this portion of the Colorado Trail.*

is on a dirt road. Turn right on the road and pass through a gate with a cattle guard at **mile 17.9**. Reach a fork in the road at **mile 18.0** (10,140) and bear left, following the road downhill. Cross a small stream via culvert under the road at **mile 18.3** (10160), where there is a hard-packed campsite north of the trail (heavy grazing by livestock may make camping unpleasant).

Continue down the road to an intersection with CO-114 at **mile 20.0** (9,725). Turn right and carefully follow the highway downhill to a wide parking area on the south side at **mile 20.4** (9,605) . There is a gate here, where the trail continues onto Segment 18. This poorly marked location is the end of Segment 17.

Pocket Gophers

The long, sinuous casts, packed with dirt, and scattered over the grasslands and meadows of the Cochetopa Gap are evidence of pocket gophers at work.

This small, thickset, and mostly nocturnal animal is a regular biological excavation service, with burrow systems that may be over 500 feet long, representing removal of nearly three tons of soil. Excess soil is thrown out in characteristic loose mounds. But it is the conspicuous winter casts that attract the attention of curious hikers.

These are actually tunnels made during the winter, through the snow and along the surface of the ground, and packed with dirt brought up from below.

Sometimes their endless burrowing activities can undermine an area to such an extent that a passing hiker can be surprised when the ground suddenly gives way under foot.

Here in Colorado, pocket gophers are found well up into the meager soils of the alpine zone and are a major factor in the soil-building process in mountain areas.

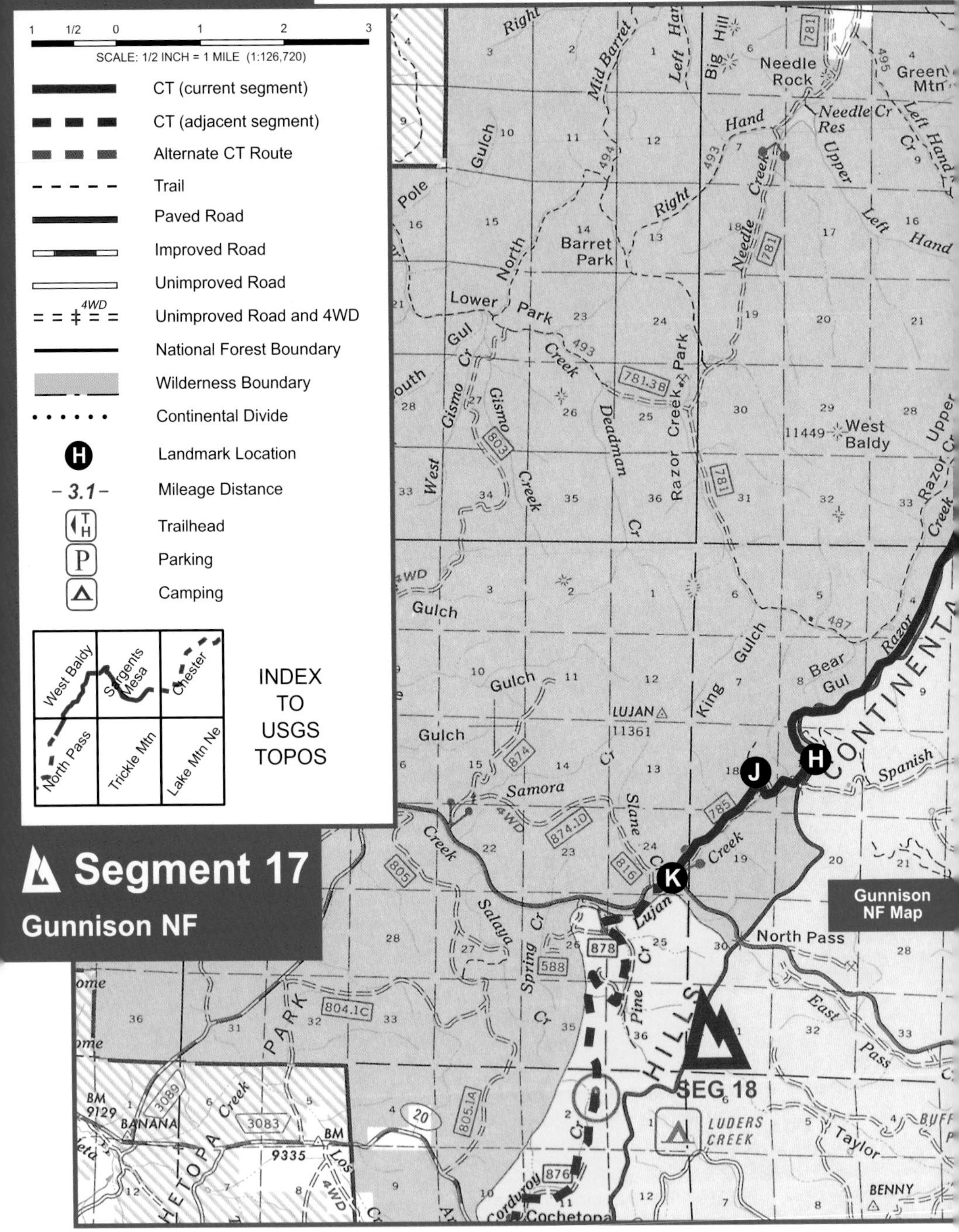
1 1/2 0 1 2 3
SCALE: 1/2 INCH = 1 MILE (1:126,720)
CT (current segment)
CT (adjacent segment)
Alternate CT Route
Trail
Paved Road
Improved Road
Unimproved Road
4WD
Unimproved Road and 4WD
National Forest Boundary
Wilderness Boundary
Continental Divide
Landmark Location
– 3.1 –
Mileage Distance
Trailhead
Parking
Camping
West Baldy
Sargents Mesa
Chester
North Pass
Trickle Mtn
Lake Mtn Ne
INDEX TO USGS TOPOS
Needle Rock
Green Mtn
Needle Cr Res
Barret Park
Lower Park
West Baldy
11449
LUJAN
11361
Samora
North Pass
Gunnison NF Map
SEG 18
LUDERS CREEK
BENNY
BANANA
BM 9129
9335
Cochetopa
CONTINENTAL

Segment 17

Gunnison NF

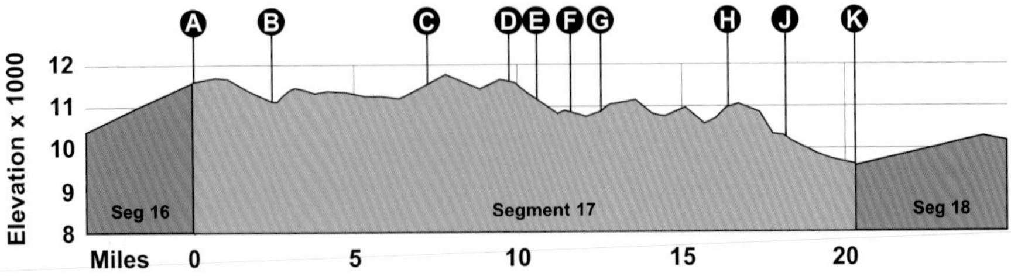
A
B
C
D
E
F
G
H
J
K
Elevation x 1000
12
11
10
9
8
Seg 16
Segment 17
Seg 18
Miles
0
5
10
15
20

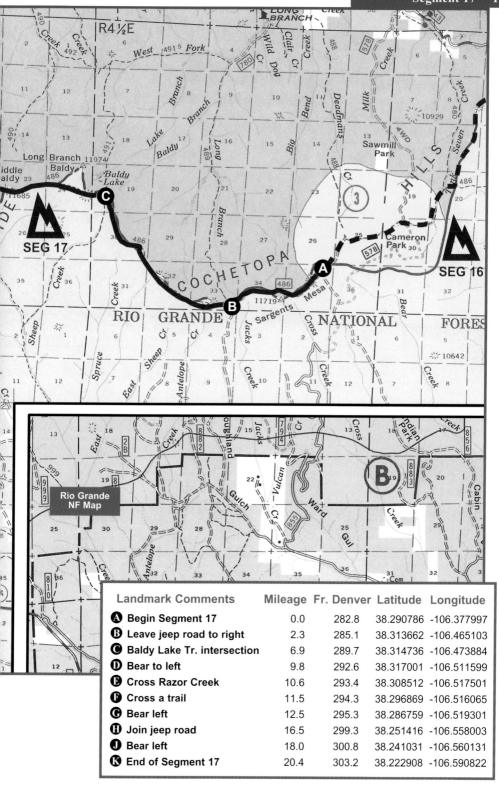

Landmark Comments	Mileage	Fr. Denver	Latitude	Longitude
A Begin Segment 17	0.0	282.8	38.290786	-106.377997
B Leave jeep road to right	2.3	285.1	38.313662	-106.465103
C Baldy Lake Tr. intersection	6.9	289.7	38.314736	-106.473884
D Bear to left	9.8	292.6	38.317001	-106.511599
E Cross Razor Creek	10.6	293.4	38.308512	-106.517501
F Cross a trail	11.5	294.3	38.296869	-106.516065
G Bear left	12.5	295.3	38.286759	-106.519301
H Join jeep road	16.5	299.3	38.251416	-106.558003
J Bear left	18.0	300.8	38.241031	-106.560131
K End of Segment 17	20.4	303.2	38.222908	-106.590822

Segment 18

Colorado Hwy-114 to Saguache Park Road

BELOW: *Hiking through the Cochetopa Hills.*

Distance: 13.8 miles
Elevation Gain: approx 1220 ft

USFS Maps: Gunnison National Forest, see pages 170-171.

USGS Quad Maps: North Pass, Cochetopa Park.

Trails Illustrated map: # 139.

Jurisdiction: Gunnison Ranger District, Gunnison NF.

Access from Denver:

Access from Durango:

Availability of Water:

Bicycling: see pg. 168-169.

Gudy's Tip

"*Water sources on these ranch roads are few and far between. And what can be found is often besmirched by cow pies. Emergency water is no longer available at Luders Campground since the pump has been removed.*" Lujan, Pine, Archuleta and Los Creeks may have small flows at times, but are unreliable in dry years and later in the summer.

About This Segment

This is not one of the most breathtakingly beautiful segments of the Colorado Trail. It is ranch country and grazing cattle are common. The grades average less than 100 feet per mile. There is not much shade and less water. However, most of the walking is easy. From this segment's start, Cochetopa Creek is the next reliable source of water, and it is 21 miles ahead. Don't bypass any water source, just because it is small. Keep your water bottles topped off whenever possible. At the end of this segment, there is a turn that many hikers report having missed. Pay close attention to the description below, especially after you turn south on Saguache Park Road.

Trailhead/Access Points

Colorado Hwy-114 Trail Access : From Saguache on US-285 in the San Luis Valley, drive west on CO-114 for approximately 30 miles to North Pass. Continue 1.1 miles down the pass to Lujan Creek Road (Saguache Co Rd-31CC/FS-785) on your right. Continue down CO-114 0.4 mile to a wide shoulder on the south side of the highway. This is the beginning of Segment 18, as well as the end of 17.

Cochetopa Pass Road (Saguache Co. Rd-NN14) Trail Access : From Saguache on US-285 in the San Luis Valley, go west on CO-114 for approximately 21 miles and take the left branch onto Saguache Co. Rd-NN14. Follow NN14 for approximately 10 miles to Luders Creek Campground. Continue another 1.8 miles to Cochetopa Pass and another 1.2 miles to where the CT joins NN14 from the north. From this point, the CT follows NN14 0.5 mile down through two switchbacks and then leaves NN14, heading south on a jeep trail. This crossing point is considered the access point. There is no parking area here. However, since there is hardly any traffic, that's not a problem.

Alternate Cochetopa Pass Road (Saguache Co Rd-NN14) Trail Access : From Saguache on US-285 in the San Luis Valley, go west on CO-114 for approximately 35 miles. Turn left onto FS-804 (BLM-3089 / Saguache Co. Rd-17GG) for approximately 5 miles until it terminates at Saguache Co. Rd-NN14 (Cochetopa Pass Rd./BLM-3083). Turn left (east) on NN14 for 6.5 miles. The access point is where the road starts to make a steep switchback turn to the left. The CT comes down the switchbacks and crosses NN14, proceeding south.

Saguache Park Road Trail Access : See Segment 19.

Supplies, Services and Accommodations

There is no convenient supply point for this segment.

Trail Description

Begin this segment at a wide parking area on the south side of CO-114, **mile 0.0** (9,605) ❹ . The trailhead is poorly marked here, but some vandalized markers may be seen on the fence at a narrow gate. Pass through the gate and cross to the south side of Lujan Creek at **mile 0.1**. The trail roughly follows the creek on the south side to **mile 0.6** (9,515) where it turns south and follows Pine Creek up a narrow valley. There are many places where one might camp along Pine Creek, but a heavy livestock population is common and might be a problem.

Join a logging trail at **mile 0.9** and continue up the valley. Ignore a side road at **mile 1.0** and cross Pine Creek at **mile 1.7**. At **mile 1.8** (9,715) **B** , turn to the right at a fork in the road and head uphill and away from the creek. Follow this road until **mile 3.6 C** , where the road becomes a single track and heads steeply up the hill. At **mile 3.8**, the climb ends at a Forest Service gate (10,260). Pass through the gate and continue ahead to an intersection with FS-876 at **mile 4.1 D** . Turn left here and follow the road. Pass through another gate at **mile 6.4** (9,780), and still another at **mile 6.6**. Intersect the Cochetopa Pass Road at **mile 6.7** (9,745) **E** ; turn right along the road. Follow the road downhill around a pair of switchbacks, then leave to the left on another jeep track at **mile 7.2** (9,630). This trail is marked as FS-864-28. Follow this road, then pass through a Forest Service gate at **mile 8.1** (9,790) **F** . Pass through an intersection at **mile 8.3**, continuing straight ahead. At **mile 8.8**, pass by the ruins of an old cabin. Ignore a faint trail that "Y"s off to the left and continue

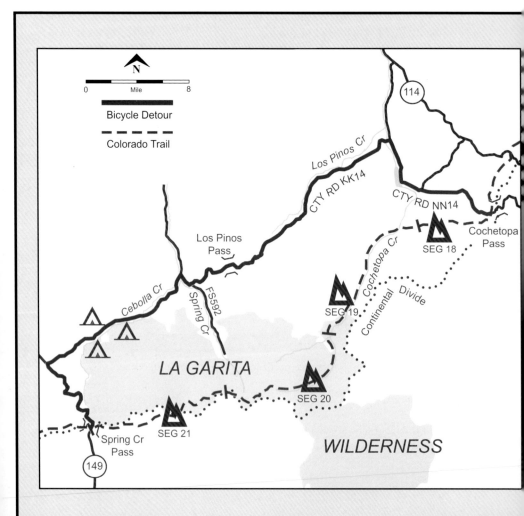

ahead to **mile 9.0** (9,610) where the jeep trail is suddenly closed off by some large boulders. This is the beginning of a short, but confusing, re-route that avoids some wetlands along the valley floor.

Turn left here and climb up a short, steep section on an intersecting jeep trail. Keep a sharp eye out to the right. The trail leaves the jeep road at **mile 9.2** (9,675). Turn right here and follow the faint trail into the trees. The trail quickly joins another jeep trail and is easily followed to **mile 9.7**, where it rejoins the original route. Turn left and follow to the west. The trail begins following a fence at **mile 10.5**. At **mile 11.0** ⑪, pass by the ruins of an old cabin (9,430). Ignore a fork that turns off to the left and continue following the fence. At **mile 11.2**, ignore another left fork. The trail now begins to drift away from the fence. Continue in a westerly direction and pass through a gate at **mile 11.9**, then bear right at an intersection, just beyond. Hit the Saguache Park Road at **mile 12.2** (9,340) ❿ . Turn left and follow the road for 1.6 miles to the end of the segment. Cross a cattle guard at **mile 13.4**, then reach the end of at the intersection with FS-787-2D at **mile 13.8** (9,530) ⓚ .

Mountain Bicycle Detour

La Garita Wilderness Detour — *Segments 18, 19, 20 and 21 (Gunnison NF):* This long, mandatory detour avoids the La Garita Wilderness Area. It is pleasant, however, and passes through a very remote part of Colorado, heavily timbered with aspen trees and spectacular in the fall. Part of the route was the planned itinerary of Aferd Packer, convicted for eating his snowbound companions in 1874. Packer's destination was the old Ute Indian Agency, passed on the detour.

Detour Description: The route begins where the CT intersects the Cochetopa Pass Road (CR NN14) at mile 6.7. Follow the road downhill in a westerly direction. Pass the Saguache Park Road at **mile 4.6**. (It is possible to add a few more miles to the ride by remaining on the CT and continuing to where it hits the Saguache Park Road at mile 12.2, then turning right and riding 2.4 miles north to this point.)

Continue west along NN14 and pass an intersection with FS-804 at **mile 5.7** (9,190), turning northwest. Pass another intersection before Dome Lakes at **mile 7.0**. Camping is allowed around the lakes. Follow the road in a more northerly direction past the lakes to **mile 10.8** and an intersection with FS-3084, also identified as CR KK14 (9,000). Turn left (southwest) and follow the road to **mile 16.4**. This is the old Ute Indian Agency location, now a Forest Service facility. Continue along the road to an intersection at **mile 20.0**. Take the right fork and continue on the Los Pinos-Cebolla Road to **mile 28.5**. Ignore a road leaving to the left and continue ahead to Los Pinos Pass at **mile 29.6** (10,510).

Head downhill to **mile 35.1** and turn left on FS-788 (8,920). Pass through a FS cattle guard at **mile 40.2** (9,180). There are several campgrounds along Cebolla Creek, as the road follows the creek upstream. After a prolonged climb, arrive at an intersection with CO-149 at **mile 50.0** (11,360). It is near this point where Packer and his party became snowbound. There is a FS campground before the intersection.

To continue on the CT, turn left onto CO-149 and pedal the 4.6 miles south to Spring Creek Pass and the start of Segment 22. To skip the challenging, high-altitude ride through Segments 22-23, refer to the Coney Summit Detour (page 194-195).

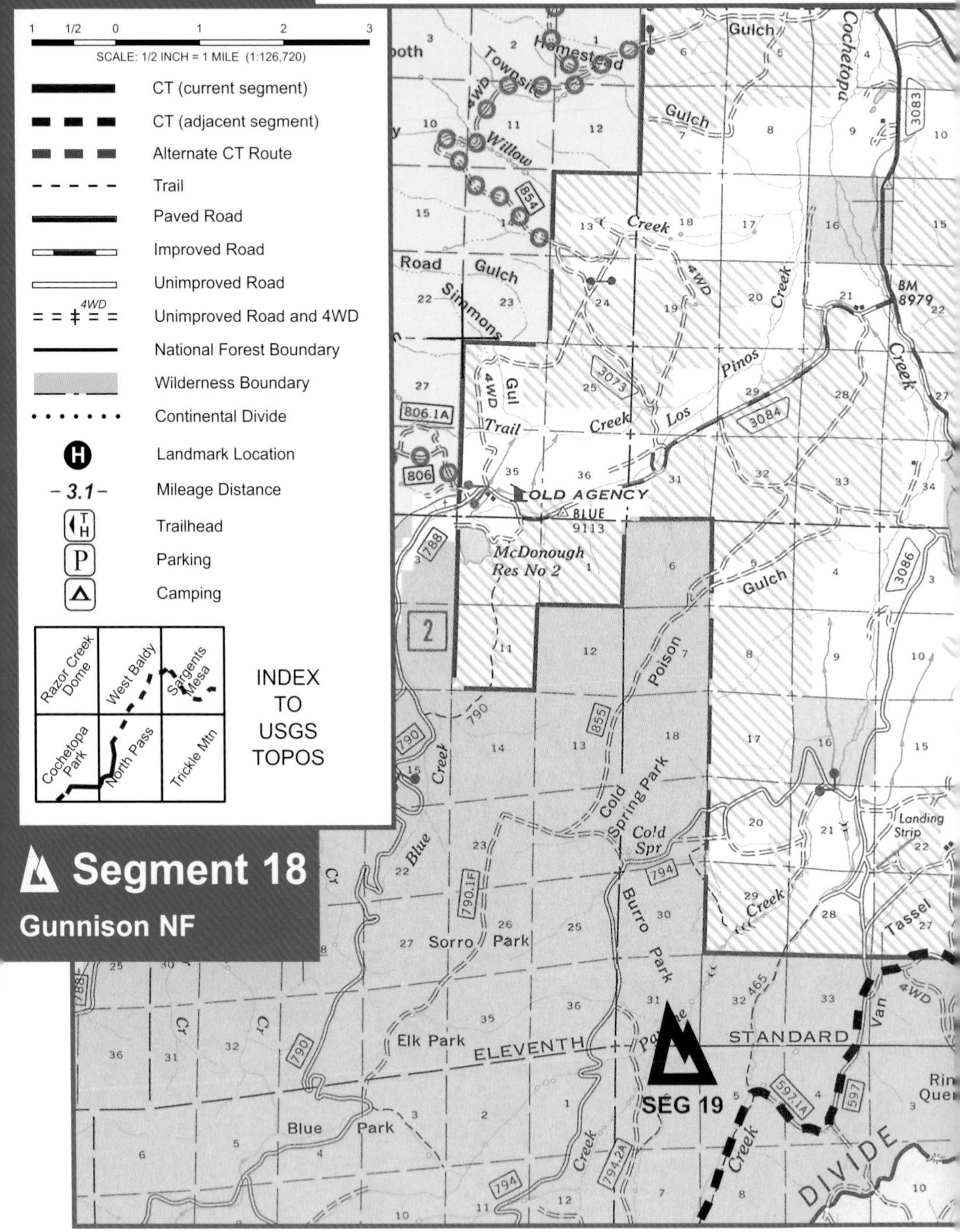

1 1/2 0 1 2 3

SCALE: 1/2 INCH = 1 MILE (1:126,720)

CT (current segment)
CT (adjacent segment)
Alternate CT Route
Trail
Paved Road
Improved Road
Unimproved Road
Unimproved Road and 4WD
National Forest Boundary
Wilderness Boundary
Continental Divide
H Landmark Location
– 3.1 – Mileage Distance
T/H Trailhead
P Parking
△ Camping

INDEX TO USGS TOPOS

Razor Creek Dome | West Baldy | Sargents Mesa
Cochetopa Park | North Pass | Trickle Mtn

Segment 18
Gunnison NF

SEG 19

OLD AGENCY
BLUE 9113
McDonough Res No 2
Cold Spring Park
Cold Spr
Sorro Park
Elk Park
ELEVENTH
STANDARD
Blue Park
DIVIDE
Burro Park

Elevation x 1000
12 11 10 9 8
Seg 17   Segment 18   Seg 19
Miles 0   5   10

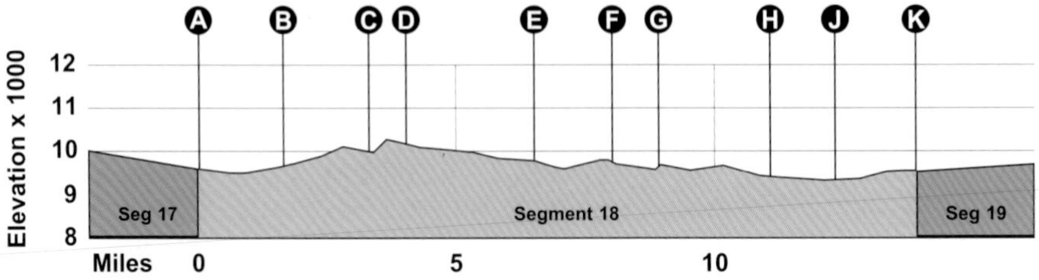

A B C D E F G H J K

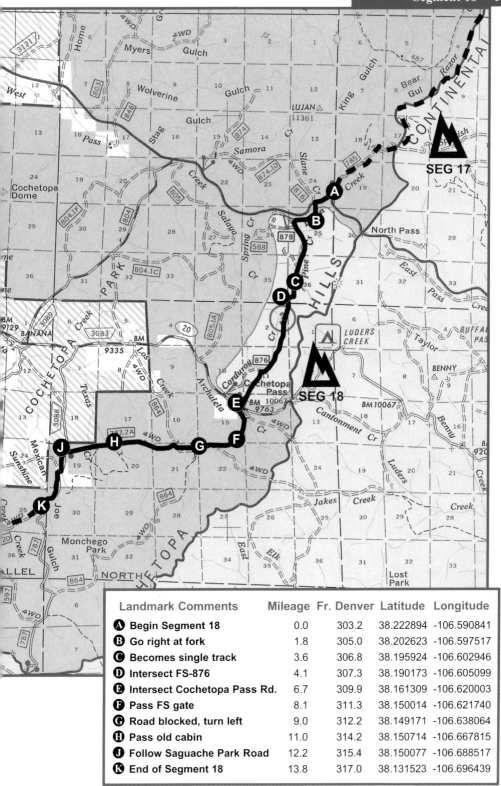

Landmark Comments	Mileage	Fr. Denver	Latitude	Longitude
Ⓐ Begin Segment 18	0.0	303.2	38.222894	-106.590841
Ⓑ Go right at fork	1.8	305.0	38.202623	-106.597517
Ⓒ Becomes single track	3.6	306.8	38.195924	-106.602946
Ⓓ Intersect FS-876	4.1	307.3	38.190173	-106.605099
Ⓔ Intersect Cochetopa Pass Rd.	6.7	309.9	38.161309	-106.620003
Ⓕ Pass FS gate	8.1	311.3	38.150014	-106.621740
Ⓖ Road blocked, turn left	9.0	312.2	38.149171	-106.638064
Ⓗ Pass old cabin	11.0	314.2	38.150714	-106.667815
Ⓙ Follow Saguache Park Road	12.2	315.4	38.150077	-106.688517
Ⓚ End of Segment 18	13.8	317.0	38.131523	-106.696439

Segment 19
Saguache Park Road to Eddiesville Trailhead

BELOW: *Hikers crossing the two-log bridge on Cochetopa Creek.*

Distance: 13.7 miles
Elevation Gain: approx 1660 ft

USFS Maps: Gunnison National Forest, see pages 176-177.

USGS Quad Maps: Cochetopa Park, Saguache Park, Elk Park.

Trails Illustrated map: # 139.

Jurisdiction: Gunnison Ranger District, Gunnison NF.

Access from Denver:

Access from Durango:

Availability of Water:

Bicycling: see pg. 168-169.

Gudy's Tip

"*The La Garita Wilderness is so remote that few travel here and you are unlikely to meet other hikers. The loneliness is offset by the complete solitude that you find.*" If you seek solitude, this is one of the least traveled segments of the CT. The trailheads are remote and can be difficult to reach after wet weather and don't expect your cell phone to work out here.

About This Segment

The CT follows a jeep/ranch road through arid cattle-grazing country until reaching Cochetopa Creek, the only reliable water source in this segment. The CT then follows the creek to the Eddiesville Trailhead. Hikers no longer have to ford the Cochetopa, a log bridge was added in the late summer of 2004 — a long-desired improvement for the CT.

Trailhead/Access Points

Saguache Park Road Trail Access   : From Saguache on US-285 in the San Luis Valley, go west on CO-114 for approximately 35 miles. Turn left onto FS-804 (BLM-3089 / Saguache Co. Rd-17GG) for approximately 5 miles until it terminates at Saguache Co. Rd-NN14 (Cochetopa Park Rd. / BLM-3083). Turn left (east) on NN14 for 1 mile, then turn right (south) on BLM-3088 (FS-787) for 3.5 miles. Note a jeep road, FS-787.2D, branching off to your right (southwest). This intersection is the end of Segment 18 and the beginning of Segment 19. No parking area is provided at this trail access.

Many hikers have reported overlooking the intersection of the Saguache Park Road and FS-787.2D. Pay very close attention!

Eddiesville Trailhead   : See Segment 20.

Supplies, Services and Accommodations

There is no convenient supply point for this segment.

Trail Description

This segment begins at the intersection of the Saguache Park Road and FS-287.2D, **mile 0.0** (9,530) **Ⓐ**. There is no formal trailhead signage. Begin by walking to the southwest on FS-287.2D. Encounter a fork at **mile 0.1** and go to the left, continuing in a generally westerly direction. At **mile 2.2 Ⓑ** , arrive at a confusing intersection that may be unmarked due to damage by cattle (9,770). Turn right here, and head towards an unusual-looking fenced area to the northwest (actual compass direction is 290 degrees). Follow the trail towards the fenced area and turn left at **mile 2.4**. The trail goes across a small wetlands area that is protected by the fence. (The trail direction here is 260 degrees — almost due west.)

At **mile 3.2**, pass through a Forest Service gate (9,840) and continue ahead to **mile 3.8 Ⓒ** , where the road ends at a "T" intersection (9,840). Turn left here and head up the valley on the Van Tassel Gulch Road. This old jeep trail climbs quickly into the forest. Top out at **mile 5.3** at an intersecting jeep trail (10,480). Continue straight ahead. At **mile 5.6 Ⓓ** , pass through another Forest Service gate (10,280). Continue descending to **mile 6.7** (9,820) **Ⓔ**. Here, once again, is an area of confusing intersections. There is a muddy stock pond ahead. Pass by the pond, heading southwest on the road closest to the water.

At **mile 7.0**, the trail suddenly leaves the road to the left and becomes a single track trail. The trail now follows along the south banks of Cochetopa Creek, where

ABOVE: *Cochetopa Creek in the La Garita Wilderness.*

BELOW: *Welcome to Eddiesville.*

there are many good campsites along the stream for the next seven miles. Pass next to a parking area for fisherman and follow the stream to the southwest. Motorized vehicles are not allowed past the fisherman's parking area. At **mile 8.5 ❻** , the trail climbs above the stream into a mixture of forest and open meadows. The CT follows this shelf above the stream to **mile 9.5** (9,985) **❼** , where the trail turns sharply to the right and downhill, descending to the stream. There are several old trails here. Head towards the stream at a point directly below a large rock formation. Here, at **mile 9.7**, you will find two excellent log bridges built by a volunteer trail crew in 2004, eliminating the last difficult water crossing along the entire trail. Hike up through the rock formation and turn left on the original trail at **mile 9.8**. Continue up the valley on the north side of the creek. Cross Nutras Creek on another new bridge at **mile 10.9** (10.045) **❽**. There are some good campsites near here. Enter the La Garita Wilderness Area at **mile 11.0**. Continue along the trail above the creek to **mile 13.6** where you leave the wilderness area at a trailhead gate. Pass through the gate and walk through a camping area to **mile 13.7** (10,355) **❾** and the segment's end at the Eddiesville Road.

Trekking With Llamas

Llamas have been raised in South America for centuries as pack animals, as well as for their fiber and meat. Increasingly on long distance trails, such as the CT, hikers are enjoying the advantages of these unique personal porters.

Llamas may be used for short hikes or may be fully loaded for traveling through the mountains on a week-long outing. An adult animal (3 years or more) can carry about 20% of its body weight in rough terrain, or about 70 pounds. They have two-toed padded feet, which do much less damage to the environment because they do not tear into or dent the ground the way hooves do. Llamas are browsers, not grazers — a style that limits over-grazing of delicate backcountry meadows.

As highly social animals, llamas travel well in a string and are easy to train. Most importantly, they are calm and trusting with people. The common stigma, that llamas spit, is true in the sense that they use that to gain advantage in their social structure — just don't get stuck between two angry llamas.

With their panniers fully loaded, and in the mountains, you should expect to go 5 to 9 miles per day. Smaller and far more maneuverable than other pack animals, their pace is perfectly suited for comfortable hiking. Being herd animals, llamas like to travel with companions and you should stay together so that they are not anxious about being separated. A good pack llama will follow its human leader willingly (nearly) anywhere, including areas where it might be hurt; so, the animal's welfare should be your primary concern at all times.

In Colorado, several outfitters offer trekking services on the CT using llamas. But as the price of pack stock continues to drop dramatically, they are coming into use by individuals, as well as by the Forest Service. Check with land management agencies, in the segments that you wish to travel, about any restrictions regarding pack animals. A Colorado Trail Foundation's web site has a lot of good info about using llamas for pack stock at *www.coloradotrail.org/Packanimals.*

ABOVE: *A llama string walks on the CT along the Continental Divide.*

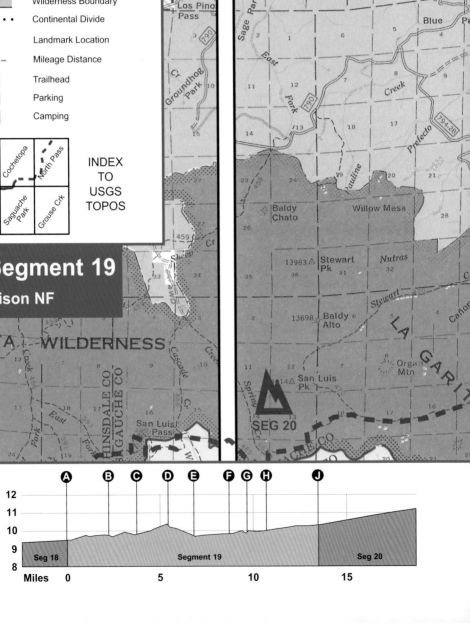

Legend:

- CT (current segment)
- CT (adjacent segment)
- Alternate CT Route
- Trail
- Paved Road
- Improved Road
- Unimproved Road
- Unimproved Road and 4WD
- National Forest Boundary
- Wilderness Boundary
- Continental Divide
- **H** Landmark Location
- – 3.1 – Mileage Distance
- Trailhead
- P Parking
- Camping

SCALE: 1/2 INCH = 1 MILE (1:126,720)

INDEX TO USGS TOPOS

Cold Spring Park | Cochetopa | North Pass
Elk Park | Saguache Park | Grouse Crk

▲ Segment 19
Gunnison NF

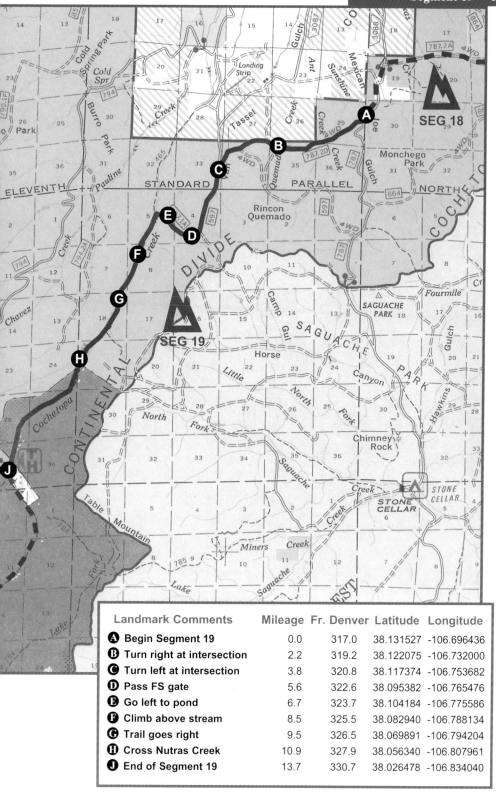

Landmark Comments	Mileage	Fr. Denver	Latitude	Longitude
Ⓐ Begin Segment 19	0.0	317.0	38.131527	-106.696436
Ⓑ Turn right at intersection	2.2	319.2	38.122075	-106.732000
Ⓒ Turn left at intersection	3.8	320.8	38.117374	-106.753682
Ⓓ Pass FS gate	5.6	322.6	38.095382	-106.765476
Ⓔ Go left to pond	6.7	323.7	38.104184	-106.775586
Ⓕ Climb above stream	8.5	325.5	38.082940	-106.788134
Ⓖ Trail goes right	9.5	326.5	38.069891	-106.794204
Ⓗ Cross Nutras Creek	10.9	327.9	38.056340	-106.807961
Ⓙ End of Segment 19	13.7	330.7	38.026478	-106.834040

Segment 20
Eddiesville Trailhead to San Luis Pass

BELOW: *Hikers follow the post and cairn-studded route near San Luis Pass.*

Distance: 12.7 miles
Elevation Gain: approx 2960 ft

USFS Maps: Gunnison NF, Rio Grande NF, see pages 182-183.

USGS Quad Maps: Elk Park, Halfmoon Pass, San Luis Peak.

Trails Illustrated map: # 139.

Jurisdiction: Gunnison Ranger District, Gunnison NF.

Access from Denver: 🚗

Access from Durango: 🚙

Availability of Water: ☕

Bicycling: 🚲 see pg. 168-169.

Gudy's Tip

"It is a temptation to climb 14,014-foot San Luis Peak, but the high incidence of lightning storms in that area can make it a dicey proposition. Be sure to check the cloud patterns and weather before ascending." It's best to depart a campsite beneath the pass quite early, drop much of your gear on the pass for the jaunt to the top, then resume your trek before afternoon thunderstorms move in.

About This Segment

This segment immediately re-enters the La Garita Wilderness Area, detouring around some private property. The trail rejoins Cochetopa Creek after about a mile and follows the valley all the way to the base of San Luis Peak (14,014). As you gain the upper valley, notice the *hoodoos* (odd-shaped rock columns) high on the north slope. Following the CT from Eddiesville Trailhead is the easiest way to get to San Luis Peak for those interested in climbing 14,000-foot mountains. From where the CT passes over the San Luis saddle, it is a fairly easy climb to the top, consisting of only 1,400 feet of vertical and 1.25 miles of horizontal distance. If you are this close, you might as well do it — the views from the top are spectacular! From the saddle near San Luis Peak, the CT stays above treeline until dipping down to San Luis Pass.

Trailhead/Access Points

Eddiesville Trailhead Access : From Saguache on US-285 in the San Luis Valley, go west on CO-114 for approximately 35 miles. Turn left onto FS-804 (BLM-3089/Saguache Co. Rd-17GG) for approximately 5 miles, until it terminates at Saguache Co Rd-NN14 (Cochetopa Pass Rd./BLM-3083). Turn right (west) and follow NN14 for 1.5 miles to Upper Dome Reservoir. Turn left (west) onto Saguache Co. Rd-15GG (BLM-3086/FS-974). Follow it around the west side of the reservoir, where it curves, and head south. Proceed south for 3 miles to an intersection with Co. Rd-14DD (FS-794). This road may also be labeled as "Stewart Creek". Follow it for about 21 miles to the Eddiesville Trailhead. This road tends to be very challenging when wet.

San Luis Pass Trail Access : See Segment 21.

Supplies, Services and Accommodations

Available in **Creede** (see Segment 21), see page 187.

Trail Description

This segment begins at the large trailhead sign in Eddiesville **A** , **mile 0.0** (10,355), an old ranch inholding that is essentially a private island within the La Garita Wilderness Area. There are still some old ranch buildings in the area. The trailhead is at the junction of Stewart and Cochetopa Creeks, and there are many campsites in the vicinity. From the Eddiesville sign, head south along a good dirt road. Cross Stewart Creek on a bridge, then turn right onto single-track trail at **mile 0.2**. There is some signage and a trail register here. About 300 feet past the register, the trail enters the La Garita Wilderness Area. At **mile 0.3**, pass through a Forest Service gate (10,410). The trail makes a sharp left turn here and begins heading southeast, just outside of the private ranch holdings. A sign at the gate identifies the Skyline Trail, the name of the old stock trail, followed by the Colorado Trail. Cross a small stream at **mile 0.4**. The trail is marked by occasional wooden posts and is easy to follow. Cross a stream at **mile 0.7 B** . There are a few good campsites near

the stream. Pass through another gate at **mile 1.3**, the end of the private inholding. There is another wilderness boundary sign here. At **mile 1.6 ⒞** , intersect the Machin Basin Trail, which come in from across the valley to the east (10,360). Continue south on the Colorado Trail, and at **mile 1.7**, the trail climbs up a short rocky stretch. Continue south. There are numerous, excellent campsites along Cochetopa Creek between here and mile 7.5, where the trail begins climbing towards San Luis Peak.

Cross a boulder field at **mile 3.6** and the pass through a Forest Service gate at **mile 3.7** (10,640) **⒟** . Cross a stream at **mile 4.9 ⒠** , and another at **mile 5.4 ⒡** , with good campsites near the latter in trees above the trail. Cross another small creek with good camp possibilities at **mile 6.7** (11,580) **⒢** . Pass the Stewart Creek Trail turnoff at **mile 7.5 ⒣** . Continue straight ahead, then cross a fork of Cochetopa Creek (11,750). Just after crossing the creek lies an excellent campsite. One CT hiker reports camping here in the fall and spotting two black bears, plus numerous elk and deer, all from the campsite. This is truly one of the wildest and most remote sections of the trail.

ABOVE: *Hoodoos in the upper valley of Cochetopa Creek.*

BELOW: *Wildflowers below the San Luis saddle.*

The trail begins climbing steeply past the creek, switchbacking upwards to the saddle, just to the south of San Luis Peak. Reach the high point of this segment at **mile 8.8** (12,600) **⒥** . From here, many people hike to the top of 14,014-foot San Luis Peak. The relative isolation of the hike will probably be diminished here, as many people climb the peak via Creede and San Luis Pass.

After crossing the saddle, the trail drops some, then contours through rock and tundra. Reach another saddle **Ⓚ** at **mile 10.1** (12,375), then drop down again. A side trail exits down Spring Creek at **mile 10.5** (12,140). Continue straight ahead and cross a small stream at **mile 10.9** (12,035) **Ⓛ** , then enter the forest briefly at a few hundred feet further. There area good campsites below in the trees (11,900). Begin climbing again and leave the trees at a large switchback at **mile 11.5**. Climb up once more to the Divide at **mile 12.1** (12,409) **Ⓜ** , then descend to the saddle of San Luis Pass at **mile 12.7** (11,940) **Ⓝ** . This is the end of Segment 20, at an old sign marking the pass.

The Fourteeners and Climbing San Luis Peak

The CT has its closest encounter with a 14er when it passes gentle-giant San Luis Peak (14,014 feet) at mile 8.8 of Segment 20. As it turns out, of the 54 peaks in Colorado that rise above the altitude of 14,000 feet, nearly two-thirds sit within twenty miles of the course of the CT. They are a common and an inspiring sight from many a ridgetop on the trail.

It seems remarkable that none of the 14ers exceeds an altitude of 14,433 feet and that all of the peaks lie within a circle having a radius of only 120 miles, centered in the Sawatch Range near Buena Vista. Even more remarkable is that nearby states that share the Rocky Mountains, and presumably share a related geologic history, have no 14ers at all.

The reasons may rest with two geological features unique to Colorado. The *Colorado Mineral Belt* is a northeast-southwest trending band of hot igneous rocks following roughly the same line as the CT. The *Rio Grande Rift* is a narrow rift valley, including the San Luis and Arkansas Valleys. Both of these features tend to push overlaying rocks upward. Interestingly, all but one or two of the 14ers are along these two features; and the highest and most numerous lie at the intersection of the two.

It's thought that although the entire Rocky Mountain region, including Colorado, Wyoming and New Mexico, went through a broad, uniform uplift, the Colorado 14ers seem to be the result of an additional local growth spurt caused by these two trends.

In any case, this happy coincidence has captured the imagination of climbers ever since Carl Blaurock and Bill Ervin became the first to climb them all in 1923. A growing number have followed in their footsteps — the Colorado Mountain Club (CMC)

ABOVE: *Camping below the saddle.*

reports that, as of the end of 2004, well over 1,000 people will have officially finished up the 14ers. But if you choose to climb San Luis Peak while passing by on your trek, you may be lucky enough to have it all for yourself. According to the CMC, San Luis Peak is one of the least climbed of the 14ers.

The climb of San Luis Peak from the saddle at mile 8.8 on the Colorado Trail is not a difficult one, with a class 1 rating and 1,400 feet of elevation gain in about 1.25 miles. Simply proceed north from the saddle, following the ridge to the gentle top. There is excellent camping in the alpine meadows below the saddle. Plan on an early start, so as to return to the saddle before early afternoon and the start of any afternoon storms. Allow about 4-5 hours round-trip.

BELOW: *Climbing up talus.*

SCALE: 1/2 INCH = 1 MILE (1:126,720)

CT (current segment)	
CT (adjacent segment)	
Alternate CT Route	
Trail	
Paved Road	
Improved Road	
Unimproved Road	
Unimproved Road and 4WD	
National Forest Boundary	
Wilderness Boundary	
Continental Divide	
H Landmark Location	
– 3.1 – Mileage Distance	
Trailhead	
P Parking	
Camping	

INDEX TO USGS TOPOS

Stewart Peak	Elk Park	Saguache Park
San Luis Peak	Halfmoon Pass	Mesa Mtn

▲ Segment 20
Gunnison NF

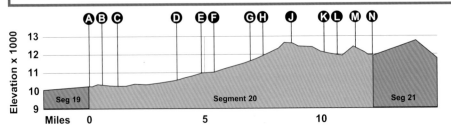

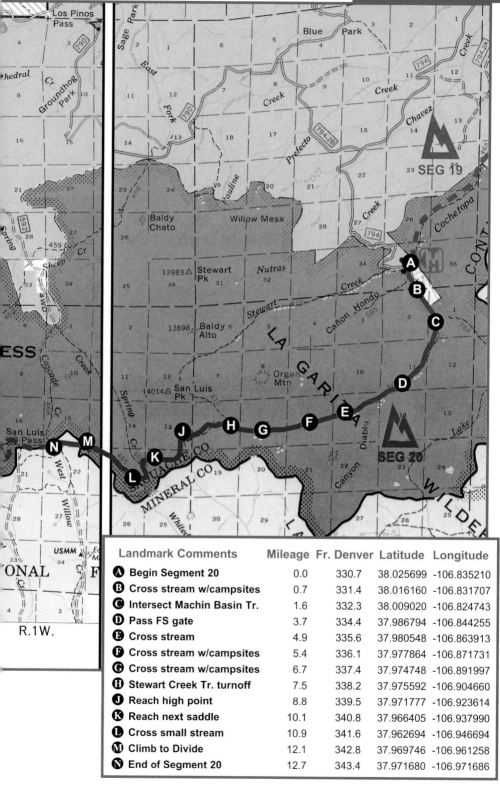

Landmark Comments	Mileage	Fr. Denver	Latitude	Longitude
Ⓐ Begin Segment 20	0.0	330.7	38.025699	-106.835210
Ⓑ Cross stream w/campsites	0.7	331.4	38.016160	-106.831707
Ⓒ Intersect Machin Basin Tr.	1.6	332.3	38.009020	-106.824743
Ⓓ Pass FS gate	3.7	334.4	37.986794	-106.844255
Ⓔ Cross stream	4.9	335.6	37.980548	-106.863913
Ⓕ Cross stream w/campsites	5.4	336.1	37.977864	-106.871731
Ⓖ Cross stream w/campsites	6.7	337.4	37.974748	-106.891997
Ⓗ Stewart Creek Tr. turnoff	7.5	338.2	37.975592	-106.904660
Ⓙ Reach high point	8.8	339.5	37.971777	-106.923614
Ⓚ Reach next saddle	10.1	340.8	37.966405	-106.937990
Ⓛ Cross small stream	10.9	341.6	37.962694	-106.946694
Ⓜ Climb to Divide	12.1	342.8	37.969746	-106.961258
Ⓝ End of Segment 20	12.7	343.4	37.971680	-106.971686

Segment 21
San Luis Pass to Spring Creek Pass

BELOW: A *lunch break with sweeping alpine views.*

Distance: 14.8 miles
Elevation Gain: approx 2940 ft

USFS Maps: Gunnison NF, Rio Grande NF, see pages 188-189.

USGS Quad Maps: San Luis Peak, Baldy Cinco, Slumgullion Pass.

Trails Illustrated map: # 139, 141.

Jurisdiction: Gunnison Ranger Dst. and Divide Ranger Dst.- Creede.

Access from Denver:

Access from Durango:

Availability of Water:

Bicycling: see pg. 168-169.

Gudy's Tip

"*Take in the views from Snow Mesa above Spring Creek. You can see the Rio Grande Pyramid and the Uncompahgre Mountains, where Ute Indians once hunted.*" Ahead is a great "U" shaped bend of the Continental Divide which holds the headwaters of the mighty Rio Grande River.

You'll get lots of exercise on the first 8 miles of this segment; hiking down into and climbing out of the various Mineral Creek drainages (East, Middle, and West). And you'll end up at almost the same altitude you started, but you will have gained roughly 2,500 feet of vertical. On the bright side, you'll get some great views and have the possibility of some really nice campsites.

A word of caution about the Mineral Creek drainages — each has a trail that comes out of the north to join the CT. While the CT may follow each of them for a short distance, if you find yourself proceeding in a northerly direction along the bottom of a drainage for over 15 minutes, consider that you might have missed a turnoff. The CT stays as close to the Divide as reasonably possible. In order to compensate for all the climbing in the first 8 miles, the 3-mile hike across Snow Mesa is flat. The last 2 miles are a 1,400-foot descent to Spring Creek Pass and the end of this segment.

San Luis Pass Trail Access 🚙 : From the north end of Creede, proceed into a steep and narrow canyon (FS-503). The San Luis Pass access point is 9.5 miles north up this canyon. Non-4WD vehicles can proceed 6.5 miles to the closed Equity Mine and a small parking area. From here, it's a 3 mile walk to the pass. Vehicles with 4WD can continue an additional 1.5 mile. No formal parking is available here. From this point, it's a 1.5 mile walk northward to San Luis Pass and the CT on a trail that prohibits motorized vehicles.

Spring Creek Pass Trailhead 🚗 : See Segment 22.

This segment begins at San Luis Pass. This obscure trailhead is the closest to Creede; but through-hikers wishing to re-supply in Creede should consider continuing on to Spring Creek Pass on CO-149, where rides are easier to obtain.

From the trail sign in the saddle, **mile 0.0** (11,940) **Ⓐ** , head west, then south as the trail makes a large switchback away from the pass. Follow the trail upwards to **mile 1.3 Ⓑ** on a ridge top (12,895). The trail drops steeply off the other side into the East Mineral Creek headwaters. Enter the trees and hit the East Mineral Creek Trail at **mile 2.6** (11,800) **Ⓒ** . Continue straight ahead and cross East Mineral Creek at **mile 2.7** (11,610). There are campsites in the area. The trail then climbs back up out of the trees to **mile 3.3 Ⓓ** to the top of a ridge that divides the drainages of East and Middle Mineral Creeks (12,180).   Cross over the ridge and drop into the Middle Mineral Creek drainage. Re-enter the forest, then cross Middle Mineral Creek at **mile 4.0** (11,610) **Ⓔ** . There are campsites in the vicinity. This routine is repeated once more as the trail climbs up out of the drainage, over a ridge at **mile 4.8** (11,860),

> This trail section is largely above tree line, and hikers should consider weather as a major factor when choosing campsites and hiking schedules. Snow Mesa can be a very unsettling experience during an electrical storm!

Viewing Ptarmigan

White-tailed ptarmigan are small alpine grouse that inhabit open tundra slopes in summer, resorting to willows and other sheltered areas in winter. They are the only bird species in Colorado to spend the entire year above treeline. The extensive alpine terrain along the old Skyline Trail is perfect habitat for viewing these hardy ground birds — if only you can spot them!

With their near-perfect seasonal camouflage, the birds attempt to escape detection from predators. Their mottled-brown summer plumage makes them almost invisible among the scattered rocks and alpine plants. In winter, only the black eyes and bill stand out against their pure white coloration.

Ptarmigan are weak flyers, as likely to scurry away when disturbed, as to burst into a short, low sail over the tundra. Despite that, they still manage to travel over surprising distances in early winter, to congregate in areas that harbor their favorite winter sustenance, dormant willow buds. In summer, they add insects, seeds, and berries to their diet.

Nesting occurs in June with 4-8 buff, spotted eggs laid in a lined depression in open ground. During breeding, males are sometimes aggressive toward any interlopers passing through their territory, flying around erratically, accompanied by hooting noises, or approaching to peck comically at the boot of a resting hiker.

A recent study by ecologist James Larison of Cornell University raises a warning flag about the future for these fascinating birds. In areas of Colorado where metals from mining operations have leached into the soil, ptarmigan have accumulated high levels of cadmium in their bodies. Ultimately this causes calcium loss and many birds suffer broken bones from brittle wings and legs.

LEFT: White-tailed ptarmigan.

ABOVE: Panorama from above Miners Creek.

then into the West Mineral Creek drainage. There is a dry campsite on the ridge. Descend again and cross a small stream at **mile 5.2** (11,980) ❶ where a small camp is possible below the trail. This is the last, good forested camp along this segment until reaching the Spring Creek Trailhead, some 9 miles ahead.

Begin climbing again and cross over a rock band at **mile 5.4** (12,020). Continue climbing up to a small saddle at **mile 5.8** (12,230) ❷. The trail contours along the treeless tundra to the west. Intersect the Mineral Creek Trail #466 at **mile 6.3** (12,320) ❸ and continue straight ahead. Resume climbing to a high point at **mile 7.6** ❹ (12,790) where the trail contours around the mountain and descends, with spectacular views of Snow Mesa and the San Juan Mountains ahead. Take a hard left at **mile 7.9** (12,570) and drop south towards a pond on Snow Mesa below. Hikers who miss this turn will find themselves far from the Colorado Trail in Rough Creek. Pass by the pond at **mile 9.5** (12,320) ❺ and head west across Snow Mesa. Cross a stream at **mile 9.8** and another at **mile 11.1** (12,260) ❻. There are campsites here, but no shelter from storms. Reach the edge of the mesa at **mile 12.8** (12,275) ❼ and begin a steep, rocky descent. Enter the trees at **mile 13.2**. Follow the clearly-marked trail as it descends to the end of the segment at CO-149 on Spring Creek Pass at **mile 14.8** (10,910) ❽. There is a large parking area here with toilets and campsites.

It is about a 10-mile side trip into **Creede** from San Luis Pass. Descend on a side trail south along the headwaters of West Willow Creek until you meet up with FS-503, then continue on it to town. Creede is an old mining town with various watering holes which recall the town's rip-roaring past.

Creede Services

Distance From CT:	
	10 miles
Elevation:	8,852
Zip Code:	81130
Area Code:	719

Dining	Several in town		
Gear	San Juan Sports	137 Creede Ave	(719) 658-2359
Groceries	Kentucky Bell Market	2nd & Main	(719) 658-2526
Info	Chamber of Commerce	on Main St	(719) 658-2374
Laundry	Creede Laundromat	101 East Fifth	no phone
Lodging	Several in town		
Medical	Creede Health Clinic	on Loma Ave	(719) 658-2416
Post Office	Creede Post Office	10 S. Main St.	(719) 658-2615
Showers	Snowshoe Lodge & BB	202 La Garita	(719) 658-2315

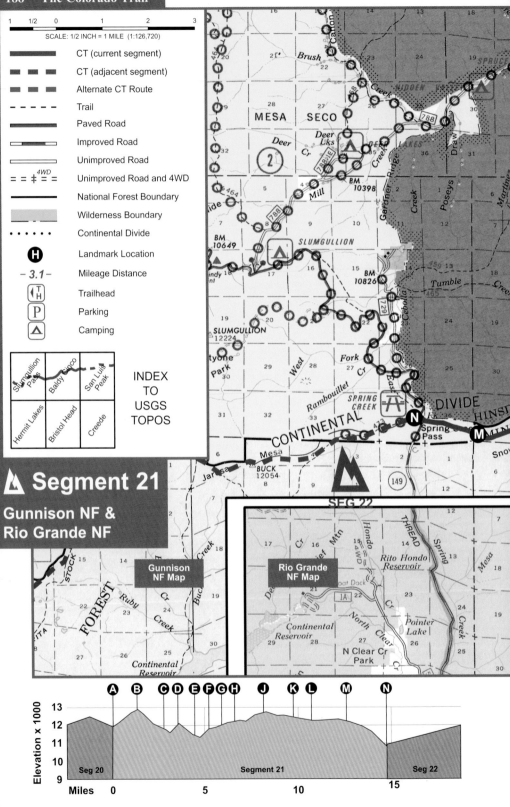

SCALE: 1/2 INCH = 1 MILE (1:126,720)

—	CT (current segment)
– – –	CT (adjacent segment)
—	Alternate CT Route
- - - -	Trail
—	Paved Road
▭	Improved Road
▭	Unimproved Road
= = ‡ = =	Unimproved Road and 4WD
—	National Forest Boundary
▬	Wilderness Boundary
• • • • • •	Continental Divide
H	Landmark Location
– 3.1 –	Mileage Distance
[TH]	Trailhead
[P]	Parking
[▲]	Camping

INDEX TO USGS TOPOS

Slumgullion Pass	Baldy Cinco	San Luis Peak
Hermit Lakes	Bristol Head	Creede

Segment 21
Gunnison NF & Rio Grande NF

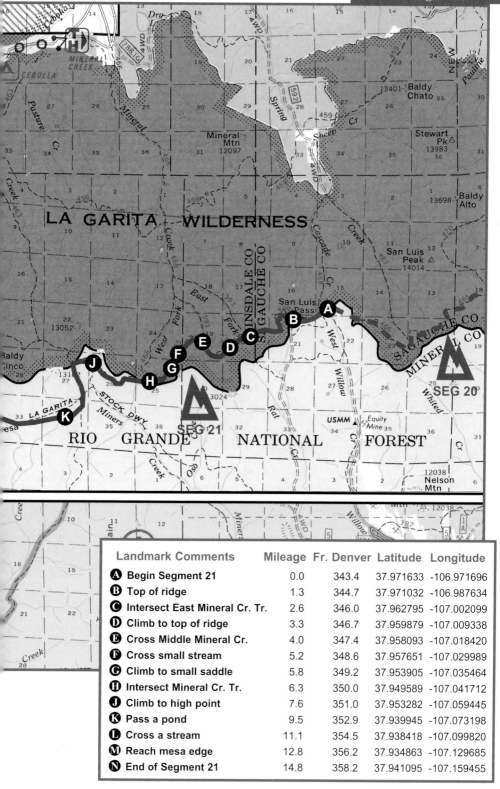

Landmark Comments	Mileage	Fr. Denver	Latitude	Longitude
Ⓐ Begin Segment 21	0.0	343.4	37.971633	-106.971696
Ⓑ Top of ridge	1.3	344.7	37.971032	-106.987634
Ⓒ Intersect East Mineral Cr. Tr.	2.6	346.0	37.962795	-107.002099
Ⓓ Climb to top of ridge	3.3	346.7	37.959879	-107.009338
Ⓔ Cross Middle Mineral Cr.	4.0	347.4	37.958093	-107.018420
Ⓕ Cross small stream	5.2	348.6	37.957651	-107.029989
Ⓖ Climb to small saddle	5.8	349.2	37.953905	-107.035464
Ⓗ Intersect Mineral Cr. Tr.	6.3	350.0	37.949589	-107.041712
Ⓙ Climb to high point	7.6	351.0	37.953282	-107.059445
Ⓚ Pass a pond	9.5	352.9	37.939945	-107.073198
Ⓛ Cross a stream	11.1	354.5	37.938418	-107.099820
Ⓜ Reach mesa edge	12.8	356.2	37.934863	-107.129685
Ⓝ End of Segment 21	14.8	358.2	37.941095	-107.159455

Segment 22
Spring Creek Pass to Carson Saddle

BELOW: *A panorama includes Lake San Cristobal from near Carson Saddle.*

Distance: 17.1 miles
Elevation Gain: approx 3680 ft

USFS Maps: Gunnison NF, Rio Grande NF, see pages 196-197.

USGS Quad Maps: Slumgullion Pass, Lake San Cristobal, Finger Mesa.

Trails Illustrated map: #141, 504.

Jurisdiction: Gunnison Ranger Dst. & Divide Rgr. Dst.-Creede.

Access from Denver:

Access from Durango:

Availability of Water:

Bicycling: see pg. 194-195.

Gudy's Tip

"Don't miss the panoramas from Antenna Summit, just after Jarosa Mesa. The view overlooking the Uncompahgre Mountains is worth the climb. Then from Coney Summit to Carson Saddle there is a steep descent on the trail, but much better than on the jeep road. If your boot tread is worn, you'll probably slip and slide here."

The CT departs west at Spring Creek Pass from the picnic ground on a jeep track, coming to a nice spring in 2.5 miles. Here the CT leaves the jeep track to the right and follows a series of cairns with sign posts, up and over Jarosa Mesa, rejoining the jeep track on the other side for a couple more miles through the tundra. Again, the CT bears right off the jeep track onto a non-motorized section and into the woods. From here to the south side of Coney Summit, the CT is designated by the Forest Service as "only open to non-motorized uses." After 0.8 mile, the trail crosses a marshy meadow which is one of the tributaries of Big Buck Creek. Water is usually available a short distance to the east. This is the last, reasonably-flat area with water along the CT for camping until reaching Carson Saddle. If you are willing to exit the CT for about 0.3 mile or so, the upper end of Ruby Creek (the next valley) has a flat camping area down by a pond. Some small, hidden springs may also be found nearby.

As the CT enters the forest on the south side of the valley, it has been rehabilitated from a dual track to a single track. Please help by staying on the single track. From the top of this ridge, the trail stays above timberline and very close to the Divide for all of the way to Carson Saddle. This area was part of the old San Juan Stock Driveway. Its markers can occasionally be seen as yellow signs on wooden posts that stick out of small stone cairns. As the CT passes Coney Summit, it joins a closed jeep track, then leaves the jeep track to the right when the CT starts down the steep descent to Carson Saddle, only to rejoin the track at the bottom of the hill. Stay on the CT, it is a much more pleasant walk.

Spring Creek Pass Trailhead 🚗 : This trailhead is located where CO-149 tops the Continental Divide at Spring Creek Pass. The pass is approximately 17 miles southeast of Lake City and 33 miles northwest of Creede. There is a Forest Service picnic area that has six picnic tables and fire rings, a toilet and an informative kiosk, as well as parking space for another half dozen or so cars near the picnic area. It is not unusual to see a camper or two in the picnic area. Water is usually available during the summer in a small irrigation ditch on the east side of the highway.

Carson Saddle/Wager Gulch Road Trail Access 🚜 : See Segment 23.

This segment begins atop the Continental Divide at Spring Creek Pass, where there is a trailhead parking area with toilets and camping facilities ❹, **mile 0.0** (10,910). Begin by leaving the parking area on a Forest Service jeep trail, headed west. The route is identified as FS-547 and there are CT confidence markers on carsonite posts. Cross a stream at **mile 2.5 ❸**, with good campsites in the area. Just past the stream, the CT leaves the jeep trail and heads off to the right following the old La Garita Stock Driveway. This wide pathway is marked with rock cairns supporting tall, four-by-four posts, many of which show the CT logo. The trail is

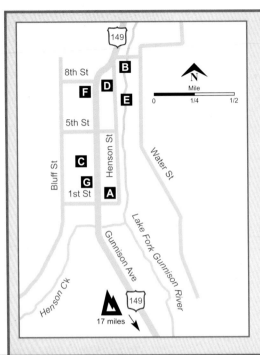

Lake City Services

Distance From CT:	
	17 miles
Elevation:	8,671
Zip Code:	81235
Area Code:	970

It is approximately 17 miles north and west to the old mining town of **Lake City** on Colorado Hwy-149 from Spring Creek Pass, probably too far for most backpackers to travel for re-supply; nor is hitchhiking especially good on this remote byway.

Supplies, Services and Accommodations

Dining		Several in town		
Gear	A	The Sportsman	238 S Gunnison Ave	(970) 944-2526
Groceries	B	The Country Store	916 Hwy 149 North	(970) 944-2387
Info	C	Chamber of Commerce	3rd & Silver	(970) 944-2527
Laundry	D	The Lost Sock	808 N Gunnison	(970) 944-5009
Lodging		Several in town		
Medical	E	Lake City Medical Center	700 Henson	(970) 944-2331
Post Office	F	Lake City Post Office	803 Gunnison Ave	(970) 944-2560
Showers	G	San Juan Base Camp	355 S Gunnison Ave	(970) 944-2559

very faint in places, but the cairns and posts are generally easy to follow. Follow these for the next 2.8 miles, leading you through the beautiful meadows along the old driveway.

Reach the high point on Jarosa Mesa at **mile 4.1** (12030). Continue following the markers west to **mile 5.6** and hit a jeep trail (11,732) **C** . Bear to the left here at a three-way intersection. The CT follows the left-most jeep track uphill, traversing the mountain with a large antennae array that is visible to the northwest. Reach a saddle at **mile 7.0** (12,075) **D** and follow the jeep trail as it turns to the southwest. Reach a high point at **mile 7.3**, then begin to descend. Turn right onto a single-track trail at **mile 7.9** (12,020) **E** . Cross a jeep trail in a grassy valley at **mile 8.6** (11,715) and follow the trail across a marshy area directly ahead. Re-enter the forest, climbing steadily up on another old jeep trail. Reach the edge of the forest at **mile 9.2** and enter a wide patch of small willows. The trail curves to the right and heads in a northwesterly direction for about 0.6 mile, then resumes its southerly direction at a switchback near the edge of the willows (12,205). Follow the trail as it continues uphill, contouring just below the Continental Divide. At **mile 12.0** (12,720), follow a series of steep switchbacks upward. Briefly reach the 13,000-foot elevation level at **mile 12.9 ❻**, then drop down slightly before resuming the climb. Reach another high point at **mile 13.8** (13,040)**❼**, then drop down slightly once again for 0.5 mile. The trail now heads through a rocky section, directly towards Coney Summit and its highest point. At **mile 14.8**, reach an intersection. The right fork leaves the Colorado Trail and climbs steeply to the 13,334-foot top of Coney Summit, then re-joins the trail a short distance beyond. The left fork is the Colorado Trail; and it contours up and around Coney Summit to the trail's highest point in its entire 483-mile length at **mile 15.5** (13,270) **❽**.

From here, the trail continues following the Divide, but heads downhill. Cross a jeep trail at **mile 15.7** (13,220), then again at **mile 15.9** (as the switchbacks cross the road twice in a short distance). The trail now runs parallel to the jeep

ABOVE: *A yurt used by a trail crew near Buck Creek.*

BELOW: *The CT climbs to over 13,000 feet in Segment 22.*

road to **mile 16.4**, where it begins following the road (12,785). Follow the road to a intersection at **mile 17.0**, then turn right. The segment ends at a triangular intersection of three jeep trails at **mile 17.1** (12,360) ❶. This is Carson Saddle, at the top of Wager Gulch. There is a small parking area, and a jeep trail descends to the north to the Cinnamon Pass Road, west of Lake San Cristobal and Lake City.

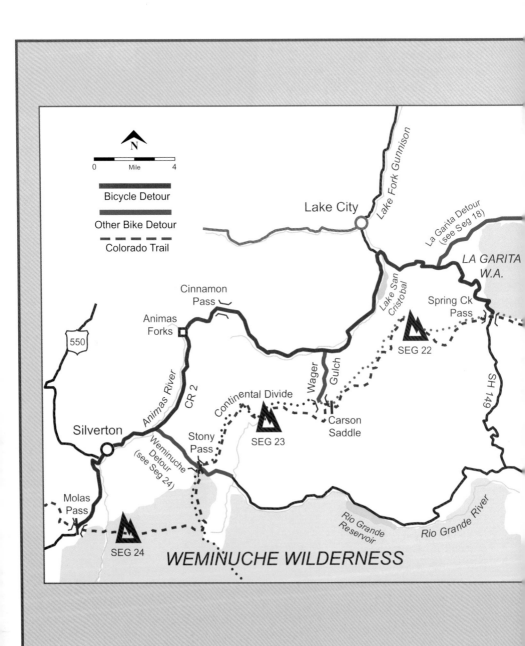

Mountain Bicycle Detour

 Coney Summit Detour — *Segment 22, 23 and 24 (Gunnison NF, San Juan NF):* This long, *optional* detour avoids a challenging, high-altitude ride through Segments 22 and 23, as well as provides the mandatory avoidance of the Weminuche Wilderness Area in Segment 24. It also can serve as a convenient continuance of the La Garita Wilderness Area Detour (see page 168-169). For those experienced riders that insist on tackling Segment 22, there is quite a bit of *hike-a-bike* on the CT from Spring Creek Pass to Carson Saddle and there is the risk of damage to the fragile alpine tundra from knobby bike tires. Riders can skip Segment 22 alone and rejoin the CT by pedaling up from Lake City via the Lake Fork/Cinnamon Pass Road and Wager Gulch to Carson Saddle. However, beyond Carson Saddle, Segment 23 is likewise mostly *hike-a-bike* alongside the Continental Divide; and you'll be required to exit the segment at the Stony Pass Road and take the required detour around the Weminuche Wilderness Area (see page 209).

Detour Description: From the top of Spring Creek Pass, turn right on CO-149 and head downhill 7.1 miles to the intersection with the Cinnamon Pass Road. (Pass by the turnoff for the La Garita Detour at about mile 4.6.) This road passes by Lake San Cristobal and is also marked as the Alpine Loop. Turn left (south) and follow the road as it passes around Lake San Cristobal. The pavement ends just past the lake at **mile 11.4**. Continue up the popular jeep route, passing by the Wager Gulch turnoff, to a fork at **mile 19.3**. Take the right fork a nd climb up on a spectacular shelf road, with the Lake Fork of the Gunnison River far below. At **mile 24.4**, pass by a small parking area. Just to the north and hidden in the trees is the Colorado Trail Education Center where outdoor classes are taught throughout the summer months.

At **mile 27.0**, pass by an intersection with a road into American Basin. Stay on the right and follow a series of switchbacks up into the tundra. Reach the top of Cinnamon Pass at **mile 28.9** and begin a steep descent on the other side. Intersect the Engineer Pass Road at **mile 31.1** and turn left. Continue bearing left at intersections at **mile 31.5** and **mile 31.9**, traversing the mountain above the ghost town of Animas Forks. Follow the road down the valley past numerous old mines and mills, past the Stony Pass Road intersection at **mile 38.7** and arrive at Silverton at **mile 43.3**. Pedal through town and get on US-550 at **mile 43.9**. Turn left and climb steeply up the highway to where the CT crosses US-550 before Molas Pass at **mile 50.0**. This is the beginning of Segment 25.

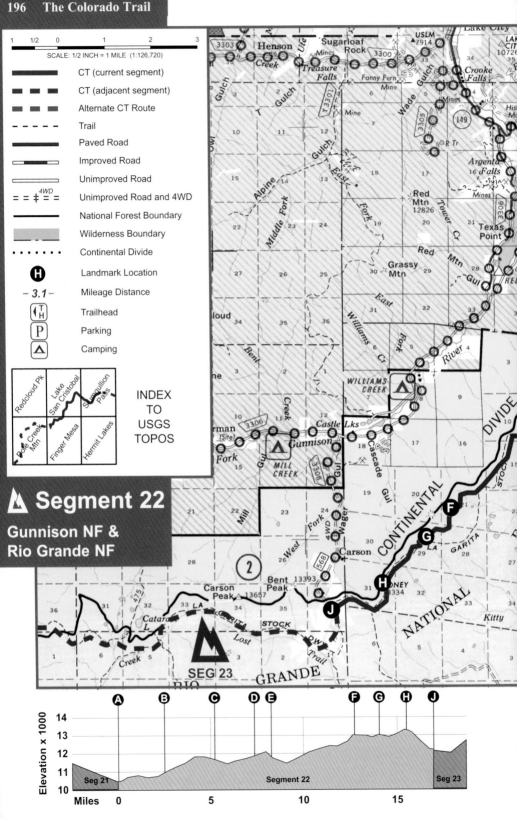

SCALE: 1/2 INCH = 1 MILE (1:126,720)

▬▬▬▬▬	CT (current segment)
▬ ▬ ▬ ▬	CT (adjacent segment)
▬ ▬ ▬	Alternate CT Route
‑ ‑ ‑ ‑ ‑	Trail
▬▬▬▬▬	Paved Road
▭▬▭▬	Improved Road
▭▭▭▭	Unimproved Road
= = ‡ = =	Unimproved Road and 4WD
▬▬▬▬▬	National Forest Boundary
▨▨▨	Wilderness Boundary
• • • • • •	Continental Divide
H	Landmark Location
– *3.1* –	Mileage Distance
[T/H]	Trailhead
[P]	Parking
[△]	Camping

INDEX TO USGS TOPOS

Redcloud Pk	Lake San Cristobal	Sanguillion Pass
Pole Creek Mtn	Finger Mesa	Hermit Lakes

▲ **Segment 22**

**Gunnison NF &
Rio Grande NF**

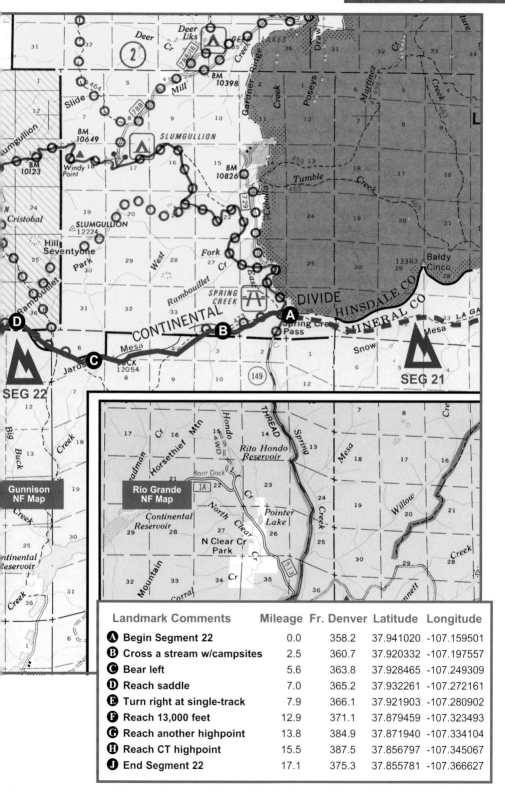

Landmark Comments	Mileage	Fr. Denver	Latitude	Longitude
A Begin Segment 22	0.0	358.2	37.941020	-107.159501
B Cross a stream w/campsites	2.5	360.7	37.920332	-107.197557
C Bear left	5.6	363.8	37.928465	-107.249309
D Reach saddle	7.0	365.2	37.932261	-107.272161
E Turn right at single-track	7.9	366.1	37.921903	-107.280902
F Reach 13,000 feet	12.9	371.1	37.879459	-107.323493
G Reach another highpoint	13.8	384.9	37.871940	-107.334104
H Reach CT highpoint	15.5	387.5	37.856797	-107.345067
J End Segment 22	17.1	375.3	37.855781	-107.366627

Segment 23
Carson Saddle to Stony Pass

BELOW: *A view of Sunshine and Redcloud Peaks from the Divide.*

Distance: 15.9 miles
Elevation Gain: approx 3120 ft

USFS Maps: Gunnison NF, Rio Grande NF, San Juan NF, see pages 202-203.

USGS Quad Maps: Finger Mesa, Howardsville, Pole Creek Mountain, Storm King Peak.

Trails Illustrated map: #140, 141 and 504.

Jurisdiction: Gunnison Ranger Dst. and Divide Ranger Dst. - Creede.

Access from Denver:

Access from Durango:

Availability of Water:

Bicycling: see pgs. 194-195.

Gudy's Tip

"*Carson Saddle has a surprising number of people in 4WD vehicles, which can be a shock after the previous isolation of the trail.*" Enjoy the spectacular, above-treeline views from along the Continental Divide on this segment, but be cautious in conditions of poor visibility. A GPS receiver can be invaluable in locating the landmark locations noted on page 203.

About This Segment

Although the CT in this segment manages to stay fairly close to the Continental Divide, things are not quite as challenging as in the previous two segments. However, if you are planning to reach this segment by car, you'll find things very challenging on both end. The CT starts on a jeep track heading south; but after a 0.5 mile, it branches off to the right, going west. At this point, it is designated as "only open to non-motorized uses" until it gets to Pole Creek. This is a very pleasant section of trail, contouring along the mountainside just below the Divide and paralleling Lost Trail Creek below. It was here that one CT hiker had the privilege of observing the birth of an elk calf and watching it struggle to its feet for the first time. After 3.5 miles, the trail passes into the Pole Creek drainage and begins a descent. After about 0.3 mile, you will come to a "Y" which may be labeled Old CT left and New CT right, or something to that effect. The Old CT follows along Pole Creek to its junction with the Rio Grande. The New CT stays very close to the Continental Divide for the next 17 miles. In fact, it crosses the CD several times before finally rejoining the Old CT at the head of Elk Creek. It is above timberline all the way to Elk Creek and the views are spectacular. In order to preserve the tundra, much of the trail is marked with cairns rather than with cut tread. From each cairn, the next can be seen in clear weather. During periods of low visibility, a GPS receiver is helpful. If your altimeter indicates that you are below 11,000 feet on this segment, you are off the trail. This segment ends at Stony Pass.

Trailhead/Access Points

Carson Saddle/ Wager Gulch Trail Access : From Lake City, drive south on CO-149 about 1.5 miles to a "Y". The right branch leads to Lake San Cristobal. Follow this road for 9.3 miles to a left turn off with a small parking area. This is the beginning of the Wager Gulch Road (BLM-3308/FS-568). This is not a road for the squeamish. It is very steep, rocky and narrow with many tight switchbacks, as well as some significant exposure. In mid-summer, the road is used by many tourists in 4WDs, and on ATVs and motorcycles. Follow this road for about 5 miles to Carson Saddle, a low point on the Continental Divide about a mile above the abandoned mining town of Carson, where it meets the CT.

Stony Pass Road : See Segment 24.

Supplies, Services and Accommodations

Services are available in **Lake City** (see Segment 22, page 192).

Trail Description

From the triangular, jeep-road intersection on Carson Saddle at **mile 0.0** (12,360) **A** go south on the jeep trail. At **mile 0.5** (12,180), exit the road on a single track trail that forks off to the right, going uphill. After a very short climb, the trail begins a gradual descent in a westerly direction. At **mile 1.2 B**, cross a small stream (12,000). There is a good campsite about 500 feet below the trail. Begin a long uphill

ABOVE: A *camp in the Pole Creek drainage.*

BELOW: *Sunset, Lost Trail Creek.*

climb, then cross a seasonal stream at **mile 1.6**. A few small campsites are possible here. A larger, seasonal stream is encountered at **mile 2.4** (12,220) **ⓒ**. Continue uphill, steeply in places, as the trail climbs to a small, unnamed pass at **mile 3.7** (12,990) **ⓓ**. There is often a small pond at this point, leftover from melting snow. Drop down from the pass into the Pole Creek drainage. Pass by Cataract Lake at **mile 4.5** where there are good campsites, as well as at several smaller lakes nearby. Begin following the Pole Creek drainage downward. Turn off of the Pole Creek Trail at **mile 5.0** (12,386) **ⓔ**. There is a sign at the intersection. This is the beginning of the "Cataract Ridge" re-location of the CT, completed in 2007. Cyclists should be aware that this is a *hike-a-bike* section, and is not all rideable. An alternate route for cyclists is to follow the Pole Creek Trail to the bottom, then take the Stony Pass Road to Silverton (see the *Coney Summit Detour*, pgs. 194-195).

The re-routed trail heads almost due west to a point on the hillside, then desends rapidly to a small lake at **mile 5.5** (12,240) **ⓕ**. This is an excellent campsite. Follow the trail around the south end of the lake, then resume in a westerly direction. The trail quickly begins climbing up a small valley, crossing a steep talus field as it heads upwards. The trail bears to the right in a saddle at **mile 6.8**, contouring around the base of 13,841-foot Half Peak. The trail continues

upward to an elevation of about 12,800', then crosses a wide, muddy field where elk wallow in the mud. This point is located on the divide, above a drainage leading into Cuba Gulch.

Begin contouring around a large, rocky hillside towards the northwest. Follow a line of cairns beginning at **mile 7.8** (12,730) **G** , staying high upon the hillside in a southwesterly direction. Reach a point on a broad ridge at **mile 8.2**, then follow cairns down the ridge into the valley below at **mile 8.5** (12,350). Cross the valley bottom and head up the other side in a westerly direction. Drop into a steep gully and cross to the other side at **mile 8.9**. Bear right after crossing the gully, following a string of cairns along its western side to a small, rocky outcropping. The grade becomes easier as the trail bears to the southwest, then crosses the divide in a small pass at **mile 9.3** **H** . The trail contours into Cuba Gulch, intersecting a cross trail at **mile 9.9**. A small, grassy meadow, 300 feet below, is a good campsite. Water may be found in the headwaters of Cuba Creek, a short distance ahead.

Contour upwards on a good trail, paying attention to cairns marking the way, to a point on the divide at **mile 10.6** (12,917) **J** . The distinct peak just to the north is Cuba. It was a major triangulation point for the Hayden Survey of the late 1800's.

The trail take a turn to the south and follows the ridge downward, crossing the top of Minnie Gulch at **mile 11.4** (12,734). The cross trail here goes from Pole Creek, to the east, to Minnie Gulch, to the northwest. The CT climbs quickly up again via a series of switchbacks to a high point at **mile 11.6**. This point is just above 13,000 feet, and is the highest point on this segment. Continue southward along the ridge, following cairns and avoiding several game trails that drop into Minnie Gulch below. Follow the well-defined trail into the saddle above Maggie Gulch, where you will cross the Maggle Gulch Trail at **mile 12.6** (12,537) **K** . Head up the other side, contouring around the mountain until the trail comes close to the top of the ridge again. Pass a small lake at **mile 13.5**, then continue upwards to a high point at **mile 13.7** (12,820). Drop down briefly, then climb up once more, before dropping down to a very well-defined trail at **mile 13.9**. Go left (southeast) and follow the trail as it contours around Canby Mountain above a large valley. Stay high on the hillside above the Stony Pass Road in a northwesterly direction, then drop to the road at **mile 15.5**. Walk up the road to **mile 15.9** (12,380) **L** , where the trail leaves the road to the southwest. This is the end of Segment 23, near the top of Stony Pass.

The Stony Pass Road

The historic Stony Pass Road was constructed in 1879 as a means to transport supplies in and ore out of the booming Silverton mining district. For a few short years, it was a busy and important route for miners and others attracted by news of new-found wealth in the San Juans. After a couple years however, the difficult route was eclipsed by the Denver and Rio Grande Western's rail route through Animas Canyon. The road quickly fell into a sorry state and gained a reputation as a "pretty rough ride."

Robert M. Ormes, of early guidebook fame, recalls struggling up it in his car, after being assured that the first car into Silverton came in this way. Finding it a lot more than his auto could handle, he encountered a man on the road who told him, *"Sure it came in this way... but, it was in some wagons."*

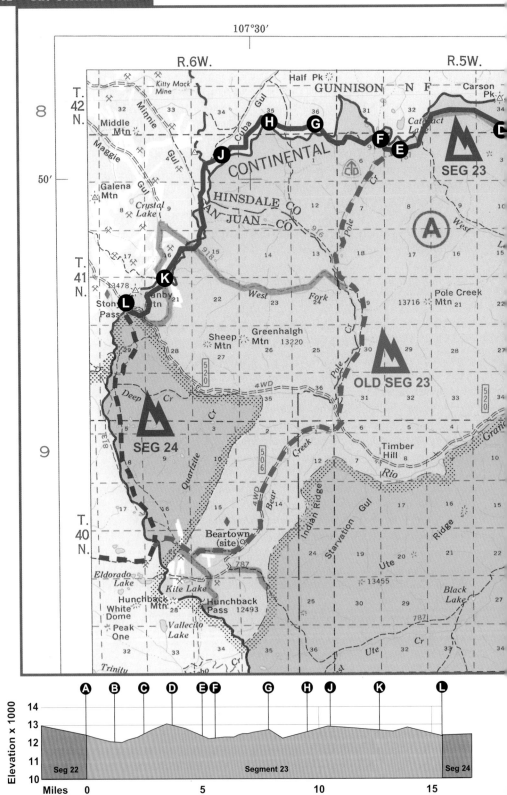

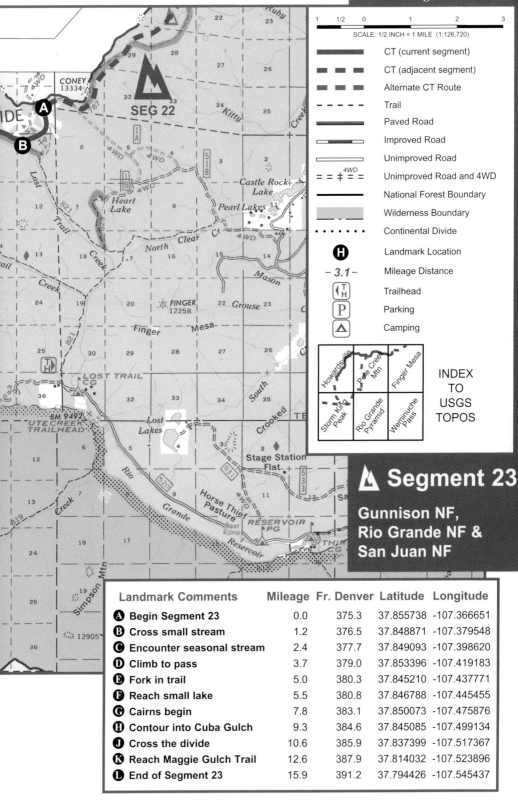

	1	1/2	0		1	2	3

SCALE: 1/2 INCH = 1 MILE (1:126,720)

	CT (current segment)
	CT (adjacent segment)
	Alternate CT Route
	Trail
	Paved Road
	Improved Road
	Unimproved Road
= = ‡ = =	Unimproved Road and 4WD
	National Forest Boundary
	Wilderness Boundary
• • • • •	Continental Divide
H	Landmark Location
– **3.1** –	Mileage Distance
T H	Trailhead
P	Parking
▲	Camping

INDEX TO USGS TOPOS

SEG 22

▲ Segment 23

**Gunnison NF,
Rio Grande NF &
San Juan NF**

Landmark Comments	Mileage	Fr. Denver	Latitude	Longitude
A Begin Segment 23	0.0	375.3	37.855738	-107.366651
B Cross small stream	1.2	376.5	37.848871	-107.379548
C Encounter seasonal stream	2.4	377.7	37.849093	-107.398620
D Climb to pass	3.7	379.0	37.853396	-107.419183
E Fork in trail	5.0	380.3	37.845210	-107.437771
F Reach small lake	5.5	380.8	37.846788	-107.445455
G Cairns begin	7.8	383.1	37.850073	-107.475876
H Contour into Cuba Gulch	9.3	384.6	37.845085	-107.499134
J Cross the divide	10.6	385.9	37.837399	-107.517367
K Reach Maggie Gulch Trail	12.6	387.9	37.814032	-107.523896
L End of Segment 23	15.9	391.2	37.794426	-107.545437

Segment 24
Stony Pass to Molas Pass

BELOW: *Hikers begin the drop into the Elk Creek Drainage.*

Distance: 19.8 miles
Elevation Gain: approx 3250 ft

USFS Maps: Rio Grande NF, San Juan NF, see pages 210-211.

USGS Quad Maps: Howardsville, Pole Creek Mountain, Silverton, Storm King Peak, Snowdon Peak.

Trails Illustrated map: #140 & 504.

Jurisdiction: Columbine District, Divide R. Dst.-Creede.

Access from Denver:

Access from Durango:

Availability of Water:

Bicycling: ✖ see page 209.

Gudy's Tip

"*Once over the Divide and in the Weminuche Wilderness, the Elk Creek drainage and its dramatic geologic walls are topped off with views of Arrow and Vestal Peaks.*" This short, impressive range of peaks is known as the Grenadiers. If you have the time, the short (but steep) trail that begins at the beaver ponds (mile 12.3) is an interesting side trip. See if you can spot rock climbers on famous Wham Ridge.

About This Segment

This segment enters the Weminuche Wilderness Area, just to the south side of the Stony Pass Road, where trail signage is severely restricted. Basically, you will walk south for 6 miles, very close to, or on, the Continental Divide. For the first mile and a half, you contour along the east slope of Green Mountain, until you come to the headwaters of Deep Creek, a tributary of the Rio Grande, and a cross trail that leads east to the Rio Grande and west to Cunningham Gulch (and eventually back to Howardsville). Continue south a half mile or so you will encounter another trail that will lead you back up on top of the CD. After another mile or so, you will encounter another trail heading west to Verdy Lake and Highland Mary Lakes. Continue south for 3 more miles, right on top of the CD, until you turn into the Elk Creek drainage. Once you enter the Elk Creek drainage, and until you get close to Molas Pass, GPS readings can be quite erratic due to the deep, narrow canyon and thick forest. This shouldn't be a problem, since it is almost impossible to get off of the CT in this area.

The view from the top of the Continental Divide at this point is one of the most striking on the CT. Savor it! The trip down Elk Creek is also very inspiring. As the CT leaves the wilderness area near the lower end of Elk Creek, one has the option of continuing on the CT or hopping a train to either Durango or Silverton. If you wish to catch the train, take the left branch of the trail. If you wish to continue on to Molas Pass, follow the right branch. Soon the CT crosses the train track and the Animas River on a foot bridge and begins the climb to Molas Pass. Emerging from the forest at the end of a long steep climb, you might consider branching right from the CT for a side trip to the Molas Lake Campground where hot showers are usually available. Otherwise, take the left branch and the CT will lead you to the end of this segment at US-550, about 0.1 mile north of the highway rest stop on Molas Pass.

> Don't miss the turn off point for the CT where it drops off the Divide and into the Elk Creek valley. Pay close attention!

Trailhead/Access Points

Stony Pass Road (FS-589,737)   : From the east end of Silverton, take the right hand branch of CO-110 toward Howardsville, which is 4 miles ahead (the left branch goes to the ski area). At Howardsville, turn right on the Stony Pass Road (FS-589) for about 2 miles to a "T" intersection with FS-737. Turn left on FS-737, which starts a steep climb, leaving the Animas River Valley. After a little over a mile and several switchbacks, there is a "Y". Take the right branch. After 2 miles is Stony Pass, with parking on the right.

US-550 - Molas Pass Trailhead   : See Segment 25.

Supplies, Services and Accommodations

Available in **Silverton** (see Segment 25 on page 214.)

Trail Description

The Colorado Trail crosses the Stony Pass Road, **mile 0.0** (12,521) **Ⓐ** , just south of an interpretive kiosk near the top of Stony Pass, and drops to a mine site. Follow the trail southward to a stream crossing in the valley bottom, then ascend to a ridge at **mile 0.6**. Bear to the right as the trail contours towards, then crosses, a steep gully, just before **mile 1.0**. Follow the trail as it heads south, just to the west side of the broad ridge. Circle to the west behind a small peak at **mile 1.4** (12,620). Drop down sharply to a small valley and cross a trail at **mile 1.8** (12,210). Continue ahead, staying east of a dirt knob to another trail intersection at **mile 2.1 Ⓑ** . The trail to the west-northwest drops down into Cunningham Gulch. Bear to the left, joining the trail in a southwest direction. The trail becomes much easier to follow at this point. Cross a small stream at **mile 2.6** (12,320). The trail climbs upwards and past a small lake and side trail at **mile 3.0**. Stay high as the trail closely follows the Divide for the next 2 miles. At **mile 5.3** (12,506) **Ⓒ** , turn right at a group of several small lakes. Take a moment and study the way ahead at this point.

The trail practically disappears as it continues to follow the Divide to the southeast, as the the main trail drops down into the valley to the east. There are several cairns high on the Divide ahead, but they may be hard to see. The faint tracks of an old two-track road are also visible. Follow the hillside upwards and stay along the Divide. Once up on the broad, grassy hill, the going gets easier. Then the trail becomes clear again, when it joins an intersecting trail coming up from the valley at **mile 6.1** (12,654) **Ⓓ** . Go to the right, continuing to the top of the Elk Creek drainage at **mile 6.4** (12,682) **Ⓔ** .

There is oftentimes snow here throughout the summer. Turn right here and descend into the Elk Creek drainage, also entering the Weminuche Wilderness Area, Colorado's largest designated wilderness. Those desiring a high altitude sidetrip can remain on the Divide past this point to another trail leading to Eldorado or Kite Lakes. To reach the high altitude lakes, continue ahead for 0.3 mile over a rocky point to an old mining trail. Turn right here to reach Eldorado Lake, or left to reach Kite Lake. Both lakes are about 0.4 miles past the intersection.

The trip down Elk Creek is nothing short of spectacular. You will pass through a nearly vertical environment with hanging waterfalls and rugged peaks. From the Divide, head downhill in a long stretch of meandering switchbacks. Pass by an old mining shed at **mile 7.4** (12,105) **Ⓕ** and continue ahead into a narrow, notch-like canyon. Carefully work your way down this canyon. The trail is often quite rough at this point because of heavy runoff each spring. Pass through the notch, then cross the creek at **mile 7.7** and **mile 8.0**, being cautious if the water is high. The trail begins to contour high above the creek. Continue ahead and enter the trees at about **mile 8.4**. Descend steeply to the creek and a sidetrail at **mile 9.0** (10,720). There are good campsites here. This side trail is used by climbers to access a saddle between Peak Two and Peak Three. Peak Two is the highpoint above the vertical wall, south of the trail.

Cross a sidestream at **mile 9.4**. There are campsites nearby. Cross another stream at **mile 9.6** (10,370) **Ⓖ** . A short side trip up this stream leads to a spectacular, but hidden, waterfall. Continue heading down the valley, which becomes wider and relatively flat. There are several good campsites along the way, but some do not meet the wilderness rules for distance from a stream or trail. At **mile 11.4**, the trail begins crossing through a huge boulder field deposited by ancient glaciers. Elk Creek goes underground here in places, then re-emerges at some beaver ponds **H** at **mile 12.3** (9,995). Vestal and Arrow Peaks are visible here, and excellent campsites may be found by following

ABOVE: *The side trail to scenic Eldorado Lake is worthwhile.*

a climbers' trail around the east side of the lake. Due to heavy use, campfires are not allowed in the basin below Vestal and Arrow. These are the last good campsites until reaching the Animas River, about three miles ahead.

Below the ponds, the trail passes through a thick forest, high above the creek. Cross a sidestream at **mile 12.5**. The trail descends steeply in places, then gets close to the creek at **mile 12.9** (9,380) in a steep inner canyon. Use caution as you follow the trail within this gorge, there are several places with steep drops to the stream below. Be particularly careful at **mile 14.1**, as you cross a small stream where it plunges to the creek. Leave the gorge and pass a trail register with a large Forest Service interpretive sign at **mile 14.4** (9,140) **J** . Leave the wilderness area at a few hundred feet beyond, then intersect a sidetrail at **mile 14.8**. This trail goes to a place where the Durango and Silverton Narrow Gauge Railroad stops to load or unload passengers.

Continue along the trail, as it contours north within the Animas River Gorge. Reach the railroad tracks by a small pond at **mile 15.1**. Follow the tracks ahead for several hundred feet, then follow the trail as it continues north between the tracks and the river. There are numerous good campsites along the river here. Campers are cautioned to hang their food; bears are commonly seen in this locale. Cross the wide river on a bridge at **mile 15.2** (8,920) **K** . This river was named by early Spanish explorers as "El Rio de Los Animas Perdidas", translated as "The River of Lost Souls." It is a class-five, whitewater river near this point. Cross a small stream at **mile 15.7**. This is the last reliable water available for about four miles, with a considerable climb ahead. A two-log bridge is available about 20 feet upstream from the trail. The next section of the trail is a seemingly endless stretch of 33 switchbacks climbing out of the Animas River gorge. Reach the top of the switchbacks at **mile 17.4** (10,300) **L** , at an unmarked intersection with a horse trail. Follow to the right here. Encounter another horse trail at **mile 18.4**. Again, bear

right. These horse trails are used by a horseback concessionaire at Big Molas Lake. Head up a short, but steep, section of switchbacks. Ignore another horse trail entering at **mile 18.6** (10,435) and continue up the hill. Encounter another horse trail at **mile 18.7** and bear to the left. The trail to the right goes to Big Molas Lake, a camping and fishing facility owned and operated by the city of Silverton. There is a small store here, where a few food items may be purchased.

Hit another intersection at **mile 18.8** (10,580) with a trail register and Forest Service trail sign. A large trailhead parking area is 0.2 miles straight ahead on the right fork. The CT itself continues to the left. Cross a small stream at **mile 19.6**. At **mile 19.7**, encounter another horse trail. Bear to the right in a westerly direction. Follow the trail upward via two large

ABOVE: *Descending into the Elk Creek drainage.*

BELOW: *Arrow and Vestal Peaks at mile 13.3, Segment 24.*

The Grenadiers

Soaring faces of hard quartzite, tumbling brooks and remote pristine campsites characterize the beautiful Grenadier Range of the western portion of the Weminuche Wilderness Area. When the CT plunges off the Divide into the Elk Creek basin, it enters a world that is a legend with generations of Colorado mountaineers.

The Grenadiers were among the last high peaks in Colorado to be conquered, most were not climbed until the 1930s on Colorado Mountain Club excursions and by members of the legendary San Juan Mountaineers group. They are unique in Colorado in that they are made up of quartzite, relatively rare in the southern Rockies; a hard and resistant rock that weathers into clean, steep north faces that often require technical climbing with ropes. At the beaver ponds at mile 12.3 on the CT, you have an excellent view of Arrow (13,803) and Vestal Peaks (13,864), the most famous of the Grenadiers and members of Colorado's Highest Hundred (or hundred highest peaks). The climbers' trail begins here, ascending steeply into the basin beneath Wham Ridge, one of the most sought-after climbs in the entire state.

The western endpoint of the short, but dramatic Grenadier Range is Mount Garfield (13,074). It looms 4,000 feet over the Animas River and D&S train tracks, and is a constant companion over your shoulder as you labor up the switchbacks to Molas Pass.

switchbacks to cross US-550 near the top of Molas Pass.   Here, the segment ends at **mile 19.8** (10,885) **Ⓜ** . There is a large parking area with toilets at 300 feet to the south of the point where the CT crosses the highway. It is 0.8 miles further to a free campground at Little Molas Lake.

Mountain Bicycle Detour

Weminuche Wilderness Detour *(Rio Grande NF, San Juan NF):* Cyclists that ride Segments 22 and 23, rather than taking the suggested Coney Summit Detour (see pages 194-195), will need to use this detour to avoid the Weminuche Wilderness Area in Segment 24. This detour crosses the Continental Divide at historic Stony Pass before dropping to join the route of the Coney Summit Detour, as it descends down the Engineer/Cinnamon Pass Road into Silverton.

Detour Description: Begin at the start of Segment 24 on the summit of the Stony Pass Road, as it descends northwest on its way to Howardsville and the Cunningham Gulch Road at **mile 4.0**. Follow it to an intersection with San Juan Co Rd-2 (the Engineer/Cinnamon Pass Road) at mile **6.5**. Turn left (southwest) and arrive at Silverton at **mile 10.3** and pass through town to meet US-550 at **mile 11.1**. Silverton is the best re-supply point for the final days of riding to Durango. Turn left onto busy US-550 and pedal up the hill to where the CT crosses the highway, just before Molas Pass at **mile 17.2**. This is the start of Segment 25.

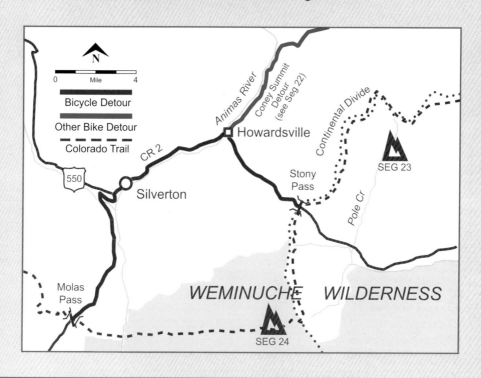

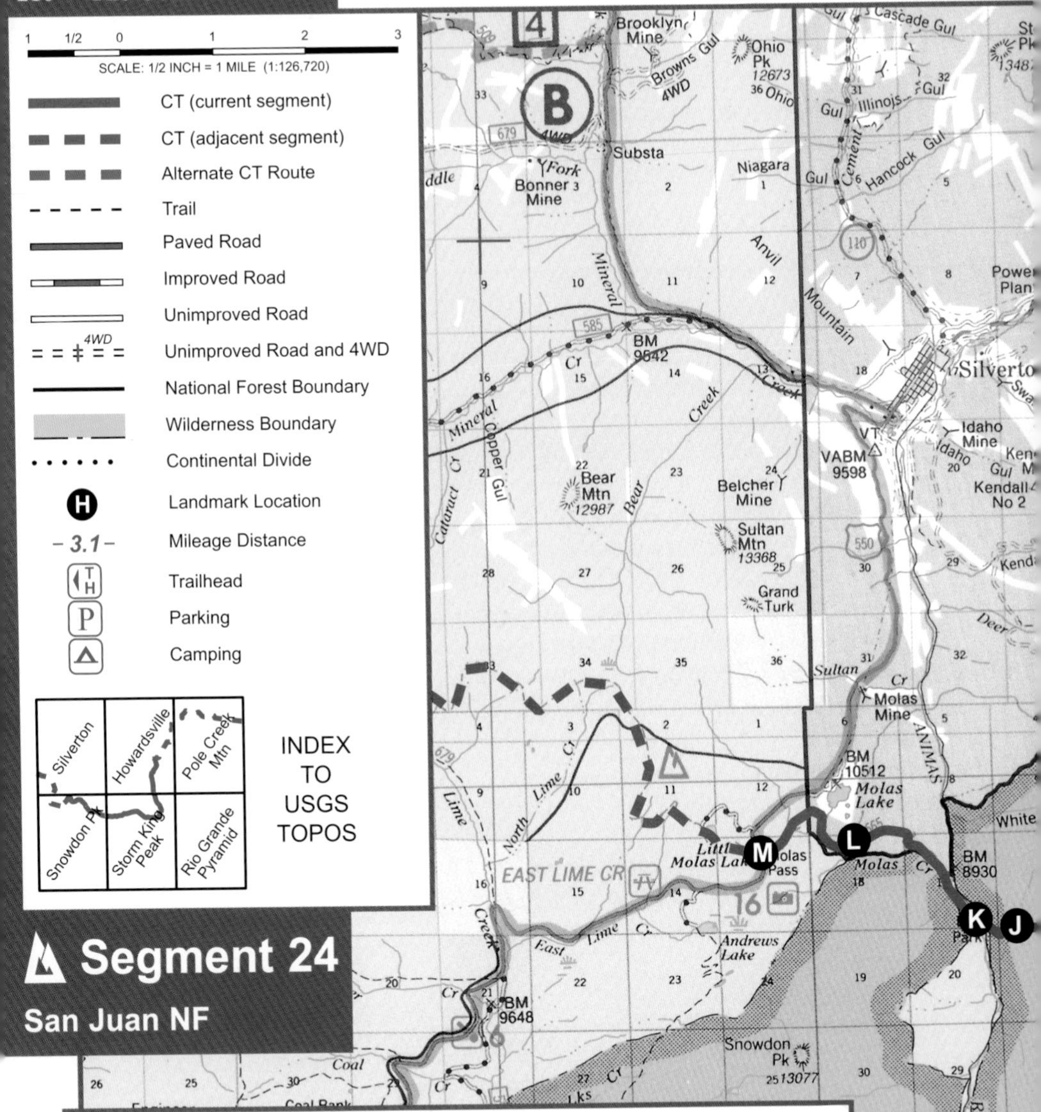

SCALE: 1/2 INCH = 1 MILE (1:126,720)
CT (current segment)
CT (adjacent segment)
Alternate CT Route
Trail
Paved Road
Improved Road
Unimproved Road
4WD
Unimproved Road and 4WD
National Forest Boundary
Wilderness Boundary
Continental Divide
Landmark Location
– 3.1 –
Mileage Distance
Trailhead
Parking
Camping
Silverton
Howardsville
Pole Creek Mtn
Snowdon Pk
Storm King Peak
Rio Grande Pyramid
INDEX TO USGS TOPOS
Segment 24
San Juan NF
Brooklyn Mine
Browns Gul
4WD
Ohio Pk
12673
Cascade Gul
Illinois
Gul
Cement
Hancock Gul
Substa
Bonner Mine
Niagara
Anvil
Mountain
Mineral
BM 9542
Mineral Cr
Creek
Silverton
Idaho Mine
Power Plant
VABM 9598
Kendall No 2
Bear Mtn
12987
Belcher Mine
Sultan Mtn
13368
Grand Turk
Copper Gul
Cataract Cr
Sultan
Molas Mine
ANIMAS
BM 10512
Molas Lake
Molas Pass
Little Molas Lake
Lime Creek
North Lime Cr
EAST LIME CR
East Lime Cr
Andrews Lake
Molas Cr
BM 8930
White
Snowdon Pk
13077
BM 9648
Coal
RIVER
SILVERTON
BM 8756

Landmark Comments	Mileage	Fr. Denver	Latitude	Longitude
A Begin Segment 24	0.0	391.2	37.794426	-107.545437
B Reach trail intersection	2.1	393.3	37.770947	-107.557225
C Reach small lakes	5.3	396.5	37.731635	-107.542556
D Intersect CDT	6.1	397.3	37.722162	-107.535595
E Leave the Divide	6.4	397.6	37.718395	-107.535471
F Pass mining shed	6.8	398.0	37.716596	-107.546066
G Cross stream	9.6	399.8	37.726563	-107.576115
H Come to ponds	12.3	403.5	37.720673	-107.625315
J Leave wilderness area	14.4	405.6	37.726746	-107.650736
K Cross river	15.2	406.4	37.733510	-107.660441
L Top of switchbacks	17.4	408.6	37.742501	-107.670004
M End of Segment 24	19.8	411.0	37.770724	-107.696186

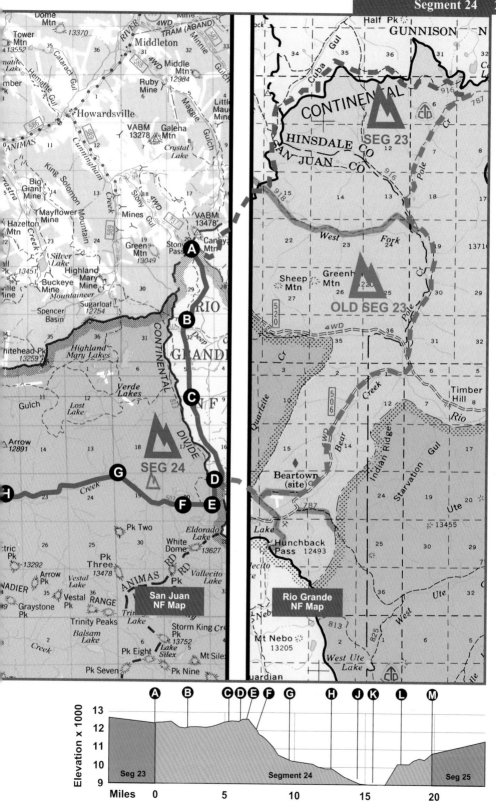

Segment 25
Molas Pass to Bolam Pass Road

BELOW: *A hiker pauses amongst a knee-high display of wildflowers.*

Distance: 20.9 miles
Elevation Gain: approx 3120 ft

USFS Maps: San Juan National Forest, see pages 218-219.

USGS Quad Maps: Snowdon Peak, Silverton, Ophir, Engineer Mountain, Hermosa Peak.

Trails Illustrated map: #104 & 504.

Jurisdiction: Columbine Ranger Dst.-West, Mancos/Dolores R. Dst.

Access from Denver:

Access from Durango:

Availability of Water:

Bicycling:

Gudy's Tip

"*There is a little store at Molas Pass (by Big Molas Lake) that offers showers and a good variety of staples. Don't miss it. Then, between Little Molas Lake and Lime Creek, wildflowers grow knee high in a kaleidoscope of colors.*" Big Molas Lake, east of the highway and north of the CT, has camping on private land. Little Molas Lake, west of the highway, has public camping.

About This Segment

This segment starts at US-550, just north of Molas Pass. It proceeds west on a trail, separate from the access road, to the south side of Little Molas Lake Campground. After a short trip through the campground, the CT departs via the west side. The area west of the campground, for several miles, is the upper Lime Creek drainage area, which was once heavily forested until a fire in 1879. Even though 130 years have past by, the forest has not returned. The CT traverses the upper reaches of this drainage for the next 9 miles, where trees will not be an impediment to the view. Even though the CT has left the Continental Divide behind, its elevation remains well above 10,000 feet for the next 50 miles.

> Hikers have reported two places in this segment where they have gotten off on the wrong trail, at mileage points 10.2 and 12.9. In both cases, they took off on the left because it appeared to be more heavily traveled. And in both cases, the CT makes a sharp right turn!

The CT crosses Cascade Creek at mile 14.6 on a very nice bridge that was built by volunteers in 1995. Prior to that, the CT forded the creek at a short distance below the bridge — a ford that was sometimes a little dicey. It put the hiker in much closer contact with the creek, so to speak, and they became acutely aware of a good size waterfall shortly below the ford! Now, many hikers miss the falls, since the new trail and bridge direct hikers well above the stream. After crossing the bridge, a short side trip down to the creek to look around might be very rewarding. This segment ends at Celebration Lake, 4WD accessible and therefore quite popular in mid-summer.

Trailhead/Access Points

US-550 - Molas Trail Trailhead : This segment begins near the summit of Molas Pass, where there is a scenic pullout. But overnight parking is not permitted. Long term parking is permitted at the nearby Molas Trail Trailhead and Little Molas Lake Trailhead. Molas Trail Trailhead is about a mile north on US-550 from the Molas Pass parking area on the east side of the highway. It is a fairly large parking area and usually has several cars in it anytime during the summer. It is approximately 5.5 miles south on US-550 from Silverton. From the parking area, a jeep track, the beginning of the Molas Trail, leads south about 0.2 mile to the CT.

Little Molas Lake Trailhead : From Molas Pass on US-550, drive north 0.4 mile and turn left (west) on a dirt road and continue 1.0 mile to the Little Molas Lake parking area. The CT passes on the south and west sides of this lake.

Bolam Pass Trail Access : See Segment 26.

Trail Description

This segment begins off of US-550, just north of Molas Pass. There is a large interpretive area with toilets on top of Molas Pass, but long term parking is not permitted there. A huge, long-term parking area is available just off US-550, one mile north (towards Silverton), near mile 20.4 of segment 24. There is another good, but smaller, parking area at Little Molas Lake Campground, located west of US-550

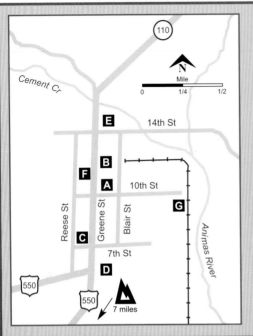

Silverton Services	
Distance From CT:	7 miles
Elevation:	9,318
Zip Code:	81433
Area Code:	970

Silverton is located approximately 7 miles north of Molas Pass on US-550. Molas Lake Campground, near Molas Trail Trailhead, carries some limited grocery items. But they do seem to have an accommodating supply of the essentials for backpackers just emerging from the wilderness, cold beer and hot showers.

Supplies, Services and Accommodations

Bus				
Bus	**A**	at The Cow Palace	1150 Greene St	(970) 387-5658
Dining		Several in town		
Gear	**B**	Outdoor World	1234 Greene St	(970) 387-5628
Groceries	**C**	Silverton Grocery	717 Greene St	(970) 387-5652
Info	**D**	Chamber of Commerce	414 Greene St	(970) 387-5654
Laundry	**E**	The Silverton Wash Tub	on Greene St	(970) 387-9981
Lodging		Several in town		
Medical		Silverton Clinic	1450 Greene St	(970) 387-5354
Post Office	**F**	Silverton Post Office	138 W 12th	(970) 387-5402
Train Depot	**G**	D&SNGRR	at the east end of 10th St	

at mile 0.9 of Segment 25. For the sake of convenience, most hikers will break their hike at one of these locations, rather than at the official trailhead on Molas Pass.

After crossing US-550, **mile 0.0** (10,885)Ⓐ, head up the trail as it diagonals away from the highway to the northwest. Pass under a power line at **mile 0.3** and continue generally west. Pass around the west shore of Little Molas Lake at **mile 0.6** and enter the campground just beyond Ⓑ (10,910). This is a free Forest Service campground that is filled on a first-come, first-served basis. It has been slated for a considerable amount of renovation in the near future, including a toilet at the CT trailhead. It is not known at the time of this writing if the campground will be open during renovation. This is a good choice for a camp, to assure an early start and to miss out on afternoon storms while crossing Rolling Pass, 10.3 miles ahead. After

passing through the campground, the CT begins a steady climb to the northwest. Cross a stream at **mile 1.6 Ⓒ**. It might be possible to make a small camp on top of some bluffs above the trail here. At **mile 2.2**, the trail begins following an old jeep trail going northeast. At **mile 2.9**, the trail leaves the jeep track and bears northwest, then eventually west at about **mile 4.0**. Here, the trail touches a saddle between West Turkshead Peak to the east and Rolling Mountain to the west (11,515). Carefully cross a small stream on a wet ledge at **mile 5.3 ⒟**. Cross Lime Creek at **mile 6.1** (11,400) **Ⓔ**, where a small campsite is possible. Cross another small stream at **mile 7.8**. At **mile 8.0**, pass above a large, excellent campsite. A small stream crosses the trail 500 feet ahead. This is the last good campsite before entering the tundra. Climb into a hanging alpine valley at **mile 9.0 Ⓕ**.

Cross a stream and begin following it up the marshy valley at **mile 9.4** (11,880), through an area with dazzling displays of wildflowers from mid-to-late summer.

ABOVE: *Sometimes, a snowy trail.*

At **mile 10.2 G**, the trail forms a "T" into the Engine Creek-Engineer Mountain Trail (12,130), a popular mountain bike loop. Many hikers have lost their way here by turning south on the heavily-used trail. Instead, turn north (right) on the lesser-traveled CT. In a few hundred feet, pass by a small lake to the west of the trail. Work your way up the rocky (and sometimes, snowy) trail to a saddle at **mile 11.0 H**, where the Mineral Creek Trail intersects from the north (12,350). Head straight ahead and begin a series of switchbacks to a high saddle at **mile 11.2** (12,520). Once over the pass, descend via more switchbacks. At **mile 12.9 I**, encounter another confusing intersection, as a trail takes off from a switchback for Silver Creek (11,450). CT travelers should continue around the switchback to the right and continue to the northwest. This is also known as the Rico-Silverton Trail. Just past this switchback, the trail crosses a small stream. There is a small, hidden lake with several campsites 0.1 mile downhill (northwest) from this location. A well-defined side trail drops down to the lake.

Continuing downhill on the trail, cross a stream at **mile 13.4**. There are no good campsites here. At **mile 14.2**, cross White Creek below a sometimes, spectacular waterfall. Continue ahead to the crossing of Cascade Creek on a sturdy bridge at **mile 14.6** (10,845) **K**. Here, the creek plunges to the valley below at the base of Grizzly Peak (13,738). There is a good campsite 200 feet from the bridge on the east side of the creek. The next mile climbs back out of the Cascade Creek drainage and contains some of the most problematic areas for maintainers of the Colorado Trail. There is one especially rough spot where water often rushes down the trail. Continue a steady climb to **mile 16.7** (11,210), where the trail rounds a ridge and a side trail intersects from the right. Continue ahead to the west and cross a small stream at **mile 17.0** with possible campsites nearby. Then at **mile 17.3** (11,250) **L**, intersect a side trail that goes down the hillside several hundred feet to a rough road (FS-579). This old mining road leads eventually out to the Bolam Pass Road (FS-578) and on to US-550 at the Durango Mountain Resort.

Cross a small stream with a possible small campsite at **mile 17.8** (11,390). Continue uphill to a seasonal stream with a good campsites at **mile 18.7**. Reach the top of a ridge and enter a large meadow area at **mile 19.1** (11,760) **M**. This vantage point has tremendous views of Lizard Head Pass ahead and Engineer Peak behind. At **mile 19.5**, the trail hits an old jeep road and follows it to the left. Stay on this old road to **mile 20.1 N** and hit FS-578B at an unmarked intersection. Go left on this road and follow it to **mile 20.7**, where the trail leaves the road to the left. Pass through a forested area and arrive at Bolam Pass Road (FS-578) near Celebration Lake (11,090), the end of this segment at **mile 20.9 P**. There are excellent campsites by the lake, but be aware that the lake water contains a lot of organic material that will quickly clog a water filter.

Safe Drinking Water

In times past, one of the great outdoor pleasures for a hiker was to dip a Sierra cup in a fast-flowing stream, like Cascade Creek, for a long drink of ice-cold water. Today, hikers know that this can be an invitation for a nasty pathogen to enter your system.

While day-hikers on the CT typically carry water for their needs, it is a constant daily bother for through-hikers to meet the need for safe drinking water. Most likely possibilities for contamination in the Colorado backcountry include *giardia lamblia*, *cryptosporidium*, and occasionally, some strains of bacteria and viruses in areas closer to towns.

While agricultural runoff is seldom a backcountry problem, chemical discharge from old mines is common in Colorado. The rule of thumb here is to look in the stream for plants, insects, and ample signs of life.

There are three proven methods that CT backpackers can use to treat water. **Boiling** is the simplest, if you have the additional fuel, and kills all known pathogens. While there is debate about shortest boil times, a minimum of 5 minutes at a rolling boil is recommended. **Iodine** (or less effective chlorine) disinfectant is not as reliable, providing some protection against giardia, and most bacteria, but not crypto. Very cold water should be left to treat overnight. **Filters** are the latest rage in backcountry water purification, if not a bit confusing. Check the specifications before you buy. A filter with pores larger than 0.2 microns will let bacteria through. A system with an iodine matrix will kill viruses.

Choose your water sources carefully, away from obvious animal hosts like beaver and cattle. Take water from as close to the ultimate source as possible, such as a spring.

ABOVE: *Pumping water.*

LEFT: *Cascade Creek.*

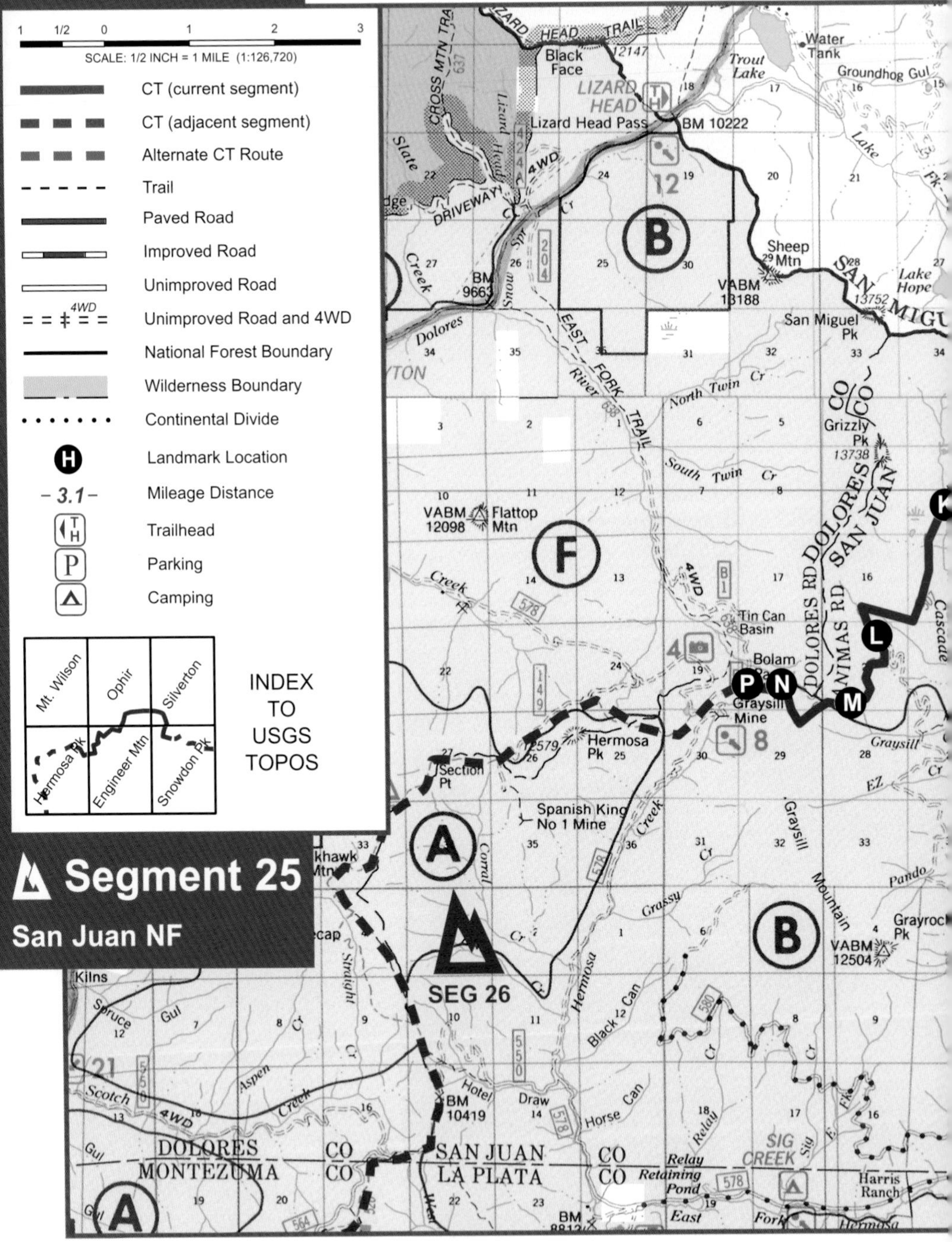

Legend / Scale

SCALE: 1/2 INCH = 1 MILE (1:126,720)

1   1/2   0   1   2   3

- CT (current segment)
- CT (adjacent segment)
- Alternate CT Route
- Trail
- Paved Road
- Improved Road
- Unimproved Road
- Unimproved Road and 4WD
- National Forest Boundary
- Wilderness Boundary
- Continental Divide
- **H** Landmark Location
- – 3.1 – Mileage Distance
- Trailhead
- P Parking
- Camping

INDEX
TO
USGS
TOPOS

Mt. Wilson | Ophir | Silverton
Hermosa Pk | Engineer Mtn | Snowdon Pk

Segment 25

San Juan NF

SEG 26

Map labels

LIZARD HEAD TRAIL
CROSS MTN TRAIL 637
Black Face 12147
Lizard Head Pass
BM 10222
Trout Lake
Water Tank
Groundhog Gul
DRIVEWAY
4WD
Slate
Dolores
BM 9663
204
Sheep Mtn
VABM 13188
San Miguel Pk
VABM 13752
Lake Hope
SAN MIGUEL
EAST FORK RIVER TRAIL
North Twin Cr
South Twin Cr
Grizzly Pk 13738
VABM 12098
Flattop Mtn
F
Creek 578
B1
Tin Can Basin
Bolam
Graysill Mine
P N
M
L
K
DOLORES RD
ANIMAS RD
DOLORES SAN JUAN
Cascade
149
579
Hermosa Pk
Section Pt
Spanish King No 1 Mine
Graysill Cr
EZ
Pando
Grayrock Pk
VABM 12504
A
B
Blackhawk Mtn
Icecap
Straight Cr
Corral
Hermosa
Grassy Cr
Black Can
550
Kilns
Spruce Gul
Scotch
4WD
21
Aspen Creek
Hotel Draw
BM 10419
578
Horse Can
SAN JUAN LA PLATA CO
DOLORES MONTEZUMA CO
564
BM 8812 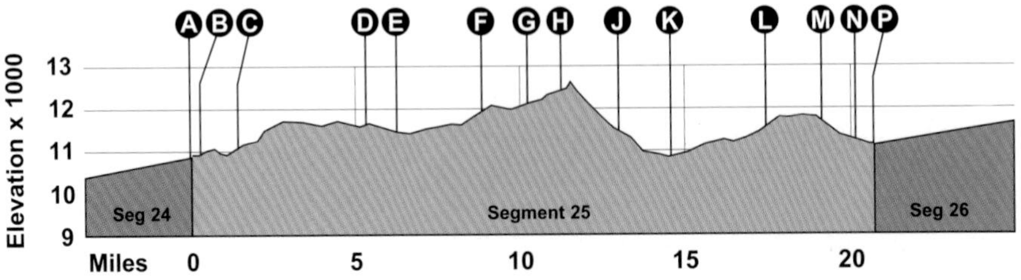
Relay Cr
Retaining Pond
Relay
SIG CREEK
Harris Ranch
East Fork
Hermosa
580

Elevation profile

Elevation x 1000

13
12
11
10
9

Miles: 0   5   10   15   20

Seg 24   Segment 25   Seg 26

Markers: A B C   D E   F G H   J   K   L   M N P

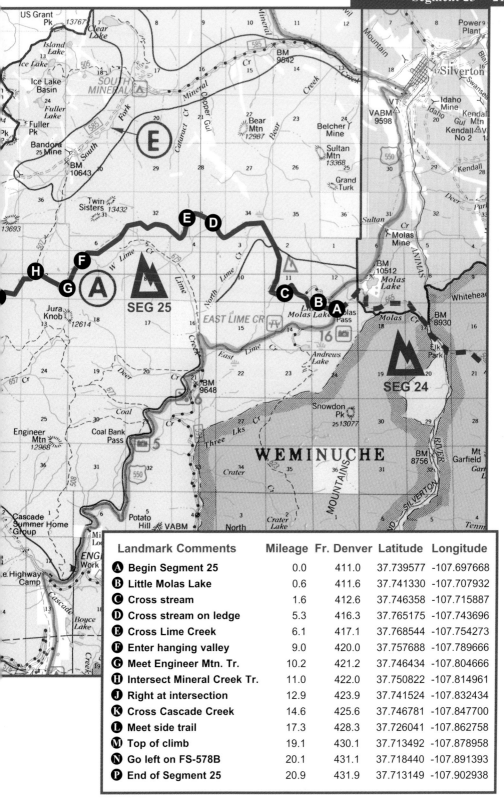

Landmark Comments	Mileage	Fr. Denver	Latitude	Longitude
Ⓐ Begin Segment 25	0.0	411.0	37.739577	-107.697668
Ⓑ Little Molas Lake	0.6	411.6	37.741330	-107.707932
Ⓒ Cross stream	1.6	412.6	37.746358	-107.715887
Ⓓ Cross stream on ledge	5.3	416.3	37.765175	-107.743696
Ⓔ Cross Lime Creek	6.1	417.1	37.768544	-107.754273
Ⓕ Enter hanging valley	9.0	420.0	37.757688	-107.789666
Ⓖ Meet Engineer Mtn. Tr.	10.2	421.2	37.746434	-107.804666
Ⓗ Intersect Mineral Creek Tr.	11.0	422.0	37.750822	-107.814961
Ⓙ Right at intersection	12.9	423.9	37.741524	-107.832434
Ⓚ Cross Cascade Creek	14.6	425.6	37.746781	-107.847700
Ⓛ Meet side trail	17.3	428.3	37.726041	-107.862758
Ⓜ Top of climb	19.1	430.1	37.713492	-107.878958
Ⓝ Go left on FS-578B	20.1	431.1	37.718440	-107.891393
Ⓟ End of Segment 25	20.9	431.9	37.713149	-107.902938

Segment 26
Bolam Pass Road to Hotel Draw Road

BELOW: *Lush growth carpets the slopes as a hiker trudges up to Blackhawk Pass.*

Distance: 10.9 miles
Elevation Gain: approx 1480 ft

USFS Maps: San Juan National Forest, see pages 224-225.

USGS Quad Maps: Hermosa Peak.

Trails Illustrated map: # 504.

Jurisdiction: Mancos/Dolores Ranger District, San Juan NF.

Access from Denver:

Access from Durango:

Availability of Water:

Bicycling:

Gudy's Tip

"*The north side of Blackhawk Pass is a valley of enchantment with vast herds of elk.*" Verdant alpine meadows near the pass, filled with lush mid-summer growth, attract wildlife — elk and mule deer, marmots and pika — and hikers, drawn by wildflowers and lovely vistas. Have your camera ready. Famous Lizard Head Peak is in view near the pass!

About This Segment

This segment of the CT continues to follow the high ground between major drainages, offering excellent viewing opportunities. In this segment, the drainages are Hermosa Creek to the south and east and the Dolores River to the north and west. It is beautiful, lonely country, staying well above 11,000 feet until after Blackhawk Pass. There are no long climbs or descents. Straight Creek, south of Blackhawk Pass, is the last reliable source of water on the CT for the next 20 miles. Plan accordingly.

Trailhead/Access Points

Bolam Pass Road (FS-578) Trail Access 🚙 *:* There are two ways to drive to this access point, both requiring a 4WD vehicle: from US-550 through the Durango Mountain Resort (formally Purgatory Ski area) and from CO-145, south of Lizard Head Pass and just north of Rico. For the US-550 approach, drive approximately 28 miles north of Durango to the Durango Mountain Resort main entrance on the west side of the road. At the upper parking area, bear right onto FS-578. Drive on FS-578 for approximately 15 miles to Bolam Pass. FS-578 follows the east fork of Hermosa Creek, west past Sig Creek Campground on to the main channel of Hermosa Creek, then north to Bolam Pass. The CT access point is at Celebration Lake.

> Test the depth of the Hermosa Creek ford before driving into it!

For the approach from CO-145, drive 6 miles north of Rico and turn right onto FS-578 for about 7 miles along Barlow Creek. At the "Y", take the left branch on to Celebration Lake and the CT access point.

Hotel Draw Trail Access 🚙 *:* See Segment 27.

Supplies, Services and Accommodations

There is no convenient supply point for this segment.

Trail Description

This segment begins at the southwest edge of Celebration Lake on FS-578 (Bolam Pass Road) at a point where the CT crosses the road from the northeast, **mile 0.0** (11,090) **Ⓐ**. There is a small parking area here at a hard-packed camping area.

Start by crossing a small stream flowing out of the south end of the lake. The trail begins a short, but steep climb that ends at a saddle at **mile 1.0** (11,530) **Ⓑ** on the southern flank of 12,679 foot Hermosa Peak. The trail circles behind the peak to the north. Pass a spring with a good campsite at **mile 1.3**. Hit a "T" intersection with a jeep trail at **mile 1.6** and turn left (southeast), following the road. Cross

A mountain bike ride, popular with the locals, begins just below the trailhead at Celebration Lake, at the intersection with the Scotch Creek and Bolam Pass Roads. Riders ride up the road to the trailhead, then follow the CT to the segment end at the Scotch Creek Road and return to their cars.

a small stream at **mile 1.8**  **C** with campsites nearby (11,485) and continue along the old jeep trail to **mile 3.0** (11,560) **D** where the trail abruptly leaves the road in a sharp right-hand turn to the west. At **mile 3.1**, pass through a flat area that would make a good, dry campsite and reach the top of a small saddle at **mile 3.9** (11,810). A short trail to the right leads to a summit with great views of the surrounding area and a rather strange summit register.

Continue ahead to **mile 4.1** (11,760) **E**, where the trail intersects the old Circle Trail coming up from Silver Creek. Go left and continue down the switchback in a southeasterly direction. Pass over a small knob (11,750) and then down some switchbacks at **mile 5.0**. The trail contours around the valley ahead and begins climbing again at **mile 6.0**. Cross a small stream at **mile 6.3** **F** and a larger one at **mile 6.4**. There are good campsites near both streams, the last sites until after passing over Blackhawk Pass.

Climb steeply to the pass at **mile 6.9** (12,000) **G** which sits between 12,681-foot Blackhawk Mountain on the west and a lower, unnamed summit to the east. Head downhill after the pass and re-enter the trees, just past a strong flowing spring at **mile 7.6** (11,480). This is the headwaters for Straight Creek. There are soft campsites near the spring. Cross the creek and continue down, then cross Straight Creek again at **mile 8.5** (11,010) **H**. There are no good campsites by this stream crossing. There is a nice viewpoint for a series of cascades, accessed via a short trail that goes uphill from this point.

Continue downhill through the forest to **mile 10.9** where the segment ends, 50 feet before the Scotch Creek Road (10,390) **J** . This is a popular, but dry campsite for trail crews working in the area.

Through-hikers should be aware that the crossing of Straight Creek at mile 8.5 is the last reliable water source until reaching Taylor Lake, some 20 miles distant over Indian Trail Ridge!

BELOW: *A hiker fills her water bottles from Straight Creek.*

Trail Crews

What makes the Colorado Trail unique is that it was developed with the efforts of thousands of committed volunteers. If you walk any significant length of the trail, you will undoubtedly meet one of the dozen or more organized volunteer work crews that toil on the CT system each year.

Each volunteer on a crew typically spends a week of his/her summer in creating trails, improving and restoring existing trails, and providing signage and information. Trail crews begin the week by meeting on Saturday, with Sunday devoted to safety training and an introduction to trail building. Trail crews work four days out of the week, with Wednesday free for hiking, fishing, climbing a 14er, or just resting in camp. The week typically ends up on Saturday with packing up the equipment.

Volunteers come from every state and several foreign countries. They must be at least 16 years old, in good physical shape, and provide their own sleeping bag, tent, utensils, and work clothing. The Colorado Trail Foundation (CTF), in partnership with the Forest Service (USFS), furnishes leaders, food, tools, and supplies. Trail crews are highly participatory and all volunteers are encouraged to join daily

camp life and enjoy the evening campfire.

The next level beyond volunteering for a trail crew is the CTF's *Adopt-A-Trail Maintenance Program*, where individuals or groups take responsibility for a section of the trail. The trail currently is divided into 53 sections for maintenance purposes, varying in length from 3 to 20 miles. Besides maintaining the tread (walking surface) and signage, adopters provide status reports and advise the CTF and USFS.

To check out the volunteer opportunities, contact **The Colorado Trail Foundation** at 303-384-3729 between 9:00 am and 5:00 pm Mountain time or view their website at *www.coloradotrail.org*.

ABOVE: A CTF trail crew.

RIGHT: A volunteer wields a Pulaski, an effective tool for clearing trail.

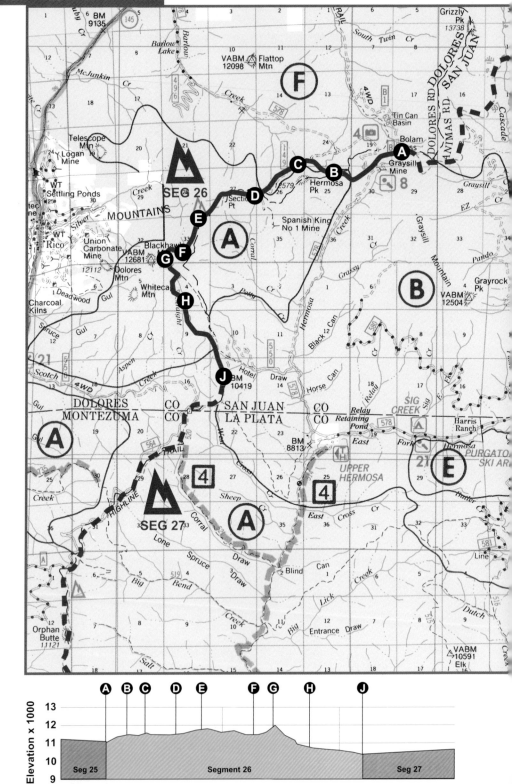

SCALE: 1/2 INCH = 1 MILE (1:126,720)

	CT (current segment)
	CT (adjacent segment)
	Alternate CT Route
	Trail
	Paved Road
	Improved Road
	Unimproved Road
4WD	Unimproved Road and 4WD
	National Forest Boundary
	Wilderness Boundary
	Continental Divide
H	Landmark Location
– 3.1 –	Mileage Distance
TH	Trailhead
P	Parking
△	Camping

INDEX TO USGS TOPOS

△ Segment 26

San Juan NF

Landmark Comments	Mileage	Fr. Denver	Latitude	Longitude
A Begin Segment 26	0.0	431.9	37.713134	-107.902960
B Reach saddle	1.0	432.9	37.711757	-107.915386
C Cross stream w/campsites	1.8	433.7	37.715285	-107.926408
D Leave road, go west	3.0	434.9	37.706120	-107.942862
E Intersect Circle Trail	4.1	436.0	37.705787	-107.959024
F Cross stream	6.3	438.2	37.687481	-107.976917
G Blackhawk Pass	6.9	438.8	37.684469	-107.979734
H Cross Straight Creek	8.5	440.4	37.675594	-107.974551
J End of Segment 26	10.9	442.8	37.650095	-107.956409

Segment 27
Hotel Draw Road to Kennebec Trailhead

BELOW: *Wildflowers blanket slopes beneath the La Plata Mountains.*

Distance: 20.6 miles
Elevation Gain: approx 3640 ft

USFS Maps: San Juan National Forest, see pages 232-233.

USGS Quad Maps: Hermosa Peak, Elk Creek, Orphan Butte, La Plata.

Trails Illustrated map: # 504

Jurisdiction: Columbine Ranger District - West, San Juan NF.

Access from Denver:

Access from Durango:

Availability of Water:

Bicycling:

Gudy's Tip

"From Indian Trail Ridge, a crest of cascading wildflowers, the views of Hermosa Valley and the La Plata Mountains are extraordinary."

This segment features sweeping vistas, culminating in a dramatic, 5-mile walk atop an alpine ridge at over 12,000 feet. Wildflower enthusiasts will find the incredible displays at their peak starting in mid-July.

About This Segment

This segment continues to follow the ridge dividing the Hermosa Creek drainage and the Dolores River drainage, all the way to Taylor Lake. (Taylor Lake drains south into the La Plata River.) The first 9 miles of this segment encounters many infrequently-used Forest Service roads and closed logging roads. The CT stays very close to the top of the ridge. If you find yourself on a road leading down away from the ridge, it is time to check with your map and compass. Also, there is no reliable source of water on the CT for the next 20 miles. In compensation, there are many great viewpoints! From mile 13.5 to mile 17 of the CT, it is not unusual to see herds of elk grazing far below in the cirque bottom to the east of the trail. From mile 14.5 to mile 19.4, the CT is above timberline. Some hikers may wish to plan their hike to avoid this section of the trail in the afternoon, in deference to the possibility of afternoon thunderstorms.

Trailhead/Access Points

There are three ways to drive to the beginning of this segment of the CT. Note that two require a 4WD vehicle: from US-550 through the Durango Mountain Resort (formally Purgatory Ski Area) and from CO-145, south of Lizard Head Pass and just south of Rico. The 2WD approach via FS-435/FS-654/FS-550 is much longer but usually accessible by normal passenger cars.

US-550 Access (Hotel Draw) : Travel approximately 28 miles north of Durango to the Durango Mountain Resort main entrance on the west side of the road. At the upper parking area, bear right onto FS-578. Follow FS-578 for approximately 8 miles along the East Fork of Hermosa Creek, continuing west past Sig Creek Campground and on to the main channel of Hermosa Creek, then north along the main channel and through a ford. About a mile after the ford, make a sharp left turn onto the Hotel Draw Road (FS-550). After about 3.5 miles, at the top of the ridge, the CT comes down the ridge from the north intersecting the Hotel Draw Road.

Test the depth of the Hermosa Creek ford before driving into it!

CO Hwy-145 Access : Drive 2 miles south of Rico and turn left onto the Scotch Creek Road (FS-550). Proceed about 5 miles to an intersection near the top of the ridge and turn left, continuing to the top of the ridge where the CT comes down the ridge on the road from the north.

FS-435/654/550 Access : From 9 miles south of Rico, turn east onto FS-435. After 6 miles on FS-435, make a sharp left turn onto FS-564. Continue on FS-564 for about 15 miles to its termination with FS-550. Follow up FS-550 for 1.3 miles to the beginning of this segment. FS-564 intersects with the CT several times in route before reaching its terminus at FS-550.

Kennebec Trailhead : See Segment 28.

Supplies, Services and Accommodations

There is no convenient supply point for this segment.

Trail Description

This segment begins 50 feet north of a small parking area on FS-550 at **mile 0.0** (10,390) **Ⓐ** . The first 10 miles or so of this segment pass through a maze of old logging trails. Much of the trail follows these old cuts and there are numerous intersections, most of which are marked with confidence markers, wooden posts, or signs, so that navigating this area is not as difficult as it may sound.

Through-hikers heading south will turn right, just before reaching the road, and follow a short section of new trail that parallels the road going south. The trail hits a closed-in logging trail in 300 feet. Follow this trail to the right as well. Encounter a fork with an unused trail, taking off to the right at **mile 0.2**. Take the left fork here. At **mile 0.6**, there will be an intersection with another logging road that turns sharply off to the left and up a hill. The trail follows this road for awhile. There is a post marking the intersection. At **mile 0.8**, encounter yet another merging logging trail. Continue straight ahead. At **mile 1.2** (10,440), turn right at a well-marked "Y" intersection . The trail encounters FS-550 at **mile 1.3 Ⓑ**. Turn right here and follow the road. This may be confusing, as this intersection is not marked. In a few hundred feet, the road intersects another Forest Service road, FS-564, and follows it to the left. There is a somewhat seasonal spring near this point. It was running strong when this was written after a wet winter. To find the spring, leave the road at this point and hike downhill to the northwest towards another old logging trail below. The spring is located within a switchback of the logging trail.

After turning onto FS-564, follow the road a short distance to **mile 1.4**, where the trail leaves the road on the left in a southwesterly direction at a well-marked

The Mancos Spur

The Mancos Spur is an alternative start or finish to the Colorado Trail. Instead of taking Segment 28 to Durango, this trail terminates in Boyle Park in the town of Mancos. There is a sign in the park with information about the spur and the Colorado Trail.

Take Main Street through town, cross Highway 160, and pick up Highway 184. Continue on Hwy. 184 for about 1/4 mile, and turn right on County Road 42. Follow CR 42 for about 4 miles to Mancos State Park (also known as Jackson Reservoir). Cross the dam at the reservoir until you reach Chicken Creek Trail, Trail #615. Go 8 miles on Chicken Creek Trail until you reach Transfer Campground. From Transfer Campground, the spur follows the West Mancos River. Where the river splits into the North Fork and the South Fork, the spur follows the North Fork. It ties into the Sharkstooth Trailhead #565. It may be difficult to follow where the spur follows some logging roads, but when you reach Sharkstooth Trail head (10 miles), you will know that you are on the right trail. Follow the Sharkstooth Trail until you reach the Colorado Trail in the vicinity of Taylor Lake (7 miles).

The spur section from Transfer Campground to the Sharkstooth Trailhead does not appear on the Forest Service map of the San Juan Forest, but Paul Peck (former ranger of the Mancos District, USFS), said that the spur was well marked. He also said it is easier to follow the spur from Taylor Lake to Mancos, than from Mancos to Taylor Lake. Nobody is maintaining this spur except for what the Forest Service can get done.

intersection. The trail climbs up along a forested ridge with spectacular views to the south, reaching the top of the ridge at **mile 2.6** (10,910). There are many good, but dry campsites in this area. At **mile 2.9**, (10,830), cross the Corral Draw Trail which drops into the Hermosa Creek drainage. Continue ahead, staying high along the ridge. Pass by more spectacular views with nice, but dry campsites around **mile 3.2**. At **mile 4.0 ❶**, intersect FS-564 again, following it to the left to **mile 4.2** where the trail leaves the road briefly within a large switchback. Cross the road again in 600 feet and follow the trail ahead, as the road departs to the right. Hit the road again at **mile 4.9** (10,740), following it for 300 feet to the left (southwest) before leaving the road again to the left. Continue to **mile 5.5** where the road is once again followed for 300 feet at another saddle. Exit again to the left and begin following the ridge, crossing the Big Bend Trail at **mile 6.3** (10,625) ❶ . There are hard, dry campsites between here and the road to the west; the last good place to camp that is accessible by car in this segment. Pass by the last road access at **mile 6.8**, then head up to **mile 7.0** where the trail joins a logging road and turns sharply to the left (southeast). Intersect the Salt Creek Trail at **mile 7.9** (10,850) ❶ and continue straight ahead. Merge with another old logging trail at **mile 8.1** and continue towards Orphan Butte, the high, bald knob visible to the south. Pass by the butte, then continue south past another logging road intersection at **mile 8.8** (10,915) ❶ .

The trail becomes less confusing at this point, as the logged area is slowly left behind. Pass a good, dry campsite at **mile 11.1** (11,060), then begin a long steady climb at **mile 11.3**. Pass a cross trail near the top of some switchbacks at **mile 12.3** (11,335) ❶ . This is actually the old trail which was replaced by volunteers in 1990 by the current route. This now goes out to a scenic overlook. Pass a seasonal spring along the side of the trail at **mile 12.5** (11,400) ❶ . This may be dry, but runs in early season or very wet years. After one last switchback, the trail turns to the south once more. At **mile 13.3** (11,520), encounter a wood sign that identifies the Highline Trail. This old route is now shared by the Colorado Trail. The long ridge to the east of here is known as "The Cape of Good Hope," an old stock driveway. Another marker identifies the Highline Trail and the Cape of Good Hope -

BELOW: *A happy hiker points the way to Indian Trail Ridge.*

ABOVE: *The "knife edge" on Indian Trail Ridge.*

BELOW: *A camper enjoys a cup near Taylor Lake after the trek over Indian Trail Ridge.*

Hermosa Park Road at **mile 14.7**. Intersect with the Grindstone Trail at **mile 15.2** (11,685) **L** at a well marked intersection. Turn left here. The Grindstone Trail leads into the Bear Creek drainage to the west. This is the closest emergency exit from the high ridge ahead, as once upon the ridge there is no easy way off.

The CT climbs steadily upward and enters the tundra at **mile 15.5** (11,820) **M**. Continue following to the south along this high, exposed ridge. Descend a steep rocky section at **mile 17.5**, then climb to the high point of the segment at **mile 18.3** (12,310) **N**. At **mile 18.9** (12,180), the trail takes a sudden sharp turn to the left and begins it's descent from the ridge, down a rocky ledge for about 300 feet. At this point, the trail becomes very pleasant, as it heads towards scenic Taylor Lake below. Pass a side trail to Taylor Lake at **mile 19.4** (11,650). Southbound hikers will appreciate the water after over 20 miles of dry trail. The segment ends at a large trailhead parking area at **mile 20.6** (11,654) **P**, the Kennebec Trailhead, where the Colorado Trail resumes on the south side of the parking area.

Indian Trail Ridge can be dangerous during afternoon thunderstorms!

Photographing Wildflowers

If you are lucky enough to traverse Indian Trail Ridge in mid-summer, you will be rewarded with a spectacular display of alpine flowers, including *arnica*, *indian paintbrush*, *bistort*, *columbine* and scores of others. Whether you shoot film or have migrated to the latest digital technology, taking photographs that provide results good enough to enlarge and display requires the right equipment, knowledge and patience. Here are some basic tips offered by the CT hikers whose photos appear in this guide:

♦   Serious wildflower photographers enjoy the control of a full-featured single-lens reflex camera (SLR), rather than a point-and-shoot camera (P&S). Being able to increase depth-of-field by "stopping down" the aperture or freezing motion on a windy day by increasing shutter speed are some of the advantages. For P&S users, learn about the "manual" controls your camera might offer.

♦   While cameras and lenses often claim "macro" or close focusing abilities, most do not magnify the image large enough to do justice to tiny alpine flowers. SLR users can invest in a dedicated "macro" lens for close focusing ability. Both SLR and P&S users can often purchase inexpensive "di-opter" lenses that screw onto to the front of their existing lens to boost magnification.

♦   Try using a small tripod and a cable shutter release to prevent blur from camera shake. Have a piece of cardboard handy for a wind block.

♦   If your scene is an expansive field of flowers, like on page 238, invest in a true wide-angle lens (35mm or less). Stop-down the aperture for greater depth of field.

♦   Try using slower, finer-grained film. Transparency (slide) film is preferred by pros over print film. Digital camera users should set a slower ISO sensitivity to avoid "noise".

♦   Shoot early or late in the day to avoid intense mid-day light. Often, overcast or even rainy days are best for subtle color saturation or for the effects of raindrops on petals (see the columbine below).

LEFT: *A hiker photographing wildflowers along the CT.*

BELOW: *Alpine blue columbine.*

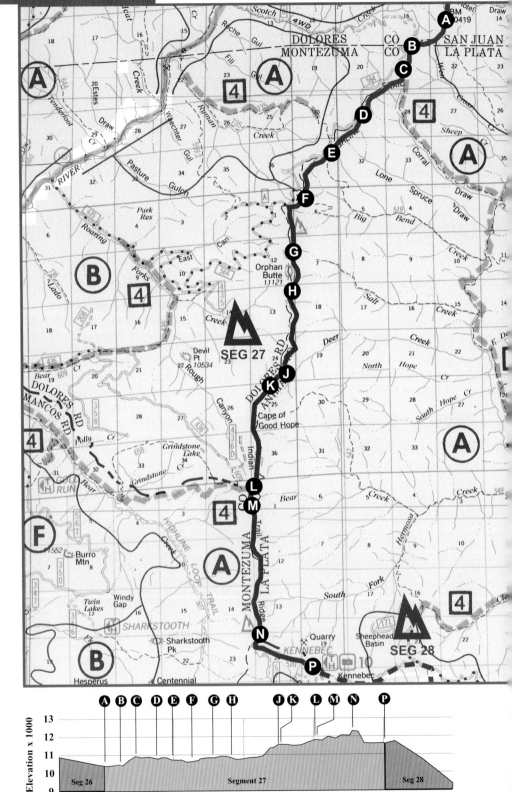

SCALE: 1/2 INCH = 1 MILE (1:126,720)

▬▬▬▬	CT (current segment)
▬ ▬ ▬	CT (adjacent segment)
▬ ▬ ▬	Alternate CT Route
- - - -	Trail
▬▬▬▬	Paved Road
⬭▬▬⬭	Improved Road
⬭▬▬⬭	Unimproved Road
= = ‡ = =	Unimproved Road and 4WD
▬▬▬▬	National Forest Boundary
▬ ▬ ▬	Wilderness Boundary
• • • • • •	Continental Divide
H	Landmark Location
– 3.1 –	Mileage Distance
TH	Trailhead
P	Parking
⛺	Camping

INDEX TO USGS TOPOS

▲ Segment 27

San Juan NF

Landmark Comments	Mileage	Fr. Denver	Latitude	Longitude
Ⓐ Begin Segment 27	0.0	442.8	37.650095	-107.956409
Ⓑ Follow FS-550 to right	1.3	444.1	37.641028	-107.963524
Ⓒ Climb up along forested ridge	2.5	445.3	37.629271	-107.972978
Ⓓ Follow road south	4.0	446.5	37.619342	-107.992278
Ⓔ Leave road to south	5.0	446.8	37.609112	-108.003560
Ⓕ Cross Big Bend Trail	6.3	448.1	37.595666	-108.013967
Ⓖ Intersect Salt Creek Trail	7.9	450.7	37.580466	-108.017796
Ⓗ Logging road intersection	8.8	451.6	37.568761	-108.019011
Ⓙ Pass trail to overlook	12.3	455.1	37.533549	-108.031811
Ⓚ Seasonal water	12.6	455.4	37.534695	-108.035367
Ⓛ Intersect Grindstone Tr, go left	15.2	458.0	37.504438	-108.038125
Ⓜ Enter the tundra	15.5	458.3	37.499024	-108.034993
Ⓝ High point on ridge	18.3	461.1	37.465445	-108.033017
Ⓟ Kennebec TH, end Seg. 27	20.6	463.4	37.451713	-108.010885

Segment 28
Kennebec Trailhead to
Junction Creek Trailhead

BELOW: *A hiker pauses atop Kennebec Pass.*

Distance: 21.5 miles
Elevation Gain: approx 1400 ft

USFS Maps: San Juan National Forest, see pages 240-241.

USGS Quad Maps: La Plata, Monument Hill, Durango West.

Trails Illustrated map: # 504.

Jurisdiction: Columbine Ranger District - West, San Juan NF.

Access from Denver:

Access from Durango:

Availability of Water: 🥤

Bicycling: see page 239.

Gudy's Tip

"If you didn't stop for a shower in one of the falls of Junction Canyon, then grab one at the Rec Center, just north of where the Junction Creek Road dead ends into Main Avenue in Durango." Durango has a large, modern recreational center, three blocks to the north of Junction Creek Road and Main, where hot showers may be obtained. There is local bus service along Main Avenue.

About This Segment

The beginning of this segment has previously been referred to as "Cumberland Basin" in the CT guidebooks. The San Juan National Forest map no longer lists "Cumberland Basin." The trailhead designation on the FS map is now "Kennebec Trailhead." So, this edition of the CT guidebook has changed to agree with the Forest Service map. There is a large trailhead sign and parking area at the intersection of FS-171 and the CT. Kennebec Pass is 0.7 mile east of Kennebec Trailhead.

This segment of the Colorado Trail is quite spectacular in many respects. It has the most vertical travel of any segment of the CT, more than 4,700 feet of vertical in one direction and 1,400 feet in the other (total up or down, depending on the direction of travel.) The views are greatly reduced, since most of this section is in dense forest and at the bottom of a narrow canyon. Although there is plenty of water in the canyon, flat camping spots are rare. Toward the south end of this segment, as the CT climbs out of the canyon, there are plenty of nice flat spots, but no water. Finally, where the canyon widens, with some nice spots and plenty of water, camping is prohibited due to popular appeal and high-density use. To reduce frustration, plan your trip down this segment carefully and stop early before all the best sites are taken.

Trailhead/Access Points

Kennebec Trailhead : From Durango, drive west on US-160 about 13 miles, or 0.5miles beyond the village of Hesperus. Turn right on La Plata County Rd-124, which eventually becomes FS-498 and then FS-571, terminating in Cumberland Basin at the Kennebec Trailhead sign. The last 2 miles are really rough and steep. A 4WD vehicle is strongly recommended.

Junction Creek Trailhead : Drive north on Main Avenue in Durango to 25th Street and turn left (west). After a couple of blocks the street turns half/right and becomes the Junction Creek Rd (La Plata Co. Rd 204) Follow it for 3 miles and take the left branch. Continue another 0.4 mile to a cattle guard and a sign announcing you are entering the San Juan National Forest. There is a 19-car FS parking lot and toilet here constructed in the fall of 2005. This is the southern terminus of The Colorado Trail. The road continues as FS-171. In about another mile there is a switchback with 7 more parking spaces. A short side trail takes you to the CT down by the Creek.

Sliderock Trail Access Point : The CT can also be accessed by 2WD vehicles at mile 2.4 of this segment. From the Junction Creek Trailhead, described above, continue on FS-171 for 17.5 miles to a side road on the left. Turn left and proceed 0.7 mile to the CT crossing of this road. There are CT markers on both sides of the road. The trail to the right leads 1.7 mile up to Kennebec Pass, via the Sliderock portion of this segment, and the trail to the left goes 19.1 miles down to Durango.

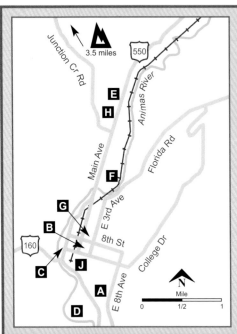

Durango Services

Distance From CT:
                        3.5 miles
Elevation: 6,512
Zip Code: 81301
Area Code: 970

Durango, an old railroad town, and now, commercial center for southwestern Colorado, is approximately 3.5 miles from the Junction Creek trailhead. The town is connected to Denver via airline and bus service, and connected to Silverton by the D&SRR in Animas Canyon.

Supplies, Services and Accommodations

Bus	**A**	Greyhound TNM&O	275 E 8th Ave	(970) 259-2755
Dining		Several sit-down and fast-food restaurants in town.		
Gear	**B**	Backcountry Experience	1205 Camino del Rio	(970) 247-5830
Groceries	**C**	City Market South	6 Town Plaza	(970) 247-4475
Info	**D**	Chamber of Commerce	111 S Camino del Rio	(970) 247-0312
Laundry	**E**	North Main Laundry	2980 Main	(970) 247-9915
Lodging		Numerous motels, hotels and B&Bs in town.		
Medical	**F**	Mercy Medical Ctr	375 E Park Ave	(970) 274-4311
Post Office	**G**	Durango Post Office	222 W 8th St	(970) 247-3968
Showers	**H**	Recreation Center	2700 Main	
Train Depot	**J**	Durango & Silverton RR	479 Main Ave	(970) 247-2733

Trail Description

Begin this segment at the Kennebec Trailhead parking lot **Ⓐ**, **mile 0.0** (11,635). The trail is marked by a display sign and leaves to the south side of the parking area, then heads southeast towards a prominent saddle. At **mile 0.4**, pass by a seasonal spring. Cross Kennebec Pass at **mile 0.7** (11,700) **Ⓑ**, then turn left at an intersection, about 400 feet past the top. The trail switchbacks hard to the left, leaving the old mining track. As you traverse north and east, reach a large talus slope at **mile 1.1** (11,370), a feature is known as The Sliderock. The trail goes for 0.2 mile across the talus, then enters a mature spruce forest on the other side. Continue on a series of switchbacks to a Forest Service road at **mile 2.4** (10,360) **Ⓒ** . This is FS-171N, leading to FS-171 (Junction Creek Road, leading to Durango). Cross the road and head downhill. The trail is easy to follow with confidence markers every mile or so. After a few switchbacks, the trail begins following a seasonal creek at **mile 3.7**. However, the terrain is generally not suitable for camping. Continue down the trail and follow another seasonal creek at **mile 4.7**. A few small, soft-surfaced campsites are possible here. Pass by a waterfall at a large switchback at **mile 5.4** (9,250) **❶**. This is a reliable spot for water year-round, but the narrow valley is not suitable for a camp. Drop down further into the inner canyon and cross Junction Creek at **mile 5.7**. The trail crosses the creek five times in all in a span of 1.5 miles. The last crossing, at **mile 7.1 ❶**, is at a bridge where there is a excellent, hard-packed campsite (8,520).

After crossing the bridge, the trail climbs steeply and steadily for the next four miles. At **mile 7.5**, the forest transitions from Engelmann spruce to a mixture of spruce, fir, and white pine. Cross a seasonal side stream at **mile 7.3**. There is a excellent, dry campsite on a ridge at **mile 8.0** (9,035) **❶**. Cross another small stream at **mile 9.1**. Reach the top of the climb at **mile 11.2** (9,560) **❶**, then begin a rolling descent. At a bend in the trail at **mile 11.5**, there is a small, but excellent campsite on a little bench above the trail (9,435) and water in a small stream 200 feet below the trail. This obscure camp was used by a commercial llama-trekking operation in years past, but is usually available. Continuing down the trail, cross a rocky section of trail, then pass through a Forest Service gate at **mile 14.2 ❶**.

At **mile 14.5**, the Colorado Trail and the Dry Fork Trail intersect (8,605). The Colorado Trail takes a hard left turn to the east. This is one corner of a very popular mountain bike ride out of Durango. Heading down the Dry Fork Trail leads to a trailhead on a county road and US-160 north of Durango. This intersection here is well marked. At **mile 16.9**, pass by a year-round spring that has some small campsites nearby (8,135). The spring has been improved for wildlife. Camping is not allowed past this point to the Junction Creek Trailhead. (Note that camping is available at the Junction Creek Campground, located 1.5 miles east of the intersection of FS-171 and CT at mile 20.3. Follow FS-171 for 1.5 miles east to the campground, a USFS fee area.)

Camping is NOT allowed beyond mile 16.9 of this segment (except at Junction Creek Campground) !

At **mile 17.1 ❶**, intersect the Hoffheins Connection Trail, (8,000), a short cut to the Dry Fork Trail. Bear to the left at this point and continue in a easterly direction to "Gudys Rest" at **mile 17.4** (7,980) **❶**. This is a scenic overlook with a bench placed in honor of Gudy Gaskill, the remarkable woman who made the Colorado Trail a reality. Take a moment here

RIGHT: *Taking in the view at Gudy's Rest.*

Viewing Dippers

A chunky, drab, wren-like bird, the water ouzel, or *dipper*, would hardly attract anyone's attention if it were not for its very unusual manner of earning a living. Dippers reside along rushing mountain streams, often perched atop a rock in the foaming center of the torrent. From this vantage point, it constantly bobs up and down, looking for aquatic insects or even small fish. Spotting a tasty morsel, it then dives headlong into the water, opens its wings, and "flies" or walks submerged through the flow.

Birds stake out a 75 to 200 meter length of stream for their territory, rarely venturing any distance from its banks. Disturbed, they fly low and rapidly, back up or down the stream, with a high, ringing alarm. During winter, dippers move to lower levels.

Nests are a bulky ball of moss, one side open, built just above the waterline in inaccessible places, such as on a rock wall or behind a waterfall.

Dippers can be found throughout the streams and rivers of western Colorado. In Segment 28, you are as likely to spot one along the lush banks of little Quinn Creek as perched on a boulder in the middle of the Animas River in downtown Durango.

Is it not enough to lean on the blue air of mountains?
Is it not enough to rest with your mate at timberline, in bushes that hug the rocks?
Must you fly through mad waters where the heaped-up granite breaks them?
Must you batter your wings in the torrent?
Must you plunge for life and death through the foam?

from a poem "The Water Ouzel" by Harriet Monroe

and look south. Some areas of Durango are visible from, including Ft. Lewis College. Through-hikers who began in Denver many miles ago may wish to pause and reflect before they re-enter the world they left behind. This is a popular day-hike destination for locals, so expect plenty of company.

Head down a series of switchbacks to re-join Junction Creek at **mile 18.9** (7,430) **L**. Cross the creek on a sturdy bridge, as the trail leaves the switchbacks and heads more to the south. At **mile 20.3**, reach an intersection near a parking area and informal trailhead on Junction Creek Road. There is a post marking the spot. (The aforementioned USFS campground is 1.5 miles east on FS-171 from this spot.) Turn to the right and follow the trail down into the narrow canyon. Continue down the trail as it parallels the creek. Cross an irrigation canal at **mile 21.3**, before reaching the trailhead at **mile 21.5** (6,990) **M**. This is the Junction Creek Trailhead, the southern terminus of the Colorado Trail. A new trailhead, with increased parking space and a toilet, was constructed in the fall of 2005. As of this writing, it is still a small trailhead, with limited parking. However, readers may find something different in the future as a major renovation and expansion is planned. The trailhead is located about 3.5 miles from Durango, via a paved road. There are several motels located near the intersection of the paved road; which becomes 25th Street, then hits Main Avenue in Durango. The downtown area is to the right at that point.

Mountain Bicycle Detour

Junction Creek Canyon Detour — *Segment 28 (San Juan NF):* For mountain bikers, this segment of the CT can involve a steep and technically difficult ride from below Kennebec Pass to the Junction Creek Trailhead. While the trail is well maintained, sharp curves and dramatic dropoffs will challenge most riders. This bypass is recommended as a popular and pleasant alternative to a descent of the CT. This route can also be combined with an ascent of the CT from the Junction Creek Trailhead for a loop ride of nearly 38 miles.

Detour Description: A side road crosses the CT at **mile 2.4** (10,360), east of Kennebec Pass. Follow the side road left for 0.7 mile to intersect with FS-171 (see alternate access route to the CT on page 235). No difficulties present themselves, other than the occasional cattle guard, as you descend some 2,400 feet on the Forest Service road. After 17.5 miles, reach the end of the Colorado Trail at the Junction Creek Trailhead. Durango is 3.4 miles further down the Junction Creek Road.

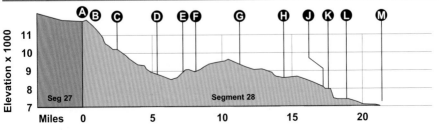

SCALE: 1/2 INCH = 1 MILE (1:126,720)

CT (current segment)	
CT (adjacent segment)	
Alternate CT Route	
Trail	
Paved Road	
Improved Road	
Unimproved Road	
Unimproved Road and 4WD	
National Forest Boundary	
Wilderness Boundary	
Continental Divide	
H Landmark Location	
– 3.1 – Mileage Distance	
Trailhead	
Parking	
Camping	

INDEX TO USGS TOPOS

La Plata | Monument Hill | Hermosa
Hesperus | Durango West | Durango East

Segment 28
San Juan NF

Landmark Comments	Mileage	Fr. Denver	Latitude	Longitude
A Begin Segment 28	0.0	463.4	37.451713	-108.010885
B Cross Kennebec Pass	0.7	464.1	37.447152	-108.001469
C Cross FS-171N	2.4	465.8	37.450557	-107.983461
D Pass waterfall	5.4	468.8	37.433220	-107.967726
E Bridge over creek	7.1	470.5	37.416366	-107.972348
F Campsite on ridge	8.0	471.4	37.406108	-107.969453
G Top of climb	11.2	474.6	37.387004	-107.960233
H Forest Service gate	14.2	477.6	37.356755	-107.975329
J Intersect Hoffheins Tr.	17.1	480.5	37.352334	-107.934653
K Gudy's Rest	17.4	480.8	37.353027	-107.931082
L Rejoin Junction Cr.	18.9	481.3	37.354717	-107.927255
M End Segment 28	21.5	484.9	37.331366	-107.902155

USFS Ranger Districts ▲

USDA Forest Service
Rocky Mountain Regional Office
740 Simms
Golden, CO 80401-4720
303-275-5350

Gunnison National Forest
Gunnison Ranger District
216 N. Colorado
Gunnison, CO 81230
970-641-0471

Pike National Forest
South Park Ranger District
320 Hwy. 285, Box 219
Fairplay, CO 80440
719-836-2031
South Platte Ranger District
19316 Goddard Ranch Ct.
Morrison, CO 80465
303-275-5610

Rio Grande National Forest
Divide Ranger District - Creede
3rd & Creede Ave., Box 270
Creede, CO 81130
719-658-2556
Saguache Ranger District
46525 State Hwy. 114, Box 67
Saguache, CO 81149
719-655-2547

San Isabel National Forest
Leadville Ranger District
810 Front Street
Leadville, CO 80461
719-486-0749
Salida Ranger District
325 W. Rainbow Blvd.
Salida, CO 81201
719-539-3591

San Juan National Forest
Columbine District
367 S. Pearl St., P.O. Box 439
Bayfiled, CO 81122
970-884-2512
Dolores District
29211 Hwy 184, P.O. Box 210
Dolores, CO 81323
970-882-7296

White River National Forest
Dillon Ranger District
680 Blue River Parkway, Box 620
Silverthorne, CO 80498
970-468-5400
Holy Cross Ranger District
24747 US Hwy. 24, Box 190
Minturn, CO 81645
970-827-5715

Useful Phone Numbers

Colorado Trail Foundation
(303) 384-3729
Statewide road conditions:
(303) 639-1111
Statewide weather reports
(303) 398-3964
Colorado Division of Wildlife
(303) 297-1192
To activate a rescue group, contact the
nearest county sheriff:

Seg 1-3	Jefferson (303) 277-0211
Seg 4-6	Park (719) 836-2494
Seg 6-8	Summit (970) 453-6222
Seg 8	Eagle (970) 328-6611
Seg 9-11	Lake (719) 486-1249
Seg 12-15	Chaffee (970) 539-2814
Seg 15-20	Saguache (970) 655-2544
Seg 21	Mineral (719) 658-2600
Seg 21-23	Hinsdale (970) 944-2291
Seg 24-25	San Juan (970) 387-5531
Seg 26	Dolores (970) 677-2257
Seg 27-28	La Plata (970) 247-1157

FACING PAGE: *Hikers near Kokomo Pass, Seg. 8.*

▲ Bibliography

Note: This bibliography is only a partial listing of the references and guidebooks to those portions of Colorado's mountains touched by the CT. Because most of the guides are updated with new printings or editions every few years, the publication dates given are those of the first edition, unless otherwise noted.

General References

Bueler, William M. *Roof of the Rockies: A History of Colorado Mountaineering.* Colorado Mountain Club Press, Golden, Colorado, 2000, third edition.
   Definitive history of Colorado mountaineering.

Chronic, Halka. *Roadside Geology of Colorado.* Mountain Press, Missoula, Montana. 1980.
   Best overall introduction to Colorado's geology.

Griffiths, Mel, and Rubright, Lynnell. *Colorado: A Geography.* Westview Press, Boulder, Colorado, 1983.
   General treatment of the geography of the whole state.

Hart, John L. Jerome. *Fourteen Thousand Feet: A History of the Naming and Early Ascents of the High Colorado Peaks.* Colorado Mountain Club, Denver, Colorado, 1972.
   The 1931 history of Colorado's 14,000-foot peaks; still available in a 1972 reprint.

Jordan, Ryan. *Lightweight Backpacking and Camping; A Field Guide to Wilderness Equipment, Technique and Style.* Beartooth Mountain Press, 2005.
   A good overall introduction to the concept of "lite-hiking".

Ladigin, Don and MIke Clelland. *Lighten Up! : A Complete Handbook for Light and Ultralight Backpacking.* Falcon Press, Helena, Montana, 2005.
   Another overall introduction to the concept of "lite-hiking".

Wolle, Muriel Sibell. *Stampede to Timberline.* Artcraft Press, Denver, Colorado, 1949.
   Classic account of the mining era in Colorado.

Zwinger, Ann H., and Willard, Beatrice E. *Land Above the Trees.* Harper & Row Publishers, New York, New York, 1972.
   Comprehensive guide to alpine ecology, including the Colorado Rockies.

Other Readings on the CT

Fayhee, M. John, and Fielder, John. *Along the Colorado Trail*. Westcliffe
Publishers, Englewood, Colorado, 1992.
   Journal account with photos of a summer on the CT.

Sumner, David. "The Colorado Trail Takes Shape." *Colorado Magazine*, July-
August 1974.
   Account of the CT during its beginnings.

Other Colorado Guides

Boddie, Caryn and Peter. *Hiking Colorado*. Falcon Press, Helena, Montana, 1997.
   A guide to 100 hikes throughout Colorado.

Fielder, John and Pearson. *The Complete Guide to Colorado's Wilderness Areas*.
Westcliffe Publishers, Englewood, Colorado, 1998.
   Includes coverage of the six wilderness areas that the CT traverses.

Gebhardt, Dennis. *A Backpacking Guide to the Weminuche Wilderness in the San
Juan Mountains of Colorado*. Basin Reproduction and Printing Company,
Durango, Colorado, 1976.
   Backpacking guide to Weminuche Wilderness with pocket maps.

Muller, Dave. *The Colorado Year Round Outdoor Guide*. Colorado Mountain Club
Press, Golden, Colorado, 2004.
   Hikes, climbs, snowshoe trips and ski trips for every week of the year.

Jacobs, Randy, and Ormes, Robert M. *Guide to The Colorado Mountains*.
Colorado Mountain Club Press, Golden, Colorado, 2000, tenth edition.
   Definitive guide to all areas of the Colorado mountains.

Jones, Tom Lorang. *Colorado's Continental Divide Trail*. Westcliffe Publishers,
Englewood, Colorado, 1997.
   Comprehensive guide to the Colorado portion of the trail.

Pixler, Paul. *Hiking Trails of Southwestern Colorado*. Pruett Publishing Company,
Boulder, Colorado, 1981.
   Day hikes in the San Juan Mountains.

Savage, Ania. *Colorado Mountain Club Pocket Guide to the Colorado
Fourteeners*. Johnson Books, Boulder, Colorado, 1997.
   Brief guide to the standard routes on the fourteeners.

Wolf, James R. *Guide to the Continental Divide Trail*. Volumes 4 and 5.
Continental Divide Trail Society, Bethesda, Maryland, 1982.
   A guide to the divide trail from Canada to Mexico, including Colorado.

⚠ Leave No Trace

The **Leave No Trace** program is a message to promote and inspire responsible outdoor recreation through education, research, and partnerships. Managed as a non-profit educational organization and authorized by the U.S. Forest Service, LNT is about enjoying places like the CT, while traveling and camping with care. The 7 LNT Principles of outdoor ethics form the framework of LNT's message:

• *Plan Ahead and Prepare*
Know the regulations and special concerns for the area you'll visit.
Prepare for extreme weather, hazards, and emergencies.
Schedule your trip to avoid times of high use.
Visit in small groups. Split larger parties into groups of 4-6.
Repackage food to minimize waste.
Use a map and compass to eliminate the use of marking paint, rock cairns or
flagging.

• *Travel and Camp on Durable Surfaces*
Durable surfaces include established trails and campsites, rock, gravel, dry
grasses or snow.
Protect riparian areas by camping at least 200 feet from lakes and streams.
Good campsites are found, not made. Altering a site is not necessary.
In popular areas:
Concentrate use on existing trails and campsites.
Walk single file in the middle of the trail, even when wet or muddy.
Keep campsites small. Focus activity in areas where vegetation is absent.
In pristine areas:
Disperse use to prevent the creation of campsites and trails.
Avoid places where impacts are just beginning.

• *Dispose of Waste Properly*
Pack it in, pack it out. Inspect your campsite and rest areas for trash or spilled
foods. Pack out all trash, leftover food, and litter.
Deposit solid human waste in catholes dug 6 to 8 inches deep at least 200 feet
from water, camp, and trails. Cover and disguise the cathole when finished.
Pack out toilet paper and hygiene products.
To wash yourself or your dishes, carry water 200 feet away from streams or lakes
and use small amounts of biodegradable soap. Scatter strained dishwater.

• *Leave What You Find*
Preserve the past: examine, but do not touch, cultural or historic structures and
artifacts.
Leave rocks, plants and other natural objects as you find them.
Avoid introducing or transporting non-native species.
Do not build structures, furniture, or dig trenches.

• *Minimize Campfire Impacts*
Campfires can cause lasting impacts to the backcountry. Use a lightweight stove
    for cooking and enjoy a candle lantern for light.
Where fires are permitted, use established fire rings, fire pans, or mound fires.
Keep fires small. Only use sticks from the ground that can be broken by hand.
Burn all wood/coals to ash, put out campfires completely, then scatter cool ashes.

• *Respect Wildlife*
Observe wildlife from a distance. Do not follow or approach them.
Never feed animals. Feeding wildlife damages their health, alters natural
    behaviors, and exposes them to predators and other dangers.
Protect wildlife and your food by storing rations and trash securely.
Control pets at all times, or leave them at home.
Avoid wildlife during sensitive times: mating, nesting, raising young, or winter.

• *Be Considerate of Other Visitors*
Respect other visitors and protect the quality of their experience.
Be courteous. Yield to other users on the trail.
Step to the downhill side of the trail when encountering pack stock.
Take breaks and camp away from trails and other visitors.
Let nature's sounds prevail. Avoid loud voices and noises.

    Leave No Trace publishes an educational booklet, *Outdoor Skills and Ethics*,
that specifically covers backcountry recreation in the Rocky Mountains. To obtain a
copy of this, or for more information about the LNT program, contact:
        Leave No Trace, Inc., P.O. Box 997, Boulder, CO 80306
    Ph: 1 (800) 332-4100 Fax: (303) 442-8217 Website: www.lnt.org

BELOW: *Tent site along the Colorado Trail.*

Index

Note:

Bolded text and page numbers indicate a Segment chapter. Page numbers in *italics* indicate maps.

FACING PAGE: *A hiker strides*
out across Snow Mesa.

Photo Credits

We are indebted to the following Colorado Trail hikers and organizations for providing the photographs and illustrations used in this guide:

Aaron Locander: 2-3, 8, 22, 27, 31, 40, 42, 44, 56, 57, 62, 68, 77 (both), 80, 106, 107 (lower), 114, 120, 123, 128, 134, 151, 156, 162 (lower), 174 (upper), 181 (upper), 186-187 (upper), 193 (upper), 200 (both), 207, 217 (both), 226, 231 (lower)
Andrew Skurka: 28, 41 (upper), 54, 60, 74, 110, 138, 166, 180 (upper), 253
Bill Manning: 25, 71, 223 (lower), 237
Hugo Ferchau: 38, 39
Jeff Stankiewicz: 48
Julie Manchester: 148, 180 (lower), 208 (lower)
Kay Hubbard: 107 (upper)
Linda Jeffers: 19, 41 (lower), 43 (2nd), 43 (3rd), 43 (5th), 47, 212, 215 (both), 216, 220, 222, 229, 230 (both), 234, 247
Paul Magnanti: 66
Rick Tronvig: 69, 112 (lower), 150 (lower), 162, 231 (upper)
Robert Muse: 129
Seth Miller: 43 (4th), 93 (both), 238
Terry Root: 43 (1st), 51, 186 (lower)
Tim Pitschka: 24, 34, 36, 63, 83, 101, 142, 154, 160
Courtesy of Colorado Mountain Expeditions: 12, 16, 84, 85, 88, 91 (both), 96, 104, 112 (upper), 118, 122, 126, 130, 137, 150 (upper), 157, 163, 172, 178, 181 (lower), 184, 190, 193 (lower), 198, 204, 208 (upper), 242
Courtesy of The Colorado Trail Foundation: 50, 76, 174 (lower), 175, 223 (upper), 254
Courtesy of Eric Wunrow: 11 (visit *EricWunrow.com*)
Courtesy of the U.S. Geological Survey: 99

ABOUT THE COLORADO TRAIL FOUNDATION

The Colorado Trail is maintained by the non-profit **Colorado Trail Foundation** (CTF) in cooperation with the U.S. Forest Service. The CTF recruits and trains volunteers for trail construction crews, supplies and supports the crews, conducts fully supported week-long treks on the trail, offers educational outdoor classroom series close to The Colorado Trail, maintains the trail through its Adopt-A-Trail program, distributes information on The Colorado Trail activities and trail crews, and creates and distributes publications. Donations to the CTF are tax deductible. Join us in building and maintaining The Colorado Trail for you and future generations.

♦ **Yes, I want to become a "Friend of the Colorado Trail"!**

Friends receive our CT newsletter, *Tread Lines*, notices of special events and summer trail crew, trek, and education class schedules.

Supporter $15 ___ Contributor $25 ___ Sustainer $50 ___
Sponsor $75 ___ Partner $100 ___ Patron $250 ___
Guardian $500 ___ Benefactor $1000 ___ Corporate $_____
I am a: Senior ___ Student ___ Individual ___ Family ___
My employer offers Matching Funds and I will apply for them ___

♦ **Yes, I am ready to volunteer!**

I want to work on a Volunteer Trail Crew. Please send information ___
I'd like information on the Adopt-a-Trail Program ___
I would like to help with other CT volunteer projects.
Please send information ___

Name(s):_____
Address:_____
City:_____ State:_____ Zip:_____
Telephone:_____ Email:_____

The Colorado Trail Foundation
710 10th Street #210
Golden, CO 80401-5843

Ph: (303) 384-3729   Fax: (303) 384-3743
Web: www.coloradotrail.org   Email: ctf@coloradotrail.org

For a FREE certificate for completing the entire Colorado Trail, contact the CTF office.

ABOUT THE COLORADO MOUNTAIN CLUB

The Colorado Mountain Club is a non-profit outdoor recreation, education and conservation organization founded in 1912. Today with over 10,000 members, 14 branches in-state, and one branch for out-of-state members, the CMC is the largest organization of its kind in the Rocky Mountains. Membership opens the door to:

Outdoor Recreation: *Over 3100 trips and outings led annually.* Hike, ski, climb, backpack, snowshoe, bicycle, ice skate, travel the world and build friendships that will last a lifetime.

Conservation: *Supporting a mission which treasures our natural environment.* Committed to environmental education, a strong voice on public lands management, trail building and rehabilitation projects.

Outdoor Education: *Schools, seminars, and courses that teach outdoor skills through hands-on activities.* Wilderness trekking, rock climbing, high altitude mountaineering, telemark skiing, backpacking and much more — plus the Mountain Discovery Program designed to inspire lifelong stewardship in children and young adults.

Publications: *A wide range of outdoor publications to benefit and inform members.* Trail and Timberline Magazine, twice-a-year Activity Schedule, monthly group newsletters, and 20% discount on titles from CMC Press.

The American Mountaineering Center: *A world-class facility in Golden, Colorado.* Featuring the largest mountaineering library in the western hemisphere, a mountaineering museum, a 300-seat, state-of-the-art auditorium, a conference center, free monthly program nights and a technical climbing wall.

Visit us at the beautiful American Mountaineering Center!

JOINING IS EASY!

Membership opens the door to:
ADVENTURE!

The Colorado Mountain Club
710 10th St. #200 Golden, CO 80401
(303) 279-3080 1(800) 633-4417
FAX (303) 279-9690
Email: cmcoffice@cmc.org
Website: www.cmc.org

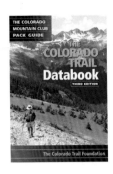